Software Reuse

Other Titles of Interest

Software Reuse

Methods, Models, and Costs

Ronald J. Leach

McGraw-Hill

New York   San Francisco   Washington, D.C.   Auckland   Bogotá
Caracas   Lisbon   London   Madrid   Mexico City   Milan
Montreal   New Delhi   San Juan   Singapore
Sydney   Tokyo   Toronto

Library of Congress Cataloging-in-Publication Data

Leach, Ronald J.
    Software reuse : methods, models, and costs / Ronald J. Leach.
       p.   cm.
    Includes index.
    ISBN 0-07-036929-1
    1. Computer software—Reusability. I. Title.
QA76.76.R47L43 1997
005.1—dc20   96-35998
                                      CIP

McGraw-Hill

A Division of The McGraw·Hill Companies

Figures 6.5 and 6.6 are excerpted from *Object-Oriented Design and Programming in C++*, by Ronald J. Leach, Academic Press, 1995.

1 2 3 4 5 6 7 8 9 0 BKP/BKP 9 0 1 0 9 8 7 6

ISBN 0-07-036929-1

The sponsoring editor for this book was John Wyzalek, the editing supervisor was Bernard Onken, and the production supervisor was Clara B. Stanley. It was set in Century Schoolbook by Ron Painter of McGraw-Hill's Professional Book Group composition unit.

Printed and bound by Quebecor Book Press.

McGraw-Hill books are available at special quantity discounts to use as premiums and sales promotions, or for use in corporate training programs. For more information, please write to the Director of Special Sales, McGraw-Hill, 11 West 19th Street, New York, NY 10011. Or contact your local bookstore.

This book is printed on recycled, acid-free paper containing a minimum of 50% recycled, de-inked fiber.

Contents

Preface

The primary intended audience for this book is software engineers and managers faced with practical problems developing software, especially schedule, cost, and quality pressures. The book can be used as a secondary reference for additional reading in an upper-level software engineering or software engineering economics course. It can also be used as the primary text in an advanced software engineering course based primarily on software reuse. Both professionals and students can read the book profitably. The typical reader of this book will have had previous exposure to the development and maintenance of software systems that are too complex to be designed and implemented by a single person.

Software reuse is one of the hottest topics in software engineering. For the past few years, nearly every conference with a heavy focus on software engineering has included at least one paper session, panel discussion, or invited talk on some aspect of software reuse. Many larger conferences have tutorial sessions on software reuse.

Software reuse is the software engineer's attempt to model the process by which an electrical engineer designs circuits—by using standard components with well-defined, well-documented interfaces. Reusable components can be found at any place in the software life cycle: requirements, design, code, test, integration, documentation, and maintenance. Reuse often allows the software engineer to be much more productive since total life cycle costs frequently can be greatly reduced.

While this book will provide a complete description of software reuse, it will focus on methods for reuse that are feasible without major investments in new software methodology as well as on cost estimation issues and on certification of reusable software components. The text will be based on experiences involving systems that are changing rapidly. This contrasts with the perspective of many writers on the topic who only consider systems that are stable over time. However, the approach of this text is consistent with software development using the rapid prototyping of spiral models of the development process.

This book emphasizes both theoretical and practical techniques for the reuse of software artifacts. Software artifacts include source code modules, requirements, designs, documentation, user manuals, test plans, test cases, test case results, and installation guides. The book is organized as follows:

Chapter 1 is an introductory chapter. In it, we present a rationale for software reuse and briefly describe some of the early results and current trends. Disincentives to software reuse, including legal and security issues, are also presented.

Chapter 2 presents more detailed discussions of several essential techniques. The primary theoretical technique discussed is domain analysis. Domain analysis is the application of systems engineering principles to the determination of common components in an organization's collection of software artifacts. The practical techniques discussed will include the development of standard interfaces, object-oriented approaches, designing for reuse, setting requirements to meet reuse standards, and some appropriate metrics.

We introduce the issue of reuse library management in Chapter 3. This chapter also includes a discussion of some of the more readily available reuse libraries, with some description of software artifacts that are at a higher level than source code. These higher-level artifacts include some designs, complete subsystems, and software written in fourth generation languages.

Chapter 4 is devoted to the certification of reusable software components. The term *certification* refers to a quality evaluation taken after the software artifact has passed through normal software testing and has been placed into service. An additional certification step is necessary because software components may be used in contexts other than the one in which they were originally developed. There will also be recommendations for appropriate standards and practices to encourage the systematic employment of software reuse.

We present a large set of cost estimation models in Chapter 5. The chapter places great emphasis on the collection and interpretation of software metrics for both evaluation of process and prediction of cost savings. Cost estimation models for reuse will include both the classical waterfall life cycle and iterative software development paradigms such as the spiral and rapid prototyping processes. We will emphasize the effect of life cycle leverage on the potential savings due to reuse. We will also describe the optimum size of reusable components (the economic reuse quantity).

Reengineering of software is discussed in Chapter 6. Reengineering involves changing a system's design to improve maintainability. Software reuse and reengineering are related because a major concern of software managers is that the cost involved in reengineering a system is affected by the amount that is reused.

Four case studies are presented in Chapter 7. These include some programs at particular installations of NASA, Battelle National Laboratories, AT&T, and Hewlett-Packard.

Chapter 8 is devoted to a discussion of some tools for software reuse. The tools discussed range from the commercial to the public domain to some that are restricted to a particular organization.

There are five appendices: a description of metrics, a glossary of terms, sources for reuse libraries, a set of suggestions for a course on software reuse, and a checklist for software reuse in a changing environment.

Some of the material—particularly the certification issues, some of the cost models including the economic reuse quantity, the heavy use of metrics in software reuse, and the reengineering model—has not previously appeared in print.

Many people deserve thanks for their part in this effort. Special thanks are due to Judith Bruner, Jack Koslosky, Ron Mahmot, and Henry Murray of the Space Center Systems Branch of NASA's Goddard Space Flight Center in Greenbelt, Maryland, for providing access to the rich history of the TPOCC project, which focused heavily on reuse. Many thanks also to Kellyann Jeletic for several interesting discussions about software process and metrics, for making me aware of the details of some of the analyses performed by the Software Engineering Laboratory at Goddard, and for reading and commenting on an earlier version of the manuscript. Clayton Sigman and Ron Mahmot of Goddard also made many insightful comments on an earlier version of the manuscript.

Linda Rosenberg of Unisys provided important resources for metrics analysis of some of the NASA/Goddard systems. Toni Zepp of Computer Sciences Corporation provided access to her electronic database of discrepancy reports for metrics analysis and comparison.

Many people provided insights into the impact of reuse on cost estimation models. Among them are Brian Bolger, Jay Carlin, Victor Church, and Gary Meyers of Computer Sciences Corporation; Dan Mandl and Larry Zeigenfuss of Goddard; and Evan Eller and Toby Perkins of Allied Signal Corporation. Many of the inputs to the cost estimation models in Chapter 5 have their roots in informal conversations with these colleagues. Ronald Cherry and Issac Jackson of the Defense Information Systems Agency (DISA), Kawanna Rice of The

Maryland Procurement Office, and Annette Johnson also provided critiques of this manuscrpt.

Michael Feldman of SIGAda and The George Washington University and Richard Conn and Hal Haft of SIGAda are owed special thanks for their many years of effort on behalf of the Ada community, especially in the area of information dissemination. These efforts have strongly influenced reuse efforts on a national level.

Special thanks are due to Christa Clark of AT&T and Terrence Fuller of Bell Northern Research for some preliminary work on software reuse and for providing brief overviews of the reuse activities at AT&T and Battelle Northern Laboratory, respectively. Patricia Collins of Hewlett-Packard provided insight into reuse programs at HP.

Dr. William Frakes of Virginia Polytechnic and State University is owed special thanks for interesting discussions and for a very stimulating seminar he gave at Howard University.

My editors at McGraw-Hill, Marjorie Spencer and John Wyzalek; the reviewer Shari Lawrence Pfleeger; and the McGraw-Hill book team, Bernie Onken, Pamela Pelton, and Clara Stanley, provided invaluable assistance in the production of this manuscript. Many thanks to all.

Ronald J. Leach

What Is Software Reuse?

In general, the term *software reuse* refers to a situation in which some software is used in more than one project. Here *software* is defined loosely as one or more items that are considered part of an organization's standard software engineering process for producing some product. Thus, *software* could refer either to source code or to other products of the software life cycle, such as requirements, designs, test plans, test suites, or documentation. The term *software artifact* is frequently used in this context.

Software reuse has several different meanings in the software engineering community. Different individuals will have different viewpoints depending on their responsibilities. For example, a high-level software manager might view software reuse as a technique for improving the overall productivity and quality of his or her organization. As such, the focus would be on costs and benefits of organizational reuse plans and on schemes for implementing companywide schemes.

Developers who use reusable code written by others probably view software reuse as the efficient use of a collection of available assets. For these consumers of existing software, software reuse is considered a positive goal since it can improve productivity. A project manager for such development would probably view reuse as useful if the appropriate reused software were easy to obtain and were of high quality. The manager would have a different view if he or she were forced to use poorly tested code that caused many problems in system integration and maintenance because of its lack of modularity or adherence to standards.

On the other hand, developers who are producers of reusable code for use in their own projects and by others might view reuse as a drain on their limited resources. This is especially true if they are required to provide additional quality in their products or to collect and analyze additional metrics.

A reuse librarian, who is responsible for operating and maintaining a library of reusable components, would have a different view. Each new reuse library component would have to be subjected to configuration management. Some degree of cataloging would be necessary for future access. Software reuse makes the job of a reuse librarian necessary.

In layman's terms, reuse can be defined as using what already exists to achieve what is desired. Reuse can be achieved with no special language, paradigm, library, operating system, or techniques. It has been practiced for many years in many different contexts.

Reusing code is often more appealing than automatic code generation. In the vast majority of projects, much of the necessary software has already been developed, even if not in house. Frequently, it's just a matter of knowing what to reuse, how to reuse it, and what the trade-offs are.

Reusability is widely believed to be a key to improving software development productivity and quality. By reusing high-quality software components, software developers can simplify the product and make it more reliable. Frequently, fewer total subsystems are used and less time is spent organizing the subsystems.

There are many examples of successful software reuse. Several success stories were cited by Charles Lillie at the Second Annual Reuse Education and Training Workshop [LILL93]. These include:

- Three hundred and twelve projects in the aerospace industry, with averages of a 20 percent increase in productivity, a 20 percent reduction in customer complaints, a 25 percent reduction in time to repair, and a 25 percent reduction in time to produce the system

- A Japanese industry study that noted 15 to 50 percent increases in productivity, 20 to 35 percent reductions in customer complaints, 20 percent reductions in training costs, and 10 to 50 percent reductions in time to produce the system

- A simulator system developed for the U.S. Navy that boasted an increase of nearly 200 percent in the number of source lines of code produced per hour

- Tactical protocol software with a return on investment of 400 percent

- A NASA report that listed reductions of 75 percent in overall development effort and cost [McGA93]

These are impressive success stories. They clearly indicate that software reuse is a technique that can have a positive impact on software engineering practice in many environments.

The phrase *reusable software engineering* encompasses the reuse of all information generated during the software development process. Among the commonly asked questions are what and how to reuse software and in which method does it prove to be the most successful.

Despite the positive outlook for reuse, some questions remain:

How should potentially reusable code be developed?

How do we locate appropriate software components?

What tools are available? Do they work?

Why is the expected quality of projects sometimes hard to achieve?

Why is the projected cost savings of software reuse sometimes hard to determine?

Why do some reused-based development projects appear to have higher life cycle costs than similar ones developed without reuse?

What changes have to be made to an organization's software development practices?

What changes do we have to make to our cost models?

Some people even ask "Why is reusability a strategy of great promise that has been largely unfulfilled?" All these questions will be addressed by the systematic approach to software reuse emphasized in this book.

This chapter will provide a brief introduction to some of the issues associated with software reuse. We will describe some of the earliest successful efforts in software reuse and indicate the role of reuse in different software development methodologies, including those based on the classic waterfall, rapid prototyping, and spiral models. We will also discuss the relationship between software reengineering and software reuse.

We will next introduce the fundamental technique of domain analysis and its relevance to reuse library management. After a digression to briefly describe some of the disadvantages of reuse and some legal issues, the chapter will close with a description of the basic understanding, state of the art, and state of the practice of software reuse.

The reader may notice that there is no explicit mention of object-oriented approaches to software reuse in this chapter. As we will see throughout this book, object-oriented techniques present many opportunities for reuse of source code components. We will describe these techniques at several points in this chapter and elsewhere in this book.

1.1   Origins of Software Reuse

As the large increase in software costs and the problems in developing quality products on schedule became more evident in the 1980s, several organizations viewed software reuse as a goal that could be achieved in limited ways right away and in broader ways through advanced development and research. Reusing software can be traced back at least as far as the early attempts of Lanergan and Poynton at Raytheon and of Matsumoto at Toshiba [MATS89]. The initial work emphasized cost savings.

One of the first papers to present the concept of formal software reuse was McIlroy's presentation [McIL68] at a NATO conference. A 1984 survey article by Capers Jones [JONE84] provides a good overview of some of the early work in the area of software reuse.

Beginning in the 1980s, the U.S. Department of Defense saw reuse as a prime candidate in its attempts to improve software productivity, and it was a major factor in the design of the Ada programming language. Many repositories of code have been developed and maintained as part of this continuing effort.

Since the adoption of the ANSI-MIL standard for Ada in 1983 [ADA83], there have been long-range research efforts to improve the ability to reuse information in the development of software. Software reuse was attracting much interest and in 1992 was described as the year's most sought after objective, or the "Holy Grail" of application development. Unfortunately, developers and analysts reported that the successful application of reuse to software projects was being hindered by a web of issues, such as training, costs, technical difficulties, and psychological resistance [RAY92]. The growing public perception of the importance of software reuse for cost reduction and quality improvement was illustrated by the publication of an article on the topic in 1993 in *Scientific American* magazine [CORC93].

It was not too long ago that hardware designers built hardware in the same way software is built today. They assembled custom circuits from individual electrical components in the same way that functions were developed from low-level components of programming languages (for example, assignment statements, conditional statements, function calls, etc.). Until a packaging technology evolved that could make the hardware environment of a chip relatively independent of the detailed workings of that chip massive reusability techniques of hardware designs were not possible.

Three steps were necessary to improve this situation:

1. Reusability of basic components, with standard interfaces and precisely defined functionality

2. Low prices for computer components, due to a repeatable manufacturing process

3. Development of tools such as VHDL, for representing architectures at higher levels of abstraction

One important concept that stands out in hardware systems is that many of the components perform unique services. These services are provided upon request, and the result is the only concern, not the internal methods of data used.

The software concept that is equivalent to this process is referred to as encapsulation, which defines a data structure along with a group of procedures for accessing it. The data structure can only be accessed by the users through careful documentation [BECK92], [LEDB85].

Some of these steps are mirrored in the evolution of compilers, database management systems, and operating systems. Most compiler designers use tools that take high-level lexical and semantic descriptions of the language being compiled to obtain initial compilers by employing lexical analyzers such as `lex`, `flex`, and `Alex`, or compiler-compilers such as `yacc`, `bison`, and `Ayacc`. These readily available tools support higher-level representations of the languages and have standard interfaces.

You have probably noted the similarity of the language of the past few paragraphs to the fundamental concepts of object-oriented design and programming. This is clearly not accidental. The concepts of object-oriented design and programming were developed in order to support the higher levels of abstraction and information hiding necessary for software development using reusable software components.

You should note, however, that most existing systems are not object-oriented and that many systems developed using the object-oriented paradigm are so new that their total life cycle costs (including the costs of analysis, requirements, design, coding, testing, integration, maintenance, and documentation) have not yet become apparent. Thus, for many organizations, the total life cycle savings due to software reuse for object-oriented systems cannot yet be completely determined. The increase in abstraction of some object-oriented systems over equivalent, procedurally oriented ones will have some effect on reuse programs, but the complete effect of the object orientation appears hard to quantify at this point.

Since there are many billions of lines of code in existing applications, most of which were developed using procedural and not object-related paradigms, any reuse method that is only capable of addressing object-oriented systems is not likely to have immediate positive effects for the majority of existing software systems. The long-term benefits of the application of such a method to procedurally developed systems remains to be seen.

However, since many of the ideas underlying the object-oriented approach frequently are consistent with the goals of software reuse, we will encounter object-oriented approaches many times in this book.

1.2   Reuse and the Software Life Cycle

Software artifacts may be reused at many phases in the software engineering life cycle, including analysis, requirements, designs, implementations, test plans, test cases, test results, error data, and documentation. This is true regardless of the software development life cycle model that is used in the organization. We will describe the classical waterfall, rapid prototyping, and spiral models in more detail in Chap. 5, when we present cost models for software reuse programs. In general, you should expect that earlier reuse in the life cycle is better than later reuse because of the potential for eliminating software development steps.

It is important to classify the places where software reuse can occur. In the next few pages, we will describe three common categorizations for reuse activities and will provide a fourth to reflect some more recent trends in software development.

Capers Jones [JONE84] lists five important subtopics under the general heading of "reusability": reusable data, reusable architecture, reusable designs, reusable programs and common systems, and reusable modules.

- Reusable data
  The concept of reusable functions implies that there is a standard data interchange format. Reusable programming requires reusable data.

- Reusable architecture
  "Since for the first 30 years of programming, designers and programmers have tended to consider each application as a unique artifact, there is no widespread architectural scheme for reusable programming" [JONE84].

- Reusable design
  Software should be designed so that sections of code can be reused. Doing so is difficult, despite appearances to the contrary [CORC93].

- Reusable programs and common systems
  Programs used by more than one customer are considered reusable. Reusable programs tend to concentrate in just a few application areas. A second aspect of reusable programs are common systems,

which are developed and shared among enterprises with multiple locations.

- Reusable modules
  Reusable modules and standard subroutines are more common now that reusable modules are beginning to be supported in the industry by library management systems.

Note that COTS (Commercial Off-the-Shelf) software is in the category of reusable programs and common systems. This is the most extreme case of software reuse. The percentage of a software artifact that is reused should be considered as a continuum ranging from an entirely new system with zero reuse to a COTS system with 100 percent reuse.

Goldberg and Rubin [GOLD90] have a more object-oriented focus. They suggest that most reuse falls into one of five categories:

- Algorithm reuse
  Algorithm reuse involves using the same algorithm across data structures. Using the data abstraction supported by object-oriented technology, algorithms that use the object-oriented data abstraction technique can be implemented at a high level of a class hierarchy and automatically become available to subclasses.

- Reuse of classes and instances
  Reuse at the object level occurs in either of two forms: refining a class via inheritance to obtain a new class or using instances of a class in the composition of a new class. With inheritance, both the protocols for the interface and implementation of the class are reused. However, with composition only the interface protocol specified in the class of the instance is reused.

- Reuse of application frameworks
  An application framework provides code for nearly all the required functionality. The framework also consists of abstract classes, the operations they implement, and the expectations for providing the concrete code in subclasses that specialize the framework for particular applications. By supporting a variety of subclasses the framework can be reused across applications. This is more commonly used in the Smalltalk family of languages than in C++. However, as C++ matures more attention is paid to reusable artifacts, which results in the frameworks being of a higher priority as well.

- Reuse of full applications
  Full applications such as text editors, network communications packages, file managers, picture editors, and database managers can be embedded within other applications. These common stand-

alone applications consist of objects that can be refined and are considered as reusable artifacts appropriate for further refinement. COTS products fall into this category.

- Reuse of interface specifications
An interface specification is the most abstract reusable artifact of a software system. It consists of a set of messages that "embody a coordinated set of behaviors." Classes whose instances perform these behaviors must also provide a behavior implementation. In turn, the instances can then be used whenever specific behavior is expected [GOLD90].

An alternative characterization of reuse is presented in the survey paper by Mili, Mili, and Mili [MILI95]. They categorize common reuse situations as the following:

- Source code components
In this case, the primary impact of reuse is at the design and later life cycle stages. The reusable software artifacts are source code components.

- Software schemas
In this case, the primary impact of reuse is also at the design and later life cycle stages. The reusable software artifacts are essentially processes developed by program design tools such as programmer's assistants [JONE84], [KRUE92].

- Reusable transformation systems
This is a high-level approach that is appropriate for developing software from specification languages. It is used at the specifications stage. See Ramamoorthy, Garg, and Prakash [RAMA88] for a discussion.

- Application generators
This technique makes use of tools such as the UNIX utilities `yacc` for parser generators and `lex` for lexical analyzers. This affects design and requirements in the sense that a system that uses these application generators must meet the requirements of the system rather than the other way around. For example, a language must be specified by a context-free grammar before a parser can be developed by the `yacc` utility.

- Very high-level languages
These are also used at the system specifications level. Some typical examples of this level of reuse are the finite state machine generator and spreadsheet software available from the ASSET library of reusable software artifacts. We will describe these examples briefly in Chap. 3 when we discuss reuse libraries.

It is not obvious where COTS fits in the classification scheme of Mili, Mili, and Mili [MILI93]. Placing it into the source code category implies that the main use of COTS is in the design phase. However, in many environments cost pressures force any initial requirements to be modified to meet the standard interface of the COTS product. In these environments, COTS has an impact on the requirements step.

As we indicated earlier, we present a more inclusive characterization for software reuse. And, as we pointed out at the beginning of this chapter, the producer of potentially reusable software products and the consumer of existing reusable software artifacts often have different perspectives on software reuse. Not all activities will be done by the producer or consumer of software reuse. The following list indicates the author's perspectives on the totality of reusable artifacts:

- Reusable architecture
- Reusable requirements
- Reusable design
- Reusable programs and common systems
- Reusable modules
- Reusable transformation systems, filters, and "glueware"
- Reusable cost models, plans, and schedules
- Reusable experiential, metrics, and measurement data
- Reconfiguration of flexible, reusable systems
- Reusable data for use by programs
- Reusable documentation
- Reusable negotiations with customers
- Reusable negotiations with software vendors
- Reusable algorithms
- Reusable classes and instances
- Reusable interface specifications
- Reusable inputs to application generators
- Reusable inputs to very high-level languages

For the sake of brevity, we will only discuss the categories that are either different from those on previous lists or else not discussed before.

Reusable transformation systems and filters would be necessary if two software systems with different interfaces had to communicate. An example of the need for such a filter is a system developed at NASA to allow satellite data arriving at ground control stations in blocks of 4800 bytes that are already formatted into proprietary "NASCOM blocks" to be changed into standard TCP/IP format packets for use with common network utility software. The use of COTS products such as the networking software available in the HP-UX version of UNIX often requires filters when these products are interfaced to existing software. The cost of such filters must be considered if existing software is to be reused.

Reusable cost models, plans, and schedules are necessary for software managers to obtain the full benefits of software reuse. Of course, we do not mean the direct reuse of a schedule for a previous project in another project. What we have in mind here is reuse of information from the typical plans and schedules for a project that has similar complexity and amounts of software reuse to the new project. Cost models will be very different from most existing models if the primary activity is integrating COTS products, writing filters or glueware between existing systems, reconfiguring existing systems, or programming applications generators. Cost modeling will be discussed in Chap. 5.

Reusable experiential, metrics, and measurement data are necessary when analyzing the effects of a systematic program of software reuse.

Reconfigurable flexible, reusable systems are often essential in the software development process. Proper configuration of an underlying operating system's kernel or a database management system often allows software systems purchased from different vendors to communicate. Changing the configuration of existing systems is a common reuse activity.

Reusable data for use by programs is common. For example, it occurs in large databases such as a digitized map of the earth or an initialization suite.

Reusable documentation should be available on every reusable system. Reusing documentation can be as simple as replacing only the changed sections in a manual or as technically sophisticated as changing hypertext or multimedia on-line materials.

Reusable negotiations with customers are important if there is a good relationship based on customers interacting with the developers to obtain a software solution that meets their essential needs at minimal cost. We will discuss this issue in Chap. 2 when we describe reuse-driven requirements engineering.

Reusable negotiations with software vendors become important if a software project uses a COTS product that requires a large amount of information sharing between the producer of the COTS product and the systems integrators. The relationship between COTS producer and system integrator often becomes much closer than a simple transaction between vendor and purchaser. This issue will be also be discussed in Chap. 2 when we describe reuse-driven requirements engineering. The papers of Waund [WAUN95], Ellis [ELLI95], and Kontio [KONT95] provide additional information on this topic.

Negotiations also become important when a reusable software component has errors that are detected only during its subsequent use. It is always easiest to conduct negotiations in an existing trusted relationship framework.

Reuse is often categorized by the nature of the environments in which the software artifacts are reused. Vertical reuse occurs when software artifacts are reused in different projects in the same application domain. An example of vertical reuse might be an edge detection routine used in several image processing programs. You should note that the term *vertical reuse* is sometimes used more narrowly to refer to reusing software artifacts at different life cycle phases in several generations of the same project. Successful vertical reuse requires detailed knowledge of the application domain.

Horizontal reuse occurs when a software artifact is reused in a different application domain from the one in which it was originally developed. As such, it requires excellent knowledge of several application domains. Multiple uses of a sort routine, database management system, or graphical user interface (GUI) illustrate the effect of horizontal reuse at the system level. Unfortunately, there are many opportunities for horizontal reuse of smaller software components. Clearly, effective horizontal reuse is much more difficult to achieve at the component level than is vertical reuse.

We now turn our attention to the most common type of software reuse: reuse of source code. In the case of source code, the "software" that is being reused can be one or more source modules, source code for a subsystem, or even source code for an entire system.

Focusing on reuse of source code is typical of the behavior of a user of a library of mathematical subroutines. The user expects to have a certain set of functions available in the library to perform certain computations. The interfaces to these functions are easy to understand, as is the output. A function to compute the sine of a real number will take a numerical argument and return a numerical value. By common convention, the name of this function will always be "sin." The type of the argument to the function and its return value are also specified in the library.

The details of the implementation of functions provided in mathematical libraries are hidden from a user. The use of these functions is easily understood by a person wishing to use the mathematical library, assuming that the person is knowledgeable about the application area in which he or she wished to write programs using this library.

The mathematical library offers all the essential features for software reuse for several reasons:

- The area under consideration is well understood. Many people understand the basic mathematical principles on which the library is based.

- The algorithms for computation of the desired mathematical quantities are well understood, the source code has been tested thoroughly, and the code for the implementation of the algorithms does not get changed frequently. The code in mathematical libraries is therefore of high quality and is relatively error-free.

- The information content of nearly every function included in the mathematics library is well matched to a mathematical concept in both size and functionality. Source code for functions is generally very short, often less than a page.

- There is minimal interaction between the different modules of the mathematics library. The interfaces are clearly documented and understood.

- In contrast to developing a new library, reuse offers substantial savings (in terms of cost and time) whenever we wish to use the existing modules in a program.

The rationale of this example of software reuse is easy to understand, even for a novice in the area. What is harder to understand is the appropriateness of software reuse in other areas that do not have as clear a potential for reuse. We will explore these issues in the next few sections.

To broaden the scope of this discussion, we will introduce the term *software artifact,* which is commonly used in the software reuse literature. A software artifact is some component of a software system at some phase of the software life cycle. Clearly, a source code module is an example of a software artifact. Other examples include requirements, designs, test plans, test suites, test results, documentation, process and quality metrics, cost estimates, and sets of maintenance reports. The higher levels of the software, especially those that occur at earlier phases of the software life cycle, can be described using either formal or informal methods.

Note that reuse at earlier levels of the software life cycle provides the maximum potential for cost saving because larger portions of the software engineering effort can be either eliminated or done more quickly. If we reuse a set of requirements for a subsystem the later artifacts of the software life cycle (designs, code, test plans, documentation, etc.) are also reused implicitly, thus providing reductions in the cost of these life cycle activities.

You should also note that we have ignored any cost associated with the reuse process. Costs that are explicitly reuse related include acquisition, analysis, component selection, measurement, certification, and maintenance costs. For small, well-understood application domains in which there are only a few, high-level components there are few costs associated with software reuse.

For larger application domains, which are too large or complex to be understood by one person or have too many potentially reusable components, reuse programs are more costly. The need for efficient access to appropriate reusable software artifacts requires some classification scheme and a retrieval mechanism. Implementation of the classification scheme and data entry into a database can be quite costly. Automatic methods are in their infancy and are not generally available in any case. Checking reusable components into and out of a library can also be troublesome and requires some degree of configuration management. For now, we will ignore both the initial cost of setting up a reuse program and the recurring costs of maintaining a reuse library. As noted, cost modeling will be studied in detail in Chap. 5.

Let's summarize the features observed in the previous example of software reuse—the mathematics library:

- The area under consideration is well understood.

- The software is well understood, is tested thoroughly, does not get changed frequently, and is of high quality.

- The information content of a function is well matched to a mathematical concept in both size and functionality.

- The interfaces are clearly documented and understood.

- There is substantial savings (in terms of cost and time) over developing a new software artifact.

All these factors contribute to the degree to which reuse is successful for the mathematics library. The special nature of this library is the standard by which the success of other reuse efforts are measured. This is somewhat unfortunate because many of the comparisons make many relatively successful reuse efforts appear to have had little benefit in terms of cost or quality.

The reason for this apparent lack of savings from reuse is the lack of leveraging of total software life cycle costs. If we can reuse a portion of the code, as we do in a reusable library module, then we reduce the testing and maintenance costs for the module. There is little effort directed toward reuse in the mathematics library because the problem domain encourages a match of the functionality of the library module and the mathematical quantity that is computed by the code. The documentation is also reusable with little effort.

The real payoff in reuse occurs with earlier uses in the life cycle. The analysis of a system to determine the potential for reuse is an absolutely essential step in the software reuse process, and unfortunately this requires the dedication of a considerable amount of resources. We will return to this point many times throughout this book. The technique of analyzing a system for its potential, called *domain analysis,* will be discussed in Chap. 2. Life cycle-based cost estimates that include the overhead of a systematic program of software reuse will be presented in Chap. 5.

1.3   Software Reuse, Rapid Prototyping, and Evolving Systems

The term *software reuse* suggests that there is an archive of reusable software artifacts that can be used as part of the development of new systems. In the most common view of software reuse the software artifacts can be high level such as requirements or design, lower level such as source code modules, or related artifacts such as test plans or documentation. The application domains and environment are relatively stable, and therefore reuse is considered to be appropriate.

However, some application domains and software environments exhibit a somewhat different behavior. These environments have a high degree of productivity because designs and code are shared between systems. We will use the term *donor system* to describe the system from which the artifact was originally created in the case where one system contributes a portion of its software artifacts to another. However, because the systems are themselves evolving, the donor system does not exhibit all the features usually associated with a reuse library.

The motivation for this discussion is the continuing evolution of ground center control systems for spacecraft control at NASA's Goddard Space Flight Center. We will discuss this software development process in detail in Chap. 7 as one of four case studies. In this particular environment, a central core of reusable software has developed over several years, with various spacecraft missions using different releases of this software to meet the special scientific needs of the individual spacecraft. The central core has evolved as a stand-alone system used in simulators and also as a support system to meet different projects' specific needs.

Note that this situation has considerable overlap with, but is not identical to, the rapid prototyping or spiral models of software development. Here the central core is not a throwaway prototype but is an integral part of several ongoing projects. However, there are a sufficient number of similarities for us to be able to apply some of the reuse methods and techniques described in this book to the prototyping or spiral software development methodologies.

Even in these rapidly evolving environments some form of software reuse is possible, with considerable opportunities for cost savings. Goldberg and Rubin [GOLD90] summarize the situation well:

> Reuse is also known as a response to the problem of rapid development without losing system robustness. The goal of reuse is to develop a set of abstractions that are not limited to a single software effort. These abstractions or artifacts can be used to make future software systems development more productive while also enhancing quality.

Two incrementally-based software development methodologies, rapid prototyping and the spiral approach, help to point out a common misconception about the cost savings associated with software reuse. If the only effect of a reuse program is to reduce code development effort, then the cost savings will occur only during the development of the code and will be only a small portion of the total cost for the system.

As the reusable component is used in other parts of the system, or in related systems, there is still the development cost savings. This savings is again a small portion of the development costs, and there is no substantial savings unless the effect of reuse is leveraged throughout the software life cycle, regardless of the software development methodology used.

The rapid prototyping and spiral development methodologies offer great opportunities for software reuse. Existing source code, even if not a perfect match for a delivered software product, is often satisfactory for prototypes and proof-of-concept systems.

Unfortunately, realistic cost models are often difficult to create in these situations. Nevertheless, software reuse is very promising in these methodologies in addition to its importance in systems developed using the waterfall life cycle model of software development.

1.4 Typical Duties of Members of a Reuse Team

Many different tasks are performed in a systematic program of software reuse. In this section we will describe some of the most common tasks and recommend some experiences that individuals should have before being given primary responsibility for these tasks.

The tasks described here are heavily weighted toward the front end of the reuse process, with particular emphasis placed on the initial process of domain analysis to determine and classify the application domain and select potentially good candidates for reuse. Depending on the size of the domain, some of these tasks may be performed by the same person, or else it may be necessary for teams to perform each job task. Note that the tasks described in this section will ordinarily be performed in addition to the normal responsibilities of a team of software engineers.

A *domain expert* is an individual who is both experienced and knowledgeable about a particular application domain. He or she must have detailed knowledge about available COTS products and the interface standards they adhere to. There must be at least one domain expert for each application domain.

A *domain analyst* is an expert on the general process of domain analysis. He or she is responsible for the development of the appropriate domain analysis classification scheme and the criteria for selection of potentially reusable components. Determining opportunities for the composition of components into higher-level structures is also an important part of the domain analysis process. The domain analyst will interact with the domain expert as part of this process.

A *domain engineer* is responsible for implementing the domain analysis classification scheme and the selection criteria determined by the domain analyst. This will usually require populating a database of information about reusable components.

A *reuse librarian* is responsible for organizing and managing the reuse library. His or her duties will involve publishing a catalog of library assets and determining appropriate access methods. In addition, he or she will be responsible for configuration management of library assets.

A *reuse asset analyst* is responsible for certifying that the asset meets certain standards for quality, modularity, documentation, and future support. He or she is responsible for determining certification standards within the framework of the organization. (Certification is generally considered to occur after the software artifact has been tested and placed into use.)

A *reuse metrician* is responsible for keeping track of the number of times that projects use components in the reuse library. He or she is also responsible for measuring the amount of reuse in projects that use components from the reuse library. Whenever a new project modifies a software component, the percentage of reuse must be measured and provided for further analysis. The reuse metrician will also keep track of any errors found in reuse library components. In many organizations, this person will often be responsible for other metrics data collection and analysis.

A *reuse economist* is responsible for the development of cost models that accurately predict the total costs of software reuse programs. As such, he or she must be able to estimate the costs of integrating and maintaining reusable software components. He or she will work with the reuse metrician in determining reuse and quality factors in new software projects. The reuse economist will be able to measure the overhead costs of producing reusable software components as well as the reduction in costs realized by the consumer of such components.

A *reuse manager* is responsible for coordinating the activities of the other members of the reuse team. He or she is responsible for reporting to management on the costs and benefits of the reuse program. He or she will also be responsible for allocating resources to the overhead of domain analysis, reuse library management, and to the producers and consumers of reusable components.

Each of these tasks will be described in more detail in Chaps. 2 and 3. We note that there are other, more specialized tasks that may be required in particular reuse situations. For example, special skills will be needed when using the reuse-driven requirements engineering technique introduced in Chap. 2. We will defer a discussion of tasks specific to this approach until then.

1.5   Reengineering and Reuse

The terms *software reengineering* and *software reuse* are often confused. Since there are many different, but related, definitions commonly used in the literature, we will fix our terminology as follows.

Software reuse refers to a situation in which some software artifact is used in more than one project or system. On the other hand, *software reengineering* is a process by which an existing system is transformed to another system that has at least the same functionality as the original system.

Part of the confusion in terminology is the widespread use of the term *business process reengineering* to change the manner in which an organization performs its activities. In this sense, business process reengineering means a revision of the software development process. This issue belongs to the general discussion of software engineering process and as such is beyond the scope of this book. We will note that business process reengineering as applied to software reuse would include the development of a systematic plan of software reuse. This systematic plan might involve software reengineering in many instances or it could be confined to evaluation of existing software artifacts, their organization into reuse libraries, and the proper and consistent use of software components in these reuse libraries.

Software reengineering involves an examination of a system to determine what its functionality is, how it is designed, how it has been constructed, and how the organization of the system might be reengineered, or changed, into another system. We will provide some hypothetical illustrations to help the reader understand the software reengineering process and be able to recognize some situations that might make reengineering worthwhile.

The first case that we will consider involves application software that was developed for an older generation of personal computers. The software filled a perceived need of the user community. However, the application had a text-based interface and made use of overlays to circumvent the limited amount of memory available on the original generation of personal computers.

In any event, the software lost most of its market share, and a major revision was needed to include a graphical user interface (GUI) and much more functionality. To keep its base of current users, any new system must be data-compatible with the existing one.

In this case, the reengineering process includes the following options:

- Develop a new system from scratch that has the desired new functionality.

- Develop a new system, using as much of the old system as possible.

The second example of the possible problems associated with software reengineering is a system that was satisfactory as a stand-alone system but now has to interface with other software applications because of changing requirements. This might occur if a control system now has to record data using a commercially available database package instead of a proprietary one. The new requirements for interfacing strongly indicate that the existing system must be changed.

In this case, we have a different set of options:

- Change the database interface of the system to match that of the commercially available database package.

- Develop a filter to transform data from the format of the existing software to that of the commercially available database package.

- Rewrite the system entirely to meet the new data format specifications.

As our last hypothetical example, we consider the case of a "legacy system" written in a proprietary language that was implemented only on a single family of computers. Assume now that there are very few, if any, models of this computer now available and that there is no in-house expertise in either the hardware or the software. Any maintenance performed on the software will be corrective because the cost of transporting programmers to the site is prohibitive for any but the most pressing problems.

The problems are obvious: no possibility for improvement of the system at reasonable cost, absolute dependence on the fortunes of a single software/hardware vendor, and skyrocketing costs.

Assuming that the functionality of the system is essential to the goals of the organization responsible for it, the only solution is some sort of reengineering analysis. To make things simple, we will assume initially that the original requirements of the system are available and understood.

This reengineering analysis will include the selection of options that are appropriate, given the goals and resources of the responsible organization. Possible options for this example include:

- Design and implement a new system that meets the existing requirements.

- Port the existing system to a new hardware platform and software environment.

- Understand the existing system and determine which, if any, subsystems or modules can be ported easily to a new hardware platform and software environment.

These choices are typical of the software reengineering process. In each hypothetical situation there was a set of alternatives ranging from minor revisions of the system to complete redesign. Other intermediate choices were often available. There is also a compelling need to change the existing system.

In each case, gaining an understanding of the system was an essential step. Since many legacy systems have nonexistent, incomplete, or inaccurate external documentation, we often have to make our decisions primarily through the analysis of source code and its internal documentation.

Software reengineering is related to software reuse in that an analysis of what portion of the system can be reused is an essential factor in determining the relative costs of different alternatives.

In Chap. 6, we will describe the software reengineering process in depth and present suggestions that can help model the reengineering process and quantify the costs of some of the decisions indicated for these illustrations.

One last word on software reengineering is in order. Occasionally, the process of understanding a system is carried one step further, so that the design of the system can be inferred from the system's responses to selected inputs. This process is often called *reverse engineering*.

1.6 Library Issues

A systematic reuse program will sometimes include creation, classification, and management of a library of reusable software artifacts.

The process of analyzing the software artifacts in an organization and classifying them so that they may be placed into a reuse library classification scheme is part of a general process called domain analysis. This is perhaps the most essential step in software reuse. We will describe it briefly in this introductory chapter and will study it in much more detail in Chap. 2.

There are two basic methods for developing the classification schemes of domain analysis: a bottom-up approach using basic building blocks and a top-down classification scheme developed by exhaustive methods.

A *classification scheme* is needed for a reuse library of any substantial size. Such a scheme must be able to express both hierarchical and syntactical relationships. The classification scheme can be built from the bottom up from basic building blocks; such a scheme is often called a *faceted classification scheme,* and the method is often called *synthesis.*

An alternative is to analyze the relevant universe and to create a top-down scheme by exhaustive methods. This is often called the *enumerative classification scheme* approach [PRIE91].

The elements of the reuse library can be organized by using imperative statements. An *imperative statement* can be represented by triples of the form <*action, object, agent*>. Here, the term *action* refers to the function (or method) used to carry out the action specified in the imperative statement, the term *object* refers to the abstract object being acted upon, and the term *agent* refers to the abstract data type that encapsulates the data structure used for the implementation.

Many reuse libraries for pure object-oriented systems omit the last field (agent) of the triple. However, the use of such descriptions as *buffer, file,* or *tree* for this argument can sometimes improve the quality of a library search.

A set of *synonyms* will be essential when setting up or searching a reuse library. Some sample terms and common synonyms are the following:

Term	Synonyms
add	increment, total, sum
assign	set
input	read, enter, get

We will need an algorithm to search a library of reusable software artifacts and return artifacts that are "near" to the desired artifact. The algorithm can be applied to libraries that consist of software requirements, designs, code modules, test plans, test suites, documentation, or any combination of these.

Finally, the reuse library must be managed. This includes certifying the correctness and performance properties of the potentially reusable artifact as well as employing configuration management to maintain consistency of the reuse library. Reuse library organization and management will be discussed in detail in Chap. 3.

1.7 Potential Disadvantages of Reuse

There are several dilemmas associated with reusability. The first dilemma is the "generality of applicability versus payoff." Many technologies are very general and can be used in a wide range of application domains. From the perspective of the producer of the reusable artifact, this usually results in a much lower payoff for each individually reused module than those systems that are narrowly focused on one or two application domains.

You should note, however, that a small, flexible, high-quality sort routine that is used many times can have a large payoff for consumers of this reusable component. As we noted earlier, use of an existing general purpose database such as a digitized representation of the earth may offer considerable cost savings compared to creating a new database.

The second dilemma, component size versus the potential of reuse, is based on the mean size of the component. As a component grows and becomes more complex, the payoff involved in reusing that component increases more than just linearly.

The component becomes more and more specific, which narrows the application and increases the cost of reusing it when modifications are required. This dilemma requires considerable attention. The last dilemma is the cost of library population. Developing a viable reusability system is an investment that does not have an early payoff. Therefore, the process of populating libraries can retard or even block the development of a working reusability system.

There are several operational problems associated with reuse libraries. Four fundamental problems must be addressed:

- Finding appropriate components
  There is more to the finding process than just locating a perfect match. Often similar components must be located because even if a target component must be partially redeveloped, rather than reused as is, it may be close enough to the ideal component to be able to reduce costs and eliminate many defects. The more specific

the larger components become, the less likely they are to be reused in multiple applications. In many cases, it is difficult to find a perfect match.

With highly specialized modules, we must examine many modules carefully and in great detail for reuse to be effective. On the other hand, if the components are so abstract that they capture only one aspect of an algorithm, only a relatively small search is needed, and the problem of finding components would then be minor.

- Understanding components
  The understanding process is required whether a component is to be modified or not. A proper model of the component's execution must exist in any reuse system, regardless of the underlying technology chosen for its implementation.

- Modifying components
  Components can spawn, change, and evolve into new components with the changing requirements. It is not realistic to expect that we can build a system that allows significant reuse without modifying some portion of the components. The percentage of modification must be determined insofar as it is used as an input to cost and quality models. Few tools are available to help modify components.

- Composing components
  The composition process introduces the most challenging requirements for components. There must be the ability to represent composite structures as higher-level, independent entities with well-defined computational characteristics as well as the capability to further combine these composite structures.

According to an anonymous project manager, "People think that source code modules can be thrown into libraries and reused whenever they need them, but this is not the case." It is clear from this statement that there is a major education issue entailed in software reuse. Managers at all levels must be convinced of the importance of reuse activities. Education of managers, analysts, and programmers is necessary before there can be major savings through systematic programs of software reuse.

It might be a good educational technique for software engineering students to have programming exercises and contests in which teams are given a set of requirements and component libraries and for which the objective is to construct a system that meets the requirements while writing the smallest amount of new code.

McClure [McCL92] points out that one of the reasons for limited success in software reuse across projects is a lack of up-front planning for reusability. Allowing for the costs of a systematic reuse program is especially important. Clearly, an effort is required to understand the desired component and determine related, useful components in a reuse library.

There are several factors that inhibit the advancement of reusability technology:

- Representation technology
  There is no representation for any level of software artifact (architectures, requirements, designs, source code, test cases, documentation, reusable data, etc.) that fosters reusability across a wide range of domains.

- Lack of a clear and obvious direction
  There is no specific strategy defined as an approach to optimizing reuse. In the meantime, management is unlikely to define a definite approach until a "best path" is fairly obvious. It is clear, however, that reuse is a multiorganization problem, and it requires massive work before there is a considerable payoff.

- The "not invented here" (NIH) syndrome
  This is a relatively easy problem to solve, at least for programmers. The issue depends on management's criteria for rewarding reuse. Once management establishes the proper culture, developers rapidly learn that reuse does not inhibit their creativity. They are now free to attack more challenging problems. Once this fact is realized, resistance to reuse often disappears. As an independent software engineer put it, "We really have no choice. With the cost pressures we face, we either push reuse here or else look for a job."

- High initial costs
  Absence of reusable library components prevents reuse technology from spontaneously arising. This effort requires a large commitment and considerable initial and recurring costs [BIGG87]. Note the difference in viewpoint of a producer and a consumer of reusable software artifacts.

- Legal and contractual issues
  There are many legal issues, especially in safety-critical applications. These will be discussed in the next section.

1.8 Legal and Contractual Issues of Software Reuse

There are several potential problem areas that arise when software reuse is practiced. They can be grouped into four categories:

- Liability in case of failure of a reused component

- Ownership of reused components

- Maintenance costing

- Security of potentially reusable components

Some of these issues are easy to understand, at least on a superficial level. Since neither the author nor most readers are lawyers we will not attempt to describe any of the finer technical points of contractual issues related to reuse.

Consider the case of a life-critical application such as a heart-monitoring system used in a critical care unit. Suppose that the display subsystem is intended to flash a warning on a screen and sound an alarm when the heart rate falls below a certain level. Suppose also that this subsystem is obtained by setting parameters within a commercially available product (a clear case of reuse).

Suppose also that the system fails because it enters an unexpected state in a reused module that was not tested by the original software engineers who created it and the patient being monitored dies or becomes irreparably brain damaged because of the failure of this subsystem.

Who is responsible for the failure? Is it the original team and organization that built the system, or is it the team and organization that incorporated it into the life-critical application? There are few precedents in the software area at this time, and most licensing agreements attempt to protect the creators of systems.

A second question arises concerning the ownership of software components that are reused. Without a clear understanding of who owns what system, later developers might be reluctant to reuse other systems. The ownership of components is also reflected in the level of bureaucratic and organizational difficulties. We will illustrate this point with a hypothetical example.

Suppose you were designing a system for which a spelling checker and a related dictionary were necessary. If you admired the relevant utilities available with your word processor, you might ask the owner of the copyright for permission to use the subsystem. It is not obvious that the copyright owner would be able to grant this permission. It might be difficult to determine the original cost of the spelling checker and dictionary and thus determine a price for the use of this portion of the word processor. It might take a relatively long time to secure this cost information, thereby causing deadlines to be missed. In this case, reuse of this spelling subsystem would be difficult.

Note that the difficulties related to determining the cost of ownership of components are related to the "NIH" syndrome.

Appropriate costing for maintenance purposes is often difficult. Consider the extreme case of the use of influential software to create a system as is, without any modifications. Let us assume that the COTS software has already been integrated with the desired system and that the combined system has been released for use. The maintenance costs for the combined system were probably modeled by largely ignoring the cost of maintaining the commercial system, assuming that the maintenance cost for this system would be amortized across many users. If the commercial system has an unexpected failure, causing the combined system to fail, where does the money come from to fix or work around the failed commercial system? It was not a budgeted item in the original maintenance cost estimate. In addition, who is responsible for lost revenues for the combined system?

In the case of a system that uses a COTS product, it is relatively clear who is responsible for fixing bugs in the COTS. Responsibility for error fixing and maintenance is much less clear in other environments. Determining responsibility for documentation and configuration management is also a problem.

The final legal or contractual barrier to reuse comes from security issues. Many software problems are solved and resolved many times in many different environments because the developers are constrained from communicating with each other. The following quotation is from a NASA security handbook [MOD92] that established four levels of security:

Level 0. Sensitivity/criticality level 0:
(1) Would have a negligible impact on NASA's missions, function, image, or reputation. The impact, while unfortunate, would be insignificant and almost unworthy of consideration.
(2) Probably not result in the loss of a tangible asset or resource.

Level 1. Sensitivity/criticality level 1:
(1) Would have a minimal impact on NASA's missions, function, image, or reputation. A breach of this sensitivity level would result in the least possible significant unfavorable condition with a negative outcome.
(2) Could result in the loss of some tangible asset or resource.

Level 2. Sensitivity/criticality level 2:
(1) Would have an adverse impact actively opposed to NASA's missions, function, image, or reputation. The impact would place NASA at a significant disadvantage.
(2) Result in the loss of significant tangible asset(s) or resource(s).

Level 3. Sensitivity/criticality level 3:

(1) Would have an irreparable impact, permanently violating the integrity of NASA's missions, function, image, or reputation. The catastrophic result would not be able to be repaired or set right again.
(2) Result in the loss of major tangible asset(s) or resource(s) including posing a threat to human life.

These security issues illustrate why, for example, the software used to control spacecraft is much less likely be part of a generally available reuse library, than is, say, a set of routines to manipulate a stack of integers. The software used to control spacecraft is at level 2 or 3 of the four NASA security levels, depending on the situation.

1.9   The Current Status of Software Reuse

There are three common ways to estimate the current status of software reuse: from the basic understanding of the technology by research experts, from the state of the art in reuse research and pilot reuse projects, and from the state of the practice in government and industry. We will describe each of these views of software reuse in turn.

1.9.1   Basic understanding

From the standpoint of basic understanding of reuse technology, only an informal and incomplete picture of what to reuse and how to reuse it is available. Reuse experts are only beginning to characterize the total scope of information that can be utilized in software construction. Intensive research is needed to enhance the capabilities to capture, modify, and reuse a wide range of information at different stages in the software development process. This is true regardless of the software development paradigm (classic waterfall model, rapid prototyping, spiral model, etc.) that is used.

Research is especially needed in the following areas:

- Determination of proper search methods for reuse libraries. It is not clear if new reuse-specific search methods are needed or if standard library science techniques can be applied. If both approaches work, it is not clear which of the two is more efficient.

- Representation methods that are both flexible enough to incorporate existing representations and powerful enough to allow capture of appropriate knowledge.

- Accurate cost models that take into account COTS products and reuse of artifacts at multiple life cycle levels and describe both consumer and producer reuse.

1.9.2   State of the art

From the standpoint of the state of the art, there are a sufficient number of reusable software artifacts that have already been applied at least in prototype form and even more that are ready for application. Prototyping is characterized as a proposed solution to the problem of balancing the increasing demands on developers with the decreasing ability to articulate the user's requirements [GOLD90].

Prototyping is an easy way to modify the software to meet changing or unclear user requirements. Modern programming languages, such as C++, Ada, and fourth generation languages, provide enhanced capabilities for encapsulating and reusing small chunks of code.

C++ and Ada have many object-oriented features. It is natural to consider objects as potentially reusable software artifacts. Indeed, reusability is touted as one of the major benefits of the object-oriented programming paradigm. It is relatively easy to reuse small source code modules that contain objects and functions that perform transformations on these objects. A state-of-the-art reuse program in an object-oriented software development environment would also have reusable object-oriented designs.

Object-oriented techniques offer great promise for reuse because of the enforced information hiding of good object-oriented software.

The REBOOT (REuse Based on Object-Oriented Techniques) project is a good example of a systematic approach to object-oriented software [KARL95]. This project is carried out by a consortium of several companies in Denmark, France, Germany, Italy, Norway, Spain, and Sweden. The effort includes process improvement, extensive use of metrics, and reusable objects.

Although specialized, purely object-oriented module interconnection languages are not widely used, they can contribute to a solid understanding of how to put modules of code together. Methods for organizing large library components to facilitate their retrieval are clearly understood and are ready for application. Programming and detailed design techniques that focus on the manipulation of objects rather than the flow of control are understood and have the capability of providing a convenient base for reuse.

Some fundamental issues are especially important in current research:

- Methods for evaluation of software artifacts for their potential reuse

- Well-defined, practical methods and guidelines for the composition of reusable software artifacts into higher-level components that can be used in software architectures

- Methods for evaluation of the quality of reusable software artifacts and their effect on systems that use them either as is or with some level of modification

- Methods of monitoring usage of reusable software components. This is becoming especially important with the growth of the Internet and the availability of public, electronically available reuse libraries. Note that the Internet problems are similar to the problems that commercial publishers have with electronic publication.

1.9.3 State of the practice

There are two kinds of reuse currently being practiced: systematic and ad hoc. Ad hoc reuse is dependent upon the informal knowledge of individuals about available software artifacts. The effects of ad hoc reuse on cost or system quality cannot be measured. More importantly, any successes of an ad hoc reuse effort cannot be repeated. We will not discuss ad-hoc reuse any more in this book.

The benefits of reuse are best achieved from a systematic software reuse approach. This involves the analysis, measurement, and management of software systems and reuse libraries introduced in this chapter and discussed at length later in this book. In short, systematic software reuse is a disciplined process of software development that makes use of existing software artifacts whenever they are available and their reuse is practical.

A systematic reuse strategy is based on two related processes: the design and development of reusable components and the utilization of reusable components. To promote these processes, managerial and technical support are needed. Managers should strive to adjust the manner in which they supervise, review, and compensate software developers. By the same token, developers must learn to overcome any personal biases they have against reusing artifacts they did not develop. Developers must understand what is involved in developing and utilizing these reusable components.

Unfortunately, most software development environments do not follow these guidelines. This is true to a lesser extent even for those organizations that are beginning software reuse programs. Clearly, some of the problems with software reuse are as much managerial as technical.

The situation is summarized by the general comments of Goldberg and Rubin [GOLD90]:

> Managers need to change the reward structures so that reuse is a requirement. Writing new lines of code when a reusable component exists should be considered unacceptable. When a software engineer's code is

accepted for the corporate library and the librarian monitors its use and notes high usage, the engineer has made a contribution as significant as that of a salesperson meeting a quota—the engineer has saved the organization time and money, which means more profit on the bottom line. Of course, this savings will be measured after one or two years, not immediately. A long-term organizational commitment must be made to the reuse process if it is to pay off.

By itself, the driving force of economic issues will continue to push organizations toward heavier applications of reuse in production software development. Another drive, creativity, is often wasted on re-creating designs of code and pushing forward to new levels of functionality, reliability, efficiency, or some other quality of a system that could just as well have been realized through reuse. As Freeman observed in 1983 [FREE83], "The highly competitive product design arena will push developers into realizing that the competition lies on heavier reuse not continuously reinventing old structures."

Freeman also reassessed the state of the practice of software reuse in 1983 [FREE83]: "In spite of the long-time existence of languages and methods that facilitate reuse, and the demonstration in several convincing ways of the economic value and practicality of production use of reuse concepts, very few organizations that produce software have any organized efforts to exploit what we already know how to do." Unfortunately, this statement is in large part still true today. An examination of the more recent references indicates some real successes in small, local environments, but few large organizations have defined detailed companywide systematic reuse processes. For example, Hewlett-Packard's reuse efforts at this time encourage local software groups of different sizes to experiment to determine reuse practices that are appropriate for their applications and business [COLL95]. Therefore, we recommend that organizations that are beginning *systematic* reuse practices start at the source code level.

Reuse at the code and reusable data levels is recommended as the first step in a systematic reuse program because of the effort needed just to produce stable, tested code. It is much easier to classify code and to create, organize, and maintain reuse libraries that consist solely of source code components or a few databases than it is to do so for multiple software artifacts such as designs, requirements, plans, and the like.

Object-oriented approaches have not led to the cost savings and reuse promised by some proponents. A major goal of object-oriented programming was to enforce modularity and thereby promote abstraction. The difficulty of obtaining major savings is relatively clear by now—it is hard to develop an abstract view of software systems of any size, whether by object-oriented or procedural methods. In general, the savings that can be identified as being due to object-oriented programming have occurred in source code development and have not been appreciable because they were not applied earlier in the software life cycle.

We should note that the current state of object-oriented programming is likely to change. The availability of high-quality software components such as the Booch components available from Rational Corporation or the Grace components available from EVB Corporation are beginning to have an effect on software development. The popular recognition of the effect of object-oriented programming in computer science education is indicated by the prominence given to a panel discussion at the 1996 Computer Science Conference sponsored by the Association for Computing Machinery (ACM). The panel addressed the changes in the data structures course, which is usually the second course in computer science, caused by the ready availability of standard software components to perform most of the operations that were usually coded by hand previously.

As we will see in Chap. 5, the major savings of a systematic program of software reuse will occur when higher-level software artifacts such as requirements, designs, and architectural frameworks are reused. This cannot be done without major investments in process improvement.

Consider the REBOOT project mentioned earlier. It has emphasized process improvement and an advanced process according to the Software Engineering Institute's Capability Maturity Model (CMM). It has developed some techniques for efficient classification of software and some standards for reusable objects. All these activities require a large investment that cannot possibly pay off when their costs are amortized over a few new software development projects. The effective savings will come in future projects after the groundwork has been done in developing the proper object models, object libraries, and higher-level views.

Any approach that is focused at the source code level will not result in maximal cost savings. Thus, beginning software reuse projects are likely to reduce costs by only a small amount.

Note that there are additional problems when object-oriented source code is reused. For example, the existing code should be encapsulated sufficiently so that there are very few conflicts possible. An example of a possible conflict is the use of a method name in two or more parents of a new class.

Finally, management support used to encourage systematic software reuse for both producers and consumers, and training techniques to facilitate reuse are not common in most organizations.

Summary

Reuse provides a great opportunity for improving the quality of software systems while simultaneously reducing their cost. It is based on the idea of reusable components that are used in the same way that an electrical engineer selects components for systems. Reuse projects have been available since the late 1960s.

Software reuse can be done at many levels of the software life cycle. Reusable software artifacts include software architecture, requirements, designs, source code, data sets, test plans, test cases, test results, and documentation. The greatest cost savings occur when there is the greatest life cycle leverage by reusing designs and requirements. The use of COTS software is an important factor in software reuse programs.

Object-oriented techniques offer great promise for reuse because of the enforced information hiding.

One of the most important techniques used for software reuse is *domain analysis*. In domain analysis, a system is examined for the presence of common verbs and nouns, which indicate actions taken on various objects in the system. Domain analysis involves classification of software components.

Software reengineering is related to software reuse in that systems must be understood before they are either reengineered or reused, either in part or as an entirety. However, reengineering usually involves more change than is desired for software reuse.

There are many issues entailed in reuse libraries, including certification of components, configuration management, library access, and approximation methods for selecting appropriate artifacts related to the one desired, if there is no exact match.

There are some disincentives to software reuse. Foremost among them is the difficulty in developing a systematic reuse process, the NIH syndrome, legal and contractual issues, and security issues.

There is a major education issue in software reuse. Managers at all levels must be convinced of the importance of reuse activities. Managers, analysts, and programmers must be educated before there can be major savings through systematic programs of software reuse.

Further Reading

Perhaps the best place to read about software reuse in the 1970s and 1980s is the influential tutorial by Biggerstaff and Perlis [BIGG89]. This tutorial includes several articles on the general topic of software reuse and a large number of articles involving case studies. It contains descriptions of some of the earliest work in the field. It also contains some articles describing related areas such as program transformation.

The May 1994 issue of *IEEE Software* magazine was devoted to the study of software reuse and contains several excellent articles, including an especially helpful article by Frakes and Isoda [FRAK94A].

There are several recent books on software reuse. *Software Reuse* by Hooper and Chester [HOOP91] is the first to consider reuse in a more systematic, nontutorial manner. The book emphasizes reuse in the context of the Ada programming language. The slightly older book by Tracz [TRAC89] is also illuminating. Another recent book by Frakes, *Advances in Software Reuse,* [FRAK93B] provides an up-to-date description of many reuse efforts reported at an international conference devoted entirely to software reuse. Lim's book, *Managing Software Reuse,* provides a good description of some of the managerial issues involved in software reuse [LIM95].

The book on software reuse edited by Karlsonn [KARL95] describes a systematic approach taken as part of the REBOOT project. This multinational project emphasizes object-oriented approaches.

There are several relevant books that describe topics related to software reuse. Arnold's *Software Reengineering,* [ARNO92] gives an excellent tutorial introduction to software reengineering. Prieto-Diaz and Arango [PRIE91B] have an excellent tutorial introduction to domain analysis, which is the basis for most software reuse efforts.

Survey articles are often the best sources for learning about major research directions. Two excellent recent survey articles by Krueger [KRUE92] and Mili, Mili, and Mili [MILI95] are readily available. Prieto-Diaz also provided a useful article on the status of software reuse in 1993 [PRIE93A].

Since reuse is such an active area of research, electronic information is an extremely important source of current information. For example, the proceedings of the (nearly) annual WISR (Workshop In Software Reuse) conference can be found in PostScript format on the Internet just by searching for the topic "software reuse" on most Internet browsers. The Department of Defense ASSET library of reusable artifacts and related information can also be found through this same search. Many of these sources are described in Chap. 2. A summary of Internet addresses can be found in App. 2.

Most of the newer books on object-oriented design and programming include at least some material on software reuse. The books by Booch [BOOC94], Coad [COAD91], and Leach [LEAC95B] illustrate some of these ideas. The influential paper by Meyer [MEYE87] was one of the first to illustrate the potential of object-oriented programming in software reuse. The paper by Voas [VOAS95B] has a different view of testability of objects and information hiding.

The interested reader might also consult the recent book by Humphrey [HUMP95], which describes a revision of the software development process from the perspective of an individual programmer. This book stresses the importance of an individual keeping track of his or her levels of reuse when developing a set of exercises that is carefully graduated in difficulty.

Exercises

1. Examine your own personal software development process. Do you always attempt to reuse code, or do you frequently begin coding from scratch? What about reusing requirements, designs, testing information, or documentation?

2. Examine your own organization's software development process. Does it always attempt to reuse code, or do you frequently begin coding from scratch? What about reusing requirements, designs, testing information, or documentation?

3. What reuse libraries, informal or formal, exist in your environment?

4. Discuss some of the issues involved in reusing code that you developed yourself for different environments (and different employers).

5. (*This problem is intended primarily for students.*) Examine all your projects in previous courses, and identify any source code that could have been reused. Develop a scheme for organizing this code.

2

Techniques

In this chapter we describe five techniques that are important components of a systematic program of software reuse. These five techniques are *domain analysis*; *object-oriented analysis, design, and programming techniques*; the *use of standard interfaces*; *designing for reuse* and *using reuse in requirements*; and *metrics*. Many of these techniques should be applied at several points in the software development life cycle, regardless of the software development model used by the organization. For that reason, you should at least skim the material in Sec. 2.3 on object-oriented approaches even if your organization does not currently develop software using the object-oriented paradigm.

Because of the complexity of domain analysis and the difficulty of understanding this topic without a detailed concrete example, we will devote the first two sections to domain analysis. Each of the remaining sections in this chapter will discuss a different topic.

We will focus on the initial stages of a reuse program in this chapter. Reuse library management, testing and certification of software artifacts as being appropriate for reuse, economic models for systematic software reuse, and software reengineering will be discussed in the next four chapters of this book. A discussion of tools to support software reuse will be given in Chap. 8.

Most developers work to achieve a representation that is sufficient for the problem to be solved. The developer wishing to produce reusable components must go beyond sufficiency to measure completeness. Ideally, reuse implies use of the abstraction without changes or at least with minimal changes. The purpose of domain analysis is to identify the abstraction in a system, even if the abstraction is not explicitly stated. If the implementation is not complete, time will be devoted to completing the abstraction rather than the application development.

Researchers are working in the areas of domain analysis, standard interfaces, object-oriented techniques, reuse-oriented design approaches, and metrics to provide techniques that will allow designers to systematically address topics such as the completeness of an abstraction. The systematic use of these techniques should greatly improve the quality of reusable software artifacts produced and yield considerable cost savings after a systematic program of software reuse is implemented.

2.1 Domain Analysis

Most researchers in software reuse believe that domain analysis is a requirement for a successful reuse program. Domain analysis is a generalization of systems analysis, in which the primary objective is to identify the operations and objects needed to specify information processing in a particular application domain. In addition, domain analysis will precisely identify domains and software artifacts within these domains that are good candidates for reuse. Ideally, one would like to be able to create domain-specific languages that permit specifications to be written in terms meaningful to the domain [FREE83].

In this section we present the fundamentals of the domain analysis technique. A detailed example will be given in Sec. 2.2.

McClure [McCL92] defines domain analysis as the "process of discovering objects and operations common across systems within the same domain." Focusing on the problem domain rather than the solution domain is what promotes reuse.

Prieto-Diaz [PRIE91B] gives a slightly different definition. "Domain analysis can be conceived of as an activity occurring prior to systems analysis and whose output (such as a domain model) supports systems analysis in the same way that systems analysis output (such as a requirements analysis and a specifications document) supports the systems designer's tasks."

Even when a company or organization uses rapid prototyping to solve a problem, discarding earlier prototypes, there are often many problems that involve similar entities. Specializing existing designs often requires far less development and testing effort than does developing the structures from scratch.

The object-oriented paradigm benefits some problem domains more than others. This paradigm can easily handle problems that use multiple instances of certain abstractions. As with designs, specializing existing classes reduces development and testing effort. Objects with multiple instances become more powerful yet are easily controlled by the independence and self-contained nature of the different instances.

Established standards in the domain contribute to reusability success. When there are enforced standards, many things can happen:

- The problem of reusing source code within a domain becomes more manageable since the domain is more likely to be narrow.

- Components in the library have a higher probability of being reused than if no standards are used.

- There are few data types and the reusable parts are small, therefore they are more likely to be reused in multiple applications.

- The cost of development and maintenance is reduced because there is less need to write filters or glueware to interface between different components.

Since the domain is well understood the amount of time it would take to create a reusable library is reduced. Also, by understanding the domain so well, the functions of a component can be understood with only the slightest description of the function.

The fact that the domain is largely static and does not change or is not expected to change for long periods of time means that the library of parts can be quite stable. In this situation, organizations can invest in the domain over a much longer period of time. Biggerstaff and Perlis state "the worst kind of domain for reusability is one where the underlying technology is rapidly changing" [BIGG89].

We take a slightly different view of reuse in evolving systems. Even if the underlying technology is changing, some degree of cost saving can be achieved by proper monitoring, configuration management for reuse libraries, and assessment of the true costs of technology insertion. Domain analysis is essential in this environment as well as in more stable ones.

Research has not yet determined the optimal strategy for the performance of domain analysis. The difficulty is that realistic situations often require the use of tools, and it is hard to perform experiments when the underlying software environments are different. However, there are some common features of successful domain engineering projects that can be described here.

Regardless of the technical details of the definition of domain analysis it is one of the cornerstones of software reuse. We will now describe the domain analysis process.

As we indicated in Chap. 1, a classification scheme is needed for any reuse library. Such a scheme must be able to express both hierarchical and syntactical relationships. Development of a classification scheme is the goal of domain analysis.

There are two basic methods for developing the classification schemes of domain analysis: a bottom-up approach using basic building blocks and a top-down classification scheme developed by exhaustive methods. A bottom-up classification scheme is frequently called a faceted classification scheme. In this case, the domain analysis method is often called synthesis. A top-down method for developing a classification scheme is called an enumerative classification scheme of domain analysis.

Ideally, two parallel, independent domain analysis projects analyzing the same application domain would result in the same classification schemes, with only minor differences in wording and terminology. If everything were perfect in our ideal world of domain analysis, the different actions and objects described in the classification schemes would be synonyms, and it would be easy to map one scheme to the other. (As we mentioned in Chap. 1, it is important to develop a set of synonyms when setting up or searching a reuse library.)

The reality is quite different, unfortunately. The two schemes may reflect the organizational methods (top-down, bottom-up) in which the domain analysis was carried out. This is not an unexpected dichotomy.

For example, a software development methodology based on the best ideas of the 1970s and early 1980s would emphasize top-down approaches and stepwise refinement. On the other hand, a software development methodology based on the best ideas of the late 1980s and the 1990s would emphasize reuse and might be bottom-up in approach, especially if the only reuse is at the software source code component level and not at the level of reusable software architectures and systems.

The reason for this is that domain analysis attempts to apply grammatical structures of a natural language such as English to each of the following:

- Requirements and internal documentation for the system, which are probably written in a natural language rather than in a formal specification language

- External documentation, which is likely to be in the form of combined text and graphics, often in the format of a CASE tool

- Designs, which may or may not be written in a natural language pseudocode

- Source code, which is written in one or more high-level programming languages. Lower-level languages may also be used in portions of the source code

- Test plans, test data, and test results, which are written in a combination of a natural language, relatively random data organization, and mathematical tables

Even if, as our high school teachers taught us, sentences could be parsed unambiguously, there is little hope of parsing documents in each of the other languages in a way that is consistent across all possible interpretations. Thus, there is an inherent ambiguity in the parsing process of domain analysis.

Fortunately, this inherent ambiguity is not a problem because the reuse library access schemes frequently will have some criteria for determining the "best match" of a library component to a requirement, if no "perfect match" is found. We will therefore accept the fact that we cannot have a perfect classification scheme and continue with the discussion of the domain analysis process.

As described in Chap. 1, the elements of the reuse library can be organized by using imperative statements. An imperative statement can be represented by triples of the form *<action, object, agent>*. The term *action* refers to the function (or verb or method) used to carry out the action specified in the imperative statement, the term *object* refers to the abstract object being acted upon, and the term *agent* refers to the abstract data type that encapsulates the data structure used for the implementation.

Many reuse libraries for pure object-oriented systems omit the last field (agent) of the triple. However, the use of such descriptions as *buffer, file,* or *tree* for this argument can sometimes improve the quality of a library search. As we will see in the next section, it is sometimes appropriate to add another field to be analyzed as part of an imperative statement.

The terminology is a strong indicator of the influence of object-oriented approaches on reuse. This is probably no accident. The formal study of systems using domain analysis occurred at about the same time as the popularization of object-oriented languages such as C++ and Smalltalk.

We will modify this approach somewhat in the next section when we study a specific example of domain analysis.

2.2   An Example: Domain Analysis of the Linux Operating System

In this section, we will illustrate the technique of domain analysis. We will apply this technique to a system that is essentially in the public domain—the Linux operating system (named after its inventor, Linus Torwalds). This example has the advantage that the source code is available from the Internet using anonymous `ftp` from several sites, including `research.att.com`. In addition, source code for the Linux system is available on CD-ROM. The CD contains documentation and advice for system administration and other utilities.

Since the source code is available you can perform some of the analyses yourself, reinforcing the ideas presented in this section. This is not possible with proprietary systems, which have typically been the targets of domain analysis.

Domain analysis involves some sort of a classification scheme to organize the representational data observed. The faceted classification schemes described in the first chapter are an example of this approach. We will describe domain analysis in sufficient detail to illustrate the process of applying it to a realistic situation.

Linux is an attempt to rewrite the UNIX kernel to be consistent with some current thinking about modularization of operating systems. UNIX is a multitasking, multiple-user operating system based on two fundamental concepts: processes and files. Every entity in UNIX falls into one of these categories. It is the most common multitasking operating system and is available on many hardware platforms.

One of the reasons for the popularity of UNIX among computer scientists is that its source code was originally made available to universities, and thus many people became knowledgeable about its organization and internal workings. Unfortunately, the UNIX kernel (the part that must remain in memory) has grown considerably over the years, and many systems designers believe that a smaller kernel would be more efficient. This is a major factor in the development of Linux.

Many versions of Linux were available on the Internet before version 1.0, which is generally considered to be the first stable version of the system. We will only consider domain analysis of version 1.0 in this section.

The Linux project is intended to interface with the applications programs and utilities written by the Free Software Foundation's GNU project. The intention is to have a complete system that exhibits UNIX-like behavior but that is in the public domain and has source code freely available for modification.

The Linux system is written in the C programming language. It does not attempt to incorporate any object-oriented features into the operating system kernel. The reasoning behind this decision was that the Linux system is intended to mimic UNIX functionality, not to introduce new technology.

The decision to avoid C++ and most object-oriented features has interesting ramifications for operating systems. For example, without the availability of general abstractions it becomes difficult to have a general set of queue operations to handle printer spooling queues, ready queues of runnable processes, terminal I/O queues, memory access queues, and disk access queues. Separate insert and delete operations must be developed for each of these types of queues.

At first glance, the avoidance of C++ and most object-oriented features appears to be a design decision that is antithetical to the notions of writing reusable, abstract software components. However, it is consistent with some of the performance issues that need to be addressed in any quality implementation of a multitasking operating system.

We will now describe the organization of the Linux kernel. There are 15 source code files:

```
exit.c
fork.c
info.c
ioport,c
itimer.c
ldt.c
mktime.c
module.c
panic.c
printk.c
ptrace.c
sys.c
time.c
traps.c
vprintf.c
```

In general, there is a major performance issue associated with operating systems. There is also a hierarchy for the speed of memory devices (registers, cache, primary memory, secondary memory such as disks, and tertiary memory such as tapes). Because of these performance issues, we will extend the triples *<action, object, agent>* common to many domain analysis processes to consider quadruples of the form *<action, object, system, medium>*. (It is convenient to use the term "system" instead of "agent.") These four terms are defined next.

The first step in our domain analysis is to place all the essential descriptive words in the Linux operating system kernel into one of the four categories: actions, mediums, objects, and systems.

These categories can be described as follows:

- A *medium* is a physical (or virtual) device on which some object resides.

- An *object* is something that can be placed on the device indicated as an appropriate medium.

- An *action* is an operation that can be applied to some object.

■ A *system* is a collection of one or more devices or objects that controls something.

The first step—placing all the essential descriptive words into one of the four categories—is done by an iterative process of reading through the source code, looking for nouns (mediums, objects, or systems) and verbs (actions). Some of the information is obtained from the names of files, functions, or the available documentation. The only documentation consulted is what is included in the source code files, the guidance provided in some of the newsgroups on the Internet, and brief discussions with my colleague Will Craven at Howard University.

Ideally, there would be an automated tool for examining the code to obtain some of the information. Since we did not have access to such tools at the time this section was written, the information was obtained manually by examining the code.

The initial reading of the code produced the lists given in Table 2.1. Each of the lists is given in alphabetical order, and there is no significance to the fact that some actions, mediums, objects, or systems appear on the same line. Unfortunately, this initial list was inadequate for reuse purposes, primarily because we had placed many of the fundamental constructions in the wrong categories. We revised this list using what should be called the "fundamental sentence of domain analysis." This sentence is as follows:

To do action A to object O that resides on medium M is the responsibility of system S.

Placing each of the constructs in the first set of lists (Table 2.1) into this sentence is the major goal of the domain analysis process. (Note that more traditional domain analysis processes will omit the information about the medium used in the system under consideration.)

This fundamental sentence makes it easy to see any words that were incorrectly classified. For example, in the initial set of lists (Table 2.1), we had listed a "file" as a medium. That this is an error becomes clear when we construct the following sentence:

To do action A to object O that resides on medium "file" is the responsibility of system S.

Other errors become evident when we repeat this step.

Because of the need for abstraction and information hiding, we should ignore such words as *how, when,* and *where* and any conditions that must occur before an action takes place. Note that this is consistent with the information hiding and increased abstraction that are the goals of object-oriented design and object-oriented programming.

TABLE 2.1   Initial Attempt to Obtain Lists of Actions, Mediums, Objects, and Systems for Linux

Action	Medium	Object	System
add	disk	argument	clock
adjust	file	binary	coprocessor
alert	keyboard	buffer	file system
call	mouse	character	input
check	printer	coprocessor	kernel
create	screen	constant	library
duplicate	tape	digit	logging
emulate		exception	output
evaluate		expression	process
execute		file	retriever
free		function	scheduler
generate		instruction	system config
get		integer	
initialize		list	
load		machine code	
modify		macro	
offset		memory	
overflow		message	
panic		module	
pause		page	
print		permission	
protect		pipe	
read		pointer	
receive		process	
reset		queue	
restore		register	
set		segment	
share		signal	
show		socket	
signal		stack	
stop		structure	
time		table	
trace		timer	
trap			
wakeup			
write			

The next set of lists is given in Table 2.2. To save space, we have included some items that were not originally included but became evident when we continued the analysis.

We now have a reasonable approximation of the relevant actions, objects, mediums, and systems for our example. We now need to determine the relationships among them and look for any overlap, which would then be the basis for possible reuse.

Ideally, this would be done with the aid of a tool. For example, we might search a thesaurus for a set of synonyms for each action and

TABLE 2.2   Second Attempt to Obtain Lists of Actions, Mediums, Objects, and Systems for Linux.

Action	Medium	Object	System
add	disk	argument	clock
adjust	keyboard	binary	coprocessor
alert	mouse	buffer	file system
allocate	printer	character	input
call	screen	coprocessor	kernel
check	tape	constant	library
create		digit	logging
duplicate		exception	output
emulate		expression	process
evaluate		file	retriever
execute		function	scheduler
free		instruction	system config
generate		integer	
get		list	
initialize		machine code	
interrupt		macro	
load		memory	
modify		module	
offset		page	
overflow		permission	
panic		pipe	
pause		pointer	
print		process	
read		queue	
receive		register	
reset		segment	
restore		signal	
set		socket	
share		stack	
show		structure	
signal		table	
stop		timer	
trace			
trap			
wakeup			
write			

then examine the synonym list to see if other actions are used there. As we indicated earlier, we had no tool available to use, and therefore we proceeded manually with the domain analysis process.

We felt that it would have been easier to have the entries in the four columns (actions, mediums, objects, and systems) in alphabetical order. Manually sorting using cut and paste was unattractive, and it was not clear how to use the sort utility available with the word processor used to create the manuscript for this book.

Since we had obtained the original lists by examining a window on an X-terminal attached to a UNIX host, we decided to use the UNIX `sort` utility, together with the UNIX print formatting utility `pr`. Initially, there were four separate files used for the storage of the relevant actions, mediums, objects, and systems for the Linux kernel.

The first step was to sort each of these files using `sort`. This was done with UNIX shell commands such as

```
sort action_file
```

After each of the files was sorted, we combined them into a single file using the `pr` utility. The result of these two steps has been shown in the listing of actions, mediums, objects, and systems in Table 2.2.

The next step was to look for relationships and repetitions between the actions, mediums, objects, and systems. Each similarity presents a possible opportunity for reuse. If there is no similarity then there is no obvious opportunity for reuse within the system itself, and it is likely that the system has been built as efficiently as possible, at least from the standpoint of reuse. If there is no similarity then the reuse will have to appear from a subsequent use of the functions of the system. Note that in each situation, the software components should be entered into a reuse library.

The technique is simple. The first column (action) is numbered. The file containing the columns and the numbered entries is then printed out quadruple-spaced. For each noun entry in a column (mediums, objects, and systems), the numbers of all relevant actions are placed underneath the appropriate entry. The results are then compared. On the original system, the information was given on two sheets of 8½-by-11 paper. Because of the reduced margins necessary here the table is slightly constricted and the spacing has been changed.

The result of this process is given in Table 2.3. Entries in this table can be understood as follows. The number 3 for the "clock" system indicates that one legitimate action for the "clock" is "alert," which occurs in position 3 in the list of actions. Other numbers are interpreted similarly.

It is natural to ask for the level of reusability included in this release of Linux. Using our domain analysis data, we have listed the amount of possible reuse within this version of Linux in Table 2.4. Recall that we have not attempted to consider the number of opportunities for future reuse in systems other than the Linux kernel. Our perspective is only that the creator of the Linux kernel (Torwalds) was a producer of reusable software artifacts, not necessarily a consumer.

We analyzed the source code for the Linux kernel, version 1.0. The approach was to examine the source code only from the perspective of possible reuse within the kernel. We did not consider any interaction of the large set of utilities that were available from the GNU project of the Free Software Foundation with this distribution of the Linux

TABLE 2.3   Final Attempt to Obtain Lists of Actions, Mediums, Objects, and Systems for Linux.

Action	Medium	Object	System
1 add	disk 1,2,3,4,5,6,7, 8,9,10,12,16,17, 18,22,5,26,29,30, 31,34,37	binary 14,17	clock 3,4,5,9,24
2 adjust	keyboard	buffer 1,2,3,6,7,8, 16,18,22	coprocessor 2,3,4, 5,6,9,16
3 alert	memory 1,2,3,4,5, 6,7,8,9,10,12,13, 14,15,16,17,18, 22,24,25,26,27, 29,30,31,32,34, 36	clock 2	file system 1,2,3, 4,5,6,7,8,10,12, 13,15,16,18,22, 24,25,37
4 allocate	mouse	exception	input 1,2,3,4,5,6, 7,8,10,13,14,15, 16,18,22,24,25, 28,30,31,34,37
5 call	printer 6,16,25,26, 32	expression	kernel 1,2,4,5,6, 10,15
6 check	screen 4,6,9,10,12, 18,25,31,34	file 2,3,5,6,7,8,10, 13,15,18,25,28, 29,30,31,34,37	library 6
7 create	tape 1,5,6,8,10,16, 17,18	function 1,2,3,5,6, 7,8,10,13,15,22, 26,28,30,21,34, 37	logging
8 duplicate		instruction 1,5,6, 10,12,15,16,18	output 1,2,3,4,5, 6,7,8,10,13,14, 15,16,18,22,24, 25,28,30,34,37
9 emulate		list 2,3,5,6,7,8,13, 16,18,28,34	process 2,3,4,5,6, 7,8,10,13,15,16, 17,18,22,24,25, 26,27,30,31,34, 36
10 evaluate		macro	retriever 2,4,5,6, 16,18
11 execute		message 1,2,6,10, 14,18	scheduler 2,3,4,5, 6,15,16,25,27
12 free		module 6	system config 2,6,29,30
13 generate		page 1,2,3,4,5,6,7, 16,19,24,27	
14 get		permission 2,6,29,30	
15 initialize		pipe 1,2,3,4,5,6,7, 13,16,18,24,26, 27,30,37	

TABLE 2.3   (*Continued*)

Action	Medium	Object	System
16 interrupt		pointer	
17 load		process 1,2,3,4,5, 6,7,8,10,12,13, 14,15,16,17,18, 22,24,25,26,27, 28,30,31,32,36, 37	
18 modify		queue 1,2,3,4,5,6, 7,8,10,16,37	
19 offset		register content 1, 2,6	
20 overflow		segment	
21 panic		signal 6,15,25,35	
22 pause		socket 1,2,3,4,5,6, 7,8,10,13,16,18, 22,25,28,37	
23 print		table 3,4,5,6,7,8, 10,13,16,18,22, 25,28,37	
24 read		timer 2,3,4,5,6,9, 24	
25 receive			
26 reset			
27 restore			
28 set			
29 share			
30 show			
31 signal			
32 stop			
33 trace			
34 trap			
35 wakeup			
36 write			

kernel. Thus, we may have missed many opportunities for reuse elsewhere in the system.

In Table 2.4, the notation *SLOC* represents the number of *source lines of code* and *NCNB* represents the number of *noncommented, nonblank* lines of code. Descriptions of these metrics are given in App. 1. All measurements are reported on a per-file basis.

Table 2.4 indicates a large potential for reusability for the functions that make up the kernel of the Linux operating system. The opportunities for reuse are probably overstated because of the requirement for operating system performance.

Additional analysis is clearly needed before we can reuse some of these components in a production-quality system. It would be inter-

TABLE 2.4 Opportunities for Reusability in the
Linux Kernel

File	SLOC	NCNB	Possible Reuse (%)
exit.c	458	472	83
fork.c	189	207	100
info.c	19	25	100
ioport.c	116	125	100
itimer.c	95	101	41
ldt.c	74	81	100
mktime.c	14	19	100
module.c	195	208	100
panic.c	13	18	100
printk.c	159	178	100
ptrace.c	316	339	100
sys.c	523	542	100
time.c	244	258	62
traps.c	103	168	96
vprintf.c	204	220	89

esting to evaluate the complete Linux operating system and the entire set of GNU utilities to determine other possibilities for software reuse. Only then could we determine the total amount of actual reuse within these systems.

This additional analysis is clearly not feasible without automated tools to help in the domain analysis process. Nevertheless, the domain analysis process suggests a well-constructed system. This is not surprising considering the typical quality of the software produced by the Free Software Foundation.

2.3 Domain Analysis Revisited

Let's summarize the domain analysis process as carried out in the previous section. We followed five steps to analyze a collection of source code components:

- Essential descriptive words were placed into one of the four categories actions, mediums, objects, and systems. This was done by reading names of files and functions and by consulting the available documentation.

- Each of the four categories was given in alphabetical order.

- We revised this list using the fundamental sentence of domain analysis: *To do action A to object O that resides on medium M is the responsibility of system S.*

- The entries in the four categories were sorted in alphabetical order and placed in separate columns on the same page (or pages for larger systems).

- The relationships and repetitions between the actions, mediums, objects, and systems were determined. Each similarity presents a possible opportunity for reuse.

The terminology suggests that an object-oriented approach to domain analysis is appropriate, even if the system being analyzed was originally written in a procedural programming language. Using an object-oriented technique such as the "fundamental sentence of domain analysis" allowed us to categorize the functionality of components in the kernel of the Linux operating system and to develop a classification scheme as part of the domain analysis process.

In the remainder of this section we will describe some other outputs that are often obtained as a result of a domain analysis process. One of the outputs will be typical of object-oriented systems, and the other will be quite general. We will defer a discussion of general issues for reuse of object-oriented software to the next section.

The first output we describe is a *system architecture*. The system architecture describes how the components are integrated as part of an entirety. This is where our (presumably) expert knowledge of operating systems is useful. A considerable amount of information can be obtained from the individual file names: exit.c, fork.c, info.c, ioport.c, itimer.c, ldt.c, mktime.c, module.c, panic.c, printk.c, ptrace.c, sys.c, time.c, traps.c, and vprintf.c.

For example, the two files printk.c and vprintf.c handle some type of input and output, whether using external devices or computer memory. Process creation and execution tracing are clearly done in the files ptrace.c and fork.c. Similar analyses apply to most other files. A simplified block diagram of the architecture of a portion of the Linux kernel is shown in Fig. 2.1.

A second output of many domain analysis processes is an object model, that is, a set of objects and a listing of all inheritance and all interface relationships between objects. When creating object diagrams for the Linux kernel, we can call on our (presumably) expert knowledge of other versions of the UNIX operating system and assume as a first approximation that there are two basic types of objects in Linux: files and processes.

A portion of an object diagram is illustrated in Fig. 2.2. The diagram is simplified to represent the files in which the source code for the different actions are located. Each of the connection lines in Fig. 2.2 represents an instance of the uses-a relationship.

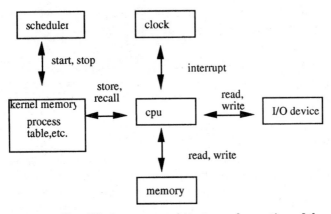

Figure 2.1 Simplified system architecture of a portion of the Linux kernel.

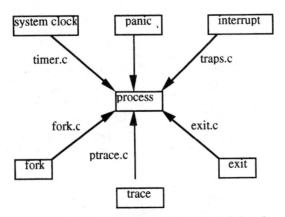

Figure 2.2 A portion of an object model for the Linux kernel.

System architectures and object models can be very useful in conjunction with a classification scheme when examining reusable software artifacts.

2.4 Object-Oriented Approaches

In most object-oriented programming languages (i.e., Smalltalk, C++, Ada, SCOOPS), an abstract, or general, class is an abstraction of some real-world entity. In an object-oriented language, the definition of a class provides a complete list of the functions that can be employed on the elements of the class. The functions belonging to a particular class are called the *member functions* for that class.

An abstract class is a reusable component because it embodies a functionality that is widely usable. The purpose of using abstract classes is to provide support for the reuse of code in quickly developing applications. General classes combined with the specialization power of inheritance provide a development environment that strongly favors reuse.

Perhaps the best way to determine an initial set of objects for a system is to use the has-a relation. The idea is to look for sentences such as

```
object 1 has a particular attribute
```

The attribute given in the has-a relation usually has a set of allowable values.

There are many techniques for developing general classes that are reusable. Use of these techniques results in classes that are abstractions of real-world entities. These techniques also result in classes that provide the basis for deriving new and more specific classes. The resulting classes have a more systematic software development process and a higher degree of generality than those developed without the techniques.

An inheritance relationship between two classes is best described as the is-a relationship. If the sentence

```
object 1 is a object 2
```

makes sense, then the two classes have an inheritance relationship. On the other hand, if the sentence does not seem to make sense, then we do not have a candidate for the is-a relation.

We should list the potential member functions and be alert for any examples of polymorphism. A function is called *polymorphic* if it can be called with different numbers or types of arguments. A common example of polymorphism is the C++ function getline(), which can be used with default arguments. Hence, the calls

```
getline(*stringp, length);
```

and

```
getline(*stringp, length, '\n');
```

will be completely equivalent, since the line-delimiting character '\n' in the second function call is the same as the default value used in the first. The compiler uses the number (and type) of the function's arguments to determine the correct version of the function to use.

The appearance of polymorphism suggests that we have chosen our inheritance relationships properly. If there is no polymorphism in any member function, then we should be suspicious that we have not described the member functions correctly, or at least not in sufficient detail.

The set of potential objects and the descriptions of their member functions should be refined at each step.

There is one final relationship that should be performed to incorporate the objects into a preliminary object-oriented design for a software system. The concern here is that the objects listed should form a complete set of the objects needed for the software system being designed. The relationship we are looking for is the uses-a relation.

We use this relationship by asking if the sentence

```
object 1 uses object 2
```

makes sense for the pairs of objects considered. Every meaningful sentence suggests either a client-server or agent-based relationship and is to be considered as part of the program's design. If we cannot find any instances of this sentence making sense, then there are two possibilities: either the objects are insufficiently specified for us to be able to describe the entire system or else the natural description of the system is as a procedural program controlling objects.

Note that objects can be related to many other objects. Multiple inheritance is possible and so are multiple objects. Thus, the previous steps should be repeated for groups of three objects, four objects, and so on, until the designer feels that the system's essential object-oriented features have been described.

Table 2.5 summarizes the recommended steps for determining objects.

Unfortunately, the techniques described in this section address only structural and organizational issues. Additional support is needed if the classes will be reused. An implementer must be able to locate the class in order to reuse it. Therefore, the documentation must be arranged to aid location of the desired functionality. An alphabetical listing based on class name is not sufficient. Some provision must be made for traversing the inheritance graph so that the various specializations of a class can be located.

In the first volume of the *Journal of Object-Oriented Programming,* Johnson and Foote described a set of rules for developing standard interfaces that can be used to develop general, reusable classes [JOHN88]. These rules, shown in Table 2.6, are to be used in addition to any guidelines for developing classes.

Rule 1 is intended to incorporate the natural recursion in data structures such as trees.

TABLE 2.5   Determination of Objects

1. Choose a candidate to be an object.

2. Determine a set of attributes of the object and their possible sets of values. Use the has-a relation. List all relevant transformations on the object.

3. Develop an initial set of transformations on the object to serve as member functions. The list of attributes and their values provides an initial set of transformations by determining the value of, and assigning a value to, each attribute of an object. Constructor, destructor, and I/O functions should also be included.

4. Determine if there is more than one example of the object. If so, then place the proposed object in a set of potential objects. If not, discard it because it fails the multiple examples test.

5. Apply the is-a relation by considering all sentences of the form
    object 1 is a object 2
    Objects considered for this relation should include the object under development and any other objects believed to be related. (The class library may be consulted during this step of the process.) Each valid sentence should lead to an inheritance relationship. Each inheritance relationship should be illustrated graphically.

6. Use polymorphism and overloading of operators (and functions) to check if we have described the objects in sufficient detail. Check the object description if no polymorphism or overloading is found.

7. Use the uses-a relation
    object 1 uses object 2
    to determine all instances of client-server or agent-based relationships. Use these relationships to determine issues of program design.

8. Review the object, its attributes, member functions, inheritance properties, polymorphism, overloading, and relationships to other objects to determine if the object is complete in the sense that no other functions, attributes, or relationships are necessary.

9. Repeat steps 2 through 8 for all combinations of relevant objects (triples, quadruples, and so on) until the object's role in any proposed system has been described adequately.

TABLE 2.6   Development of Class Hierarchies

Rule	Description
Rule 1	Introduce recursion when appropriate
Rule 2	Eliminate case analysis
Rule 3	Reduce the number of arguments
Rule 4	Reduce the size of methods
Rule 5	Make class hierarchies deep and narrow
Rule 6	Make the top of the hierarchy abstract
Rule 7	Minimize accesses to variables
Rule 8	Make subclasses specializations
Rule 9	Split large classes
Rule 10	Factor implementation differences
Rule 11	Separate methods that do not communicate
Rule 12	Send messages to components instead of self
Rule 13	Reduce implicit parameter passing

Rule 2 suggests that a class should not include a case statement that takes differing actions based on the type of an argument. "For example, a draw procedure with multiple actions depending on whether the argument is a triangle, square, etc., is contrary to the object-oriented paradigm." These pieces of functionality should be removed and placed in separate subclasses for each type.

Rule 3 serves to reduce the size of interfaces, as does *rule 4*. Rule 4 also makes the individual methods (transformations of the object, also known as member functions) easier to understand and reuse.

Unfortunately, *rule 5* is somewhat controversial. Some recent experiences testing object-oriented programs indicate that class hierarchies should be broad and not deep. See Booch [BOOC94] for more information.

Rule 6 addresses the placement of logic. The top class in a hierarchy should provide a general description of the functionality of the subclasses. It will not ordinarily be a parent of a set of instances.

As stated in *rule 7,* access to instance variables should be only through member functions. Even functions within the same class definition should access the variables of that class only through the accessory functions. This can eliminate any dependency on the data representation.

Rule 8 recommends using specialization as a guiding principle for deriving classes. Many languages allow subclasses to override inherited methods. The perceived need to override inheritance indicates that the newly derived subclass is not a true subclass.

Rule 9 increases modularity at the expense of more interconnections.

Rule 10 states that if a set of subclasses of a class all implements the same function but in two separate ways, a new level of classes should be inserted between the class and its subclasses. Two classes should be developed as subclasses of the original class, and each should serve as a superclass for one of the two sets of subclasses.

The purpose of *rule 11* is to allow noncommunicating modules to be independent functions. Such functions generally cause little or no difficulty when integrated into larger systems.

Rule 12 encourages addressing components rather than the object as a whole. By sending messages to a component instead of the whole object, the component can be replaced by any compatible object to provide different functionality.

The last rule, *rule 13,* warns against implicit parameter passing. When attempting to split one class into two classes, methods that access the same instance variable may also be split between the two new classes. This practice could lead to the undesirable situation of using the instance variable as a parameter.

Following these thirteen rules can lead to classes that are suitable for software reuse. Note that these rules are by no means standard. For example, a different set of rules can be found in Leach [LEAC95A]. Other information can be found in Karlsonn [KARL95].

There is one point that should be made about the design of classes in object-oriented programs. It is likely that classes in such programs have not been tested in the same way that functions in procedurally organized programs are usually tested. Much of the confidence in the use of these classes arises from the high level of abstraction, especially in the use of abstract classes (in C++ those with only virtual functions) and the likelihood that the classes have been reused many times. It therefore makes sense to minimize the possibility of interconnections between different objects.

We suggest following the observations of Booch [BOOC94] that most object-oriented programs benefit from being designed with a few broad, shallow families of classes. This suggestion about shallow class families means that the longest inheritance chain between a base class and a class that is derived from it should not be very deep. The restriction to a few families of classes (and hence only a few base classes) implies that the impact of any changes to the base class for any family of classes will be minimal for the entire system.

Of course, we wish to minimize the interfaces between classes and to have all classes be as coherent as possible. Parnas, Clements, and Weiss [PARN85] list several goals of the modular structure of a complex system. The object is the module-level structure in an object-oriented system. The interfaces of an object present the public face of that object. These goals can be used to judge the quality of the interfaces presented by an object.

Goals for modular reuse:

- The module's structure should be simple enough to be understood.

- One should be able to change the implementation of a module without interfering with other modules. The more likely it is that a change will be needed, the less the impact should be on the module.

- One should be able to understand a module's responsibility without understanding its operation. A reader with a well-defined concern should be able to locate the responsible module.

- There should be a small enough number of submodules to easily argue that there is no overlap; but all possibilities are covered.

- Most classes have a small number of methods, making it easy to understand the structure of the object. An object-oriented design principle says that if too many methods are present then the object should be decomposed into two or more new objects using inheritance.

- If all clients have used only the interface of the object in their implementation then it is possible to change the implementation without affecting the client classes. If the interface of the class includes a complete set of functionalities, then there should be few changes to the object that will affect the interface. For object-orientation to be successful, class implementers must take the time to fully implement a class rather than just provide those operations required for the current project.

We will not pursue these issues further but will instead be content with a brief listing of some features of high-quality modular objects.

The completeness of the interface will be related to the definition of the object itself. If designers cannot agree on the full functionality of the class, then major changes may require the introduction of new operations or the division of one function into several.

Given meaningful function names, a software engineer should be able to obtain a clear understanding of the functionality of the object from its interface.

Function names should use common terminology in the field and should require the expected arguments.

The names of classes should be descriptive. As we stated earlier, if the name is not descriptive of or meaningful about the complete functionality, the object should be decomposed into multiple classes.

There should not be a large number of subclasses derived from any one class. This often results from providing one subclass for each of several types as opposed to deriving a new functionality. A small number of subtypes should make it easy to observe the coverage of all the subclasses.

Reusable components should be self-contained and portable. The software base must be easily extensible to allow the evolutionary growth of the available components. One way of achieving this is by developing tools to browse, select, and retrieve components from the software base efficiently [LUQI88].

2.5 Standard Interfaces

The use of standard interfaces is absolutely essential for software reuse. Without standards, there is no way to enforce information hiding between modules.

Standards can be international, national, or local to the organization. They can also be as specific as the interface defined for a particular COTS product. Clearly, the more general the standard the more likely that the software component can interface with other components and therefore the greater the chance of reuse.

The simplest way to get reuse is to have the software written in the latest standard version of the implementation language, as soon as appropriate compilers and tools become available. It probably doesn't make sense to rush to the newest version of an implementation language if the support environments are of lower quality than those that the developers are used to using in the earlier version of the language.

Newer versions of languages generally include more support for software engineering. This is clearly the case in the FORTRAN world (FORTRAN 90 versus FORTRAN 77 versus FORTRAN IV), the C world (ANSI C versus classic Kernighan & Ritchie C), the Ada world (Ada95 versus Ada83), and in most other languages. For example, FORTRAN 77 includes several structured programming concepts that are not available in FORTRAN IV, and ANSI C contains provisions for function prototypes that are not present in classic Kernighan & Ritchie C.

Ada95 (formerly known as Ada9X) includes much more support for both object-oriented programming and distributed computing than did the older-language version, Ada83. Some of these features were added in response to the influence of object-oriented techniques and languages.

Other application-specific standards are also useful. Consider the case of computer graphics. The hodgepodge of conflicting standards in the early 1980s has been replaced by a smaller set of standards, making programs more portable at the same time that software components can be reused.

The standards for file formats have also encouraged reuse. The ability to transfer pictures and documents across a variety of platforms has made the World Wide Web a reality and has been very helpful in the development of applications programs such as Microsoft Word that have file format standards that allow documents to be developed in pieces on different hardware platforms and then assembled seamlessly.

The evolution of spacecraft control center software at NASA's Goddard Space Flight Center illustrates the point. In the early 1980s, each new generation of hardware required new coding because there was no consistent version of FORTRAN supported by the various hardware vendors and because the operating systems of the time were proprietary. (The long lead time for spacecraft project development meant that relatively standard languages such as FORTRAN 77 were not placed into service until several years after their appearance in the marketplace.)

The lack of standards for graphics display software was even more serious because of the time-critical requirements for acquisition and the display of telemetry data. There were many graphics standards available during this time: ACM SIGGRAPH CORE, GKS, PHIGS, NALPS, IGES, and so on.

Each spacecraft control system had to be distributed and fault-tolerant, with several degrees of redundancy.

In the late 1980s and early 1990s, UNIX became relatively standard. TCP/IP and Ethernet became standards with good performance, and they, along with UNIX, became the basis for distributed spacecraft control software. These standards and adoption of the Open Software Foundation's Motif package as a standard for user interface software, allowed software to be developed in an evolutionary manner, with some possibility for reuse.

The stabilization of the underlying operating system, graphical standards, networking and communications standards, and user interface standards allowed the software analysts to have enough time to investigate the possibility of reusing greater portions of the spacecraft control center software. The results of their effort include the TPOCC (Transportable Payload Operations Control Center) system, which we will discuss in detail as one of four case studies in Chap. 7.

For another illustration, consider the survey performed by the Department of Defense before undertaking the development of the Ada programming language in the 1980s. There were over 1600 different languages and dialects used at that time for defense-related applications and systems. Clearly, reuse was out of the question until there was more standardization of languages.

The standards discussed so far in this section are macro standards, in the sense that they do not address interfaces at lower levels such as source code modules. However, the same principles apply at lower levels.

For example, in weakly typed languages such as C, the organizational coding standards should describe the following: precision of arguments (int, float, double), any attributes of the arguments (long, short, unsigned, unsigned long, unsigned short), use of constant values as opposed to the use of the #define statement, use of global variables, and so on. Any language trickery that allows access to an enumerated type by the integer index of one of the enumerated entries should be avoided.

Programs written in other languages, such as C++, should have a clear standard for the use of constant pointers and nonconstant pointers. This point can be especially troublesome for the programmer transitioning from C to C++ and should be part of a training package for such programmers.

In any programming language, programmers should be encouraged to minimize the interface between modules and to maximize each module's cohesion by having each module perform a single action, with little or no side effect. Coding standards should be modified, if necessary, to allow seamless use of COTS software whenever the use of such software in an application is satisfactory.

The certification process for reusable software components should ensure that the interface standards have been followed before the component is inserted into a reuse library. This process will be discussed in Chap. 4.

You should note one thing about the use of these coding standards in reuse programs. Rigid coding standards may require a greater up-front cost when transforming existing code in order to meet the coding standards before placement of the code artifact into a reuse library. However, this up-front cost will be made up for by ease of integration of the reusable component into new systems. Without this up-front effort to transform potentially reusable source code components into ones with standard interfaces, there will be little, if any, actual benefit to the reuse program. Cost issues will be discussed in Chap. 5.

Indeed, programmers who have negative experiences attempting to reuse source code modules with poorly constructed, nonstandard interfaces, especially to nonstandard applications, libraries, or operating systems, are likely to resist any future efforts in software reuse.

Fortunately, there seems to be little resistance to the use of common data format standards, primarily because they are ubiquitous. Common data standards are the basis for integration of productivity packages. Typical productivity packages are Microsoft Office for Windows, DOS, and Macintosh-based systems and the Island system for UNIX workstations. Each of them includes a word processor, spreadsheet, and drawing system.

Common data formats also allow easy conversion of files from different applications such as from Microsoft Word to WordPerfect, and conversely. The standards for graphics file formats (TIFF, GIF, PICT, etc.) and database formats (DBF) also encourage easy movement of data across applications. Any reusable software that uses graphics or database files must adhere to these standards.

These common formats also allow easy transformation of documents to different hardware platforms. This was important during the writing of this book, since some of the text was created in Microsoft Word on a DOS-based portable and converted, using standard conversion routines, to Microsoft Word for a Macintosh. Some of the data analysis was done originally on a UNIX system, with the data saved as an ASCII file with the fields separated by commas (the so-called comma-delimited format). The data were then imported into spreadsheets and database files for use on several different personal computers, including IBM-compatible and Macintosh systems. The data transformations were flawless.

2.6 Designing for Reuse

Up to this point, we have described software reuse as an activity that involves the analyzing, organizing, cataloging, and evaluating of software artifacts that can be placed into a reuse library, as well as the ensuring of efficient access to the library. We now take a different approach—that reuse can also be encouraged by designing new systems so as to increase the potential for reuse of some of their components, or even the system as a whole.

Designing for reuse is a relatively new concept. As such, there are few projects that have been completed in which the goal of reusing considerable portions of the system in the future is reflected in the design of the system. Not surprisingly, these successful projects occur most frequently in organizations with sophisticated software development practices. The effect of Ada and object-oriented technologies is evident in these projects ([BIEM95], [CSC91], [NASA92B], [RUBI90].)

We will next present some general guidelines incorporating the common experiences of successful projects that were designed for reuse. Some of the information is available in a March 1995 technical report from the Software Engineering Laboratory at NASA's Goddard Space Flight Center [SEL95] and an earlier report from Computer Sciences Corporation. [CSC91]. Humphrey [HUMP95] reports many instances of improvements in productivity through systematic software reuse.

The guidelines will focus on general coding issues. Since the experiences presented in these reports involve both an object-oriented language (C++) and the object-oriented features of Ada, we will organize the guidelines according to the functionality addressed and not by the language used. Some of the guidelines are reminiscent of those described in Sec. 2.3.

The major guidelines are as follows:

- Use object-oriented design and the object-oriented programming features of a language such as Ada or C++ to increase modularity.
- The code must adhere to coding standards and must use standard formats for data and interfaces to standard software.
- The use of abstract data types increases the likelihood of future reuse. Thus, Ada generics and C++ templates should be used.
- The level of abstraction should be thin. That is, there should not be

many levels in which an Ada generic package is built on top of another Ada generic package, which in turn is built on top of another Ada generic package, and so on. The extra abstraction comes at the expense of additional testing and integration problems. Of course, the same admonition applies to C++ templates.

- Language features such as inheritance should be used sparingly because of potential testing difficulties.

- Language features such as polymorphism should be used when they make programs more readable. Even in this case, polymorphism should be used sparingly because of potential testing difficulties.

- Features such as variant records should be avoided if possible because of their potential for misuse and differences in their implementation by different compiler vendors.

- The code should be carefully documented. In particular, the programmers should not rely on the supposed "self-documentation" obtained from the use of long variable and function names.

- Everything developed as part of a system "designed for reuse" should be subject to domain analysis and should be entered into a reuse library.

- Performance issues must be addressed in the detailed design phase. The designer must be aware of the effect of dynamic binding of objects on program performance. For example, the organization of calls to functions in Ada generic packages (either user- or system-defined) must take into account the size of the libraries and their effect on a computer with a virtual memory system that uses paging.

- The documentation for the system that is "designed for reuse" should also include a "reuser's guide" that includes some of the design rationale for the system. Such information can be invaluable for a new system.

For more information on the effect of Ada generic package organization on program performance and Ada package organization suggestions see Buchman [BUCH89]. The observations in Buchman's paper also apply to the organization of C++ templates. However, the remarks about Ada libraries are relevant only to Ada83 and not to Ada95 or C++ because of semantic differences in the treatment of library organization and compilation order. (For example, Ada95 has removed some of the library management problems observed in Ada83.)

Some of these principles also apply to software written in procedural languages. The following is a reasonably complete set of relevant principles for procedurally oriented software:

- Coding standards should be used, as should standard data formats and standard interfaces to other software.

- Features such as variant records should be avoided if possible because of their potential for misuse and differences in their implementation by different compiler vendors.

- Semantic analysis tools such as the UNIX lint utility should be used to determine type conflicts between function calls and function definitions.

- Actions that should be atomic (not interruptible), such as calls to the operating system, should not be "wrapped" in enclosing functions. This is dangerous because the use of such a "wrapper" can leave an essential system resource in an inconsistent state if the wrapper function is temporarily suspended because of a switch between two concurrently executing processes.

- Potential problems in pointer access, such as depending on uninitialized memory having only null bytes as its contents, should be tested for.

- The code should be carefully documented. In particular, the programmers should not rely on the supposed "self-documentation" obtained from the use of long variable and function names.

- Everything developed as part of a system "designed for reuse" should be subject to domain analysis and should be entered into a reuse library.

- Performance issues must be addressed in the detailed design phase. The designer must be aware of the effect of dynamic binding of objects on program performance. For example, the run-time binding of dynamically linked libraries (which are common in the UNIX operating system) must be considered.

- The documentation for the system that is "designed for reuse" should also include a "reuser's guide" that includes some of the design rationale for the system. Such information can be invaluable for a new system.

There is one final point to be made about designing for reuse. Nearly every organization considering software reuse is motivated by cost savings and quality issues. As we have seen, the classification problems of systematic domain analysis are difficult to treat and require a considerable amount of both automated searches and human intervention.

For some organizations, an easier way to develop some systems is to eliminate the use of components developed in house, even potentially reusable ones, by using only COTS products. This is the ultimate level of reuse. We will describe cost models for COTS-only systems in Chap. 5.

2.7 Using Reuse to Drive Requirements Analysis

The traditional view of requirements is that it precedes the development of a system's design. This is obvious for the classic waterfall model of the software development process. But it also applies to the initial design and requirements activities for software developed using the spiral or rapid prototyping software development models.

What is not so clear is that a systematic reuse program forces the potential reuse to change any "ideal" requirements in order to meet cost pressures. That is, a system's requirements are determined in an iterative process. When the requirements are set so as to meet the (perceived) needs of clients and potential users, the requirements gathering process usually terminates. We will call the result of this standard activity the "ideal requirements."

In many software development organizations today, cost pressures require as much use as possible of COTS products and available building blocks. This will be true in nearly all such organizations in the future.

Suppose that the ideal requirements specify that a complex database entry be updated within some specific time requirement. Suppose also that the organization already licenses a commercial database that misses meeting this requirement by 10 percent.

The organization now has several choices:

- Reconfigure the database software for better performance.
- Test other commercial database products to see if any meet the ideal requirements.
- Purchase faster hardware.
- Reduce the computing load on the computer system.
- Provide a performance analysis of the entire system to locate places where system performance can be improved.
- Change the requirements from the ideal requirements to determine if lesser performance would be acceptable, especially since it is essentially free.

Clearly, many organizations will select the last alternative in many situations. This is an example of how the drive for reuse cost savings, which in this case are due to COTS, can cause changes in requirements.

The high-level description of the process is simple:

1. *Develop an initial set of requirements.* This should be done in concert with the customer. If no customer is known, then the requirements should be chosen according to the perceived needs of the system's end users. For simplicity, we will only describe the interaction of the development team with a known customer. The modification for new systems with no fixed customer but likely end users is similar and will thus not be discussed.

2. *Determine if there is an existing reusable system that meets the set of requirements.* If there is such a system, stop the requirements process and return the existing reusable system.

3. *Determine if there is an existing reusable system that meets "nearly all" the requirements.* If such a system exists, provide the customer with a description of the existing system's requirements, how they differ from the original requirements, and the expected costs of using the existing system to "nearly meet" the customer's requirements. If the customer accepts the modified requirements and is willing to accept the reused existing system at the estimated cost, stop the requirements process and return the existing reusable system.

4. *If no existing system meets or "nearly meets" the customer's requirements, then the set of requirements should be separated into sets of requirements for subsystems.* The decomposition into subsystems should be guided by the process of domain analysis, since the goal is to determine which subsystems have the greatest probability of being available as a COTS product.

5. *Steps 2 through 4 should be carried out for each subsystem.* The process will terminate for each subsystem as specified in these steps. The only additional activity is to determine if the reused subsystems meet appropriate interface standards. This should be done during a check of the certification of the reused subsystem. (It is assumed that each reused subsystem was previously certified as to its interface standards.)

6. *New software development is limited to subsystems in which no agreement can be made between the customer's fixed requirements and the existing reusable subsystem's requirements.*

7. *After agreement between customer and the software team on the final set of requirements for the subsystems, the existing subsystem building blocks are integrated along with any new code into the new system, which is then configured, tested, documented, and delivered to the customer.*

Incidentally, this is not an unrealistic academic scenario. Several of NASA's future ground support systems for spacecraft control and telemetry data handling are being designed with requirements influenced by these cost savings factors. A recent paper by Bracken et al. reports on experiences in the innovative IMMACS project with a software development process based heavily on COTS and reuse to drive the requirements [BRAC95].

In Karlsonn's book [KARL95], *Software Reuse,* the term *developing with reuse* indicates the influence of reuse and existing software artifacts on the development process of new systems in the context of the REBOOT project. The REBOOT project distinguishes between this influence and "developing for reuse," which involves the development of new, potentially reusable software artifacts. Developing for reuse involves adherence to standards, the use of standard interfaces, and object-oriented approaches.

2.8 Metrics for Reuse

The use of metrics is absolutely essential for a systematic process of software reuse. Without metrics, there is no way to evaluate the status of reuse programs, assess the quality of the components selected for reuse, or track the costs and cost savings associated with reuse.

Everyone interested in improving the use of metrics in his or her organization would benefit from reading the experiences of Grady and Caswell [GRAD87]. The title of their book is informative: *Software Metrics: Establishing a Company-Wide Program.* It is clear from their experience that a company- or organization-wide commitment is essential to an effective use of metrics in order to discover "where the organization is" and "where the organization is going."

The experience of the author at NASA's Goddard Space Flight Center is typical. A manager informed me that "reuse was the highest priority in the division" for an appointment as a NASA/ASEE (American Society for Engineering Education) Summer Faculty Fellow. This conversation was followed up by complete access to both people and metrics data, so the project was a success. Anything less than complete access, lack of commitment, or information hiding by unmotivated individuals, would have doomed the project to failure.

In the remainder of this section we will describe a minimal set of metrics that should be collected, analyzed, and used to evaluate the status and success of any reuse program. Additional discussion of the role of metrics in the certification of reusable software components will be given in Chap. 4.

For simplicity, we will assume that every organization in the software business has cost data that is broken down by project. The project data will also include effort and resource information and should contain some degree of error analysis, such as errors per 1000 noncommented, nonblank lines of code or some similar measurement. The error data is often referred to as errors/KNCNB.

The problem that must be addressed is the accurate determination of the costs and benefits of reuse in this particular software development environment.

Metrics should be collected at source code level and correlated with defect data to detect any unusual problems that can be avoided by coding standards. The idea here is to set a warning flag for each metric, and if the value of this metric for a source code module exceeds this flagged value the module is examined further.

This data should be relatively easy to collect over the history of a project both before and after delivery. However, there is a new requirement for metrics data collection in a systematic reuse process: the metrics should be collected for the purpose of analyzing the success of the reuse process. This is the responsibility of the "reuse metrician."

The obvious question for an organization is "Which metrics should we collect?" Perhaps the best answer is given by the GQM (Goals, Questions, Metrics) paradigm of Basili and Rombach [BASI88].

Typical goals include:

- Characterizing the costs of reuse for a software artifact
- Quantifying software-related costs
- Characterizing software quality
- Characterizing the languages used
- Characterizing software volatility

There are clearly many questions that can be asked about progress toward these goals. Typical questions include the following (only two questions will be listed per goal):

- How many times do we expect to reuse the software artifact?
- Is the software being considered for reuse mature and well tested?
- What are the costs per project? (for costs)
- What are the costs for each life cycle activity? (for costs)
- How many software defects are there? (for quality)
- Is any portion of the software more defect-prone than others? (for quality)
- What programming languages are used? (for languages)
- What object-oriented programming language features are used? (for languages)

- How many changes are made to requirements? (for volatility)
- How many changes are made to source code during development? (for volatility)

The clarity of these questions makes the choice of metrics easy in many cases. However, there are several hidden issues that in some cases complicate the process of data collection.

For example, if there is no tracking mechanism to determine the source of a software error it will be difficult to determine if some portion of the software is more defect-prone than others. However, if you believe that this question must be answered in order to meet your stated goals, then you must either collect the data (which will certainly cost money, time, and other resources) or else change your goals for information gathering.

The following are a few essentials for collection and analysis of metrics data in support of a systematic process of software reuse:

- The metrics data must be collected and stored by reusable software component. This might be in addition to a larger aggregation of metrics data for projects.
- The metrics data for potentially reusable software components must include cost estimates for both up-front development cost and complete life cycle cost estimates.
- Metrics should be collected on the same basis that is typical for the organization, with extensions to be able to record and analyze reuse productivity and cost data.
- Predictive models should use the reuse data, and the observed resource and quality metrics must be compared with the ones that were estimated.
- Metrics that measure quality of the product, such as errors per 1000 source lines of code; perceived readability of source code; and simplicity of control flow should be computed for each module and used as part of an assessment of reuse effectiveness.
- Metrics that measure the process, such as resources expended, percentage of cost savings, and customer satisfaction, should be computed for each module and used as part of an assessment of reuse effectiveness.

For example, the percentage of potential reuse indicated in the domain analysis of the Linux operating system should be compared with the observed percentage of reusable components. Also, error data

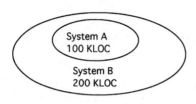

Figure 2.3 A simple software reuse situation.

for reusable modules and systems built with significant reuse should be compared with error data for systems built without reuse.

Note that reuse measurement is easiest when one system is used in its entirety within another system and without any changes. The percentage of reuse in the larger system is simply the percentage of existing code that is used in the larger system. This situation is illustrated in Fig. 2.3, where software system A consists of *100,000 lines of code* (or 100 KLOC) and is completely contained in the larger system B, which consists of 200,000 lines of code.

In Fig. 2.3, note that the perspective of the designers of system A is that their system is entirely reused. From the perspective of system B, only 50 percent of the code has been reused. Note that the project manager for system B wants system A to be of extremely high quality because reusing a high-quality subsystem makes his or her job easier. A higher-level manager who is responsible for both systems A and B might be willing to absorb the costs of providing extra quality for system A. However, a manager whose responsibility ends when system A is delivered may not be willing or able to provide additional quality, regardless of later use of the system. This difference in viewpoint causes many problems when determining the cost of reuse programs.

Not surprisingly, many organizations have difficulty developing reuse metrics data collection procedures when their systems are evolving over time and when they can identify different levels of reuse.

One such possibility is illustrated in Fig. 2.4. In this figure, system A1 contains 100 KLOC and evolves into system A2, which contains 150 KLOC. System A1 is a subsystem of system B1, which consists of 200 KLOC. System B2 contains system A2 as a subsystem, and B2 itself consists of 300 KLOC. The diagrams reflect that all the older systems are contained in the newer ones and that A1 and A2 are completely contained in B1 and B2, respectively. The percentage of reuse is generally measured as 100 percent from the perspective of system A2, since all of system A1 is reused. System B2 is considered to have 100 KLOC from reuse of the subsystem A1 but 150 KLOC from subsystem A2, assuming that A2 will also be used in some other application. Thus, both 33 percent and 50 percent are appropriate measures of reuse, depending on other usage factors.

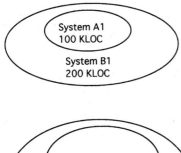

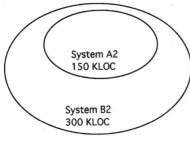

Figure 2.4 Reuse measurement in evolving systems.

Even in this situation, reuse measurement is not difficult if the systems have both been developed using the same naming conventions for files, directories, and subsystems. A simple way to collect this data is to use the following high-level algorithm.

```
Algorithm for determining the reuse level of two
releases of the same system:

The inputs are the names of two directories
where the two versions are kept.

The directories are called OLDDIR and NEWDIR.

For each file in OLDDIR, recursively search
the directory NEWDIR for a file with the same name.
    {
    Compute the difference between the pair of
    files for each desired metric.
    Report the relative change and the value of
    each desired metric on the older file.
    Mark each file as being read.
    }

Search NEWDIR for each unmarked file.

For each unmarked file, compute the value of
each desired metric on the file.

Organize the data depending on the aggregates
desired.

Report the data and store in a convenient format.
```

In the simplest situation, where only the differences between the
number of lines in a file is required and the files can be placed on a
UNIX system, the standard UNIX `find` and `diff` utilities can be
used to obtain this information easily. The UNIX `find` utility recursively searches a directory and its subdirectories for all files that
match the desired pattern. It is an extremely flexible utility.

The UNIX `diff` utility compares two files for differences between
sets of lines. It computes these differences in a useful manner. If a file
named `file_new` is created from a file named `file_old` by inserting
a different line at the beginning of the original file, then `diff` will report a difference on line 1 of the files and will not indicate any other
differences. This is far more useful than reporting that every line of
the two files is different, since line 1 of the file `file_old` becomes
line 2 of the file `file_new`, line 2 of the file `file_old` becomes line 3
of the file `file_new`, and so on. The total number of different lines
can be counted by using the line counting option of the standard
UNIX utility `wc`.

It is easy to illustrate the comparison algorithm given in this section. We can write a program using a single statement in the UNIX
shell that in turn invokes a shell script.

The single statement uses the power of the UNIX `find` utility. This
utility searches the directory OLDDIR for a file of the appropriate
name and type. (In this case we are searching for source code written
in the C programming language.) For each such file, the shell script
named `doit` is executed. The purpose of the parentheses and curly
braces is to allow the script `doit` to access its command-line arguments. The backslash is used to inform the shell that the final semi-
colon is to be interpreted as the end of the set of arguments to `doit`.

```
find $OLDDIR -name '*.c' -print -exec doit() {} \;
```

The Bourne shell script `doit` to perform a typical analysis using
`diff` is given later in this section. The positional variable $1 repre-
sents the single file name used as an argument to `doit`. This variable
is automatically available to shell scripts in UNIX.

Note that the script as presented does not handle source code in subdirectories properly. This is because the argument passed to `doit` is a
complete path name that is relative to the initial directory, such as
`./sub_dir/file.c`. As such, its name will not be matched by a file in
the directory NEWDIR. The name of the last portion of the path name,
with no occurrences of the slash (/), is required for a comparison.

It is easy to remove everything in the relative path name except the
final part after the last slash using the awk pattern matching language or by a simple C program. We omit the details and will be satis-

fied with a simpler script. Note that the script only works for files that are all inside the same directory, without any subdirectories.

```
#
#This Bourne shell script is called doit.
#It searches a directory for a file whose
#name matches its argument. It then uses the diff
#utility to compare file sizes.
#The script only works for systems with all C
#language files in the same directory and not in a
#subdirectory.
#
echo $1 >> out
find $NEWDIR -name $1 -print |diff $1| wc -l >> out
wc -l $1 >> out
echo "\n" >> out
```

This script has been set up to write the name of each argument (which will be the name of an input file from the directory OLDDIR) to the output file that we have named out. After execution of this script, the output file will contain the name of each appropriate file in the original directory, with each file name appearing on a separate line. Each line of the output file will contain either one or two numbers, depending on the appearance of the file name in the new directory NEWDIR. The arithmetic to determine the percentage of reuse is now easy to do.

The remaining step is to examine the files in the directory NEWDIR that are not part of the directory OLDDIR and therefore cannot have been reused from the system in OLDDIR. This can also be done using the find utility with a different shell script. As before, the shell script does not work on subdirectories.

```
find $OLDDIR -name '*.c' -print -exec doit2() {} \;

#
#This Bourne shell script doit2 uses its argument.
#It searches a directory for all files whose
#name does not match its argument. It then uses
#the wc utility to compute file sizes.
#The script only works for systems with all C
#language files in the same directory and not in a
#subdirectory.
#

echo $1 >> out
find $NEWDIR -name -not $1 -print | wc -l >> out
echo "\n" >> out
```

Most other situations require the collection of more complex metrics, but the essential idea is similar. We can use a similar algorithm to determine the amount of system A that is reused in system B even if the two systems are not directly related.

It should be noted that the metrics suggested here are a minimal set and do not help us estimate the relative impact of reuse on the quality of the final software product. This topic will be discussed in Chap. 4, when we study certification of reusable software components.

There is one final point to be made regarding the measurement of software reuse. Including old source code in a new project need not reflect the actual amount of reuse if some of the old code is not actually used in the new system. Thus, including large packages of "dead code" may make the amount of reuse appear large, but in fact including such code may make a system less reliable than if only the necessary components were reused in the new system.

Summary

There are five techniques—domain analysis, object-oriented techniques, standard interfaces, designing for reuse, and metrics—that are part of a systematic plan of software reuse. Several of these techniques should be applied at many places in the software life cycle.

Domain analysis is the analysis of software artifacts to determine the appropriate classification of the artifacts for potential inclusion into a reuse library. This process involves the determination of the verbs that describe the actions of the system and the nouns that describe the objects acted on by the verbs.

The set of nouns can be broken down further into objects, mediums, and systems. Perhaps the best way to understand the analysis is to attempt to describe every action of the system using the sentence

To do action A to object O that resides on medium M is the responsibility of system S.

This description allows us to ignore the details of how, when, or where the action is being performed.

Domain analysis of the Linux operating system points out some opportunities for potential software reuse.

System architectures and object models can be very useful in conjunction with classification schemes. While efficient, easy-to-use tools are preferable, it is possible to perform domain analysis with simple tools or even no tools at all during the data collection process.

The object-oriented approach to software design and implementation is appealing because object-oriented design encourages information hiding and data abstraction. Much of the reuse literature focuses on the use of object-oriented programming.

Standard, well-documented interfaces are absolutely essential for systematic reuse. These interfaces can be at the level of selection of standard programming languages, standard software platforms (commonly available operating systems, communications packages and standards, GUIs, etc.), data standards, or coding standards that enforce the types of interfaces between modules.

An important new idea is "designing for reuse." This makes heavy use of object-oriented technologies such as those supported by C++ and Ada.

Metrics are vital to any systematic software reuse program. Metrics allow software managers and designers to evaluate the status of reuse programs, assess the quality of the components selected for reuse, and track the costs and cost savings associated with reuse.

A systematic measurement program should follow approaches such as the GQM (Goals, Questions, Metrics) paradigm. One of the most important metrics is the projected number of times that the potentially reusable software artifact will be reused. Metrics should be used to measure both software quality and the efficiency of the software development process.

Further Reading

There are few books that treat each of the major topics of this chapter together. The tutorial by Biggerstaff and Perlis [BIGG89] and the book by Hooper and Chester [HOOP91] present good overviews of some general techniques for software reuse, including those described in this chapter.

The best reference on domain analysis continues to be the tutorial book by Prieto-Diaz and Arango [PRIE91B].

For more information on the UNIX operating system, consult the books by Andleigh [ANDL90], Leach [LEAC94A], or Stevens [STEV92]. Complete on-line documentation of the relevant original technical papers (primarily from AT&T Bell Laboratories) in troff-eqn-tbl format can be found in the papers directory that is generally included with the standard software distribution of most UNIX vendors.

Unfortunately, there was little information on the Linux operating system in book form at the time this book was being written. However, there is a considerable amount of Linux information available on the Internet newsgroup comp.os.linux.

There are many books on object-oriented approaches to design and programming, such as those by Booch [BOOC94], Coad and Yourdon [COAD91], and Leach [LEAC95A]. The paper by Meyer [MEYE87] was one of the first to illustrate the potential role of object-oriented programming in reuse.

Testing of object-oriented programs is in its infancy compared to testing techniques for procedural programs. Some of the best information on testing object-oriented programs can be found in Jorgenson and Erickson [JORG94] and McGregor and Korson [McGR94]. Information on testing of procedural programs can be found in Beizer [BEIZ83], [BEIZ90], DeMillo et al. [DEMI87], Harrold, McGregor, and Fitzpatrick [HARR92], and Howden [HOWD87].

Information on the status of many proposed standards can be located in the relevant newsgroups on the Internet. Copies of existing, approved standards can be obtained from the relevant standards organizations.

We are not aware of any additional materials on the subject of designing for reuse. Undoubtedly, there are internal technical reports that can be helpful. Consult your own organization's technical library.

There are many references on software metrics. Excellent overviews can be obtained from a number of books, including those by Fenton [FENT91]; Fenton and Pfleeger [FENT96]; and Conte, Dunsmore, and Shen [CONT86]. The paper by McCabe [McCA76] is extremely important for understanding metrics that apply to program control flow. Grady and Caswell's book *Software Metrics* [GRAD87] is useful from a managerial or organizational viewpoint. One of the best references on which metrics to collect is Basili and Rombach [BASI88].

There are two recent papers that are especially relevant to the topics of this chapter. A 1995 publication by Waund [WAUN95] provides a good description of lessons learned when using only COTS products to develop a software system. A 1996 paper by Pfleeger describes some pitfalls in reuse measurement [PFLE96].

Exercises

1. (*This problem is intended primarily for students.*) Examine the source code that you have written so far using the domain analysis techniques of this chapter. Did your organization of the code change?

2. Apply domain analysis to the most recent code you have written.

3. Finish the domain analysis of the kernel of the Linux operating system by completing the object model.

4. Examine some source code that is available to you. Compute some metrics on the average interfaces of your modules. If you do not have any metrics tools available, count the number of arguments to procedures and functions. Count the number of global variables as part of the interface of each procedure or function. Is there any difference between the metric values computed for the reusable code and the values for code not intended to be reusable?

5. Describe the interface standards for some relatively large system (your own or others). Does the software conform to commonly accepted standards. If so, which standards?

6. What percentage of your code is object-oriented? What percentage of your organization's code is object-oriented? How have these percentages changed in the past three years?

7. Consider a software project that you worked on and that took much longer than you expected to complete. Identify the problem elements of that project. Evaluate the percentage of the project that meets appropriate coding, data format, and other standards. Is there any overlap between the problem areas and the portion that adhered to standards?

3

Reuse Libraries

In this chapter we will describe general techniques useful when creating, modifying, using, or managing reuse libraries. We will briefly discuss several reuse libraries that are readily available either from commercial or governmental sources.

The first question that arises is whether a reuse library is even necessary. In a mature, well-understood application domain, with many existing high-quality subsystems and COTS products, a formal reuse library may not be necessary if the domain is small enough. For example, if there are only ten high-level subsystems and three appropriate COTS products available a domain expert can easily determine all potentially reusable components without any additional reuse library infrastructure.

Most application domains, however, are larger than the hypothetical one just described. The number of potentially reusable components is often quite large, and frequently many COTS products can be applied to at least some of the domain's requirements. Often the number of components is so large that no one person or group can be expected to be familiar with all of them. Potentially reusable software components often vary in quality and as such have different effects on the quality of resulting systems.

Thus, many application domains require the additional infrastructure of reuse libraries if there is to be efficient, systematic reuse. Any horizontal reuse (that is, reuse across application domains) will certainly require some sort of reuse library unless the components are database management systems, GUIs, or other relatively large programs.

As we indicated in Chap. 1, there are two tasks that must be performed in order to manage reuse libraries. The first, performed by a reuse librarian, is organizing and managing the reuse library. The second, performed by a reuse asset analyst, is certifying that the asset meets certain standards for quality, modularity, documentation, and future support.

This chapter is broadly grouped into two parts. The first part discusses general issues for creating and searching libraries of reusable software components. This portion of the chapter consists of four sections. In Sec. 3.1, we introduce some general issues in searching reuse libraries. Section 3.2 contains some options for the organization of special purpose reuse libraries. Section 3.3 includes some managerial issues such as access control, inclusion and removal of library components, and configuration management. We also discuss reuse libraries that may use multiple languages or that are relatively language independent. Section 3.4 indicates some directions for research in the area of reuse libraries. Nothing presented in the first four sections of the chapter is language-specific.

The material in the remainder of this chapter is broadly grouped into several major sections, organized by the source language in which the components are written. The current state of software engineering practice does not appear to warrant organizing the material in this chapter by functionality, since there are frequently many constraints on the language used to implement software systems. The software engineer or researcher desiring to locate existing software components to use in a system is likely to confine his or her search to components written in the desired development language. This of course poses potential problems in interoperability if it is necessary to use components that are written in different languages.

We will not attempt to provide a complete survey of available resources in this chapter. This is clearly impossible in any case, given the rapid changes in technology. Instead, we will provide an overview of some common systems and repositories for reusable software components. A more complete listing of several readily available reuse libraries is provided in App. 2 of this book.

Unfortunately, most of the material in reuse libraries are source code components. This is probably an accurate reflection of the current state of the practice of software reuse, as we described it in Chap. 1. It is easy to conclude from this that reuse is best kept at code level. However, you should focus your attention on the higher-level reusable assets, and consider the relative lack of such assets in publicly available reuse libraries as a reflection of competitive pressures and the need to keep certain domain-specific proprietary information confidential rather than place it into a library.

We chose not to describe libraries of reusable FORTRAN source code components in this book. For the reasons given in Chap. 1, reuse has been successful in mathematical libraries. Nearly all modern programming in FORTRAN is either mathematical in nature or else involves the use of legacy systems. Special purpose mathematics libraries, generally optimized for particular high-performance computer architectures, are generally available directly from compiler vendors and well-known numerical software developers. The developers of such software are generally informed about the latest algorithms and their implementation and examine the appropriate Internet sites, such as the National Center for Supercomputing Applications (NCSA), as needed.

3.1 General Reuse Library Issues

Reuse libraries can be classified into general purpose and application-specific. This classification is reflected in the way the libraries are organized, created, and used.

A general purpose reuse library frequently extends the offerings available from a particular compiler vendor.

Standardization efforts strongly influence the availability of certain general purpose software components. For example, the Ada language reference manual specifies the contents of an optional calendar package. Any optional package (the name for a relatively small, separately compilable, reusable software component in Ada) that handles time will make use of this particular package. Similar statements hold for the ANSI standard C and draft ANSI standard C++ libraries. C++ class libraries are extremely powerful sources of reusable source code components with high levels of abstraction.

The effective use of these general purpose libraries in a particular software development environment is likely to be highly dependent upon the education and training of the software engineers who will be using them. Browsers and other tools to help navigate reuse libraries are more likely to be available on commercial, general purpose systems than on special purpose ones.

On the other hand, reuse libraries that arise from particular application domains are much more likely to have had some form of domain analysis than are general purpose libraries. Thus, it is likely that the most frequent users of such libraries will be those most familiar with the relevant application domain. A reuse librarian will be responsible for the reuse library's management.

In any case, the process of searching reuse libraries for appropriate components is still complex. Search algorithms are similar to the following:

Input

```
1. A set of specifications for a set of
   one or more software components.
```

2. A reuse library including a search procedure.
3. A method for determining if there is a match to specifications.
4. A method of evaluating the degree to which components are "similar" to another component.

Algorithm

```
search library
if perfect match then
   return matched component or components
else
   {
   determine set of similar components
   determine best component match
   return best match and a discrepancy
     report
   }
```

A moment's thought shows that there are many difficulties involved in implementing such an algorithm.

Consider the simplest case for the first input, which is a single specification for one software component. Assume for simplicity that there is a single perfect match in the reuse library. If the specification is written in a formal specification language, and the reuse library has all its specifications written in the same language, then the search process can probably be carried out using automated methods. A thesaurus of similar terms will generally be required. If different artifacts in the reuse library were written using different specification languages, then any automated search process would require a translator between the specification languages.

A good illustration of this difficulty is in determining source code that matches the specification for an object. In this case, the specification might be a package specification (in Ada) or a header file with a listing of the member functions and data (in C++). The source code is presumed to be elsewhere, either in a package body (in Ada) or in a source code file containing the code for the member functions whose prototypes are in the definition of the object (in C++).

The matching process in this situation depends to a large extent upon the software artifact in the reuse library having the same organization as the specified input. This is clearly not always the case. Consider the reorganization of the standard class library for most C++ compilers for personal computers. Most data structures such as stacks and queues are now implemented on top of some abstract classes such as lists. This organization has changed over several releases of the compilers. An examination of the reorganization of class libraries makes it clear that not all searches that succeeded in, say, version 3.0 of Turbo C++, would succeed for the current version of the same library. These class libraries are discussed later in this chapter.

The terms *semantic gap* and *semantic difference* are often used to describe the differences between library components and the specifications of the component to be searched for. A considerable amount of work goes into obtaining useful, quantifiable measurements of semantic gaps. The semantic gap often cannot be resolved by comparing external descriptions of the components.

Determination of the differences between components using only external information is called *black-box or opaque reuse* because the inner details of the software artifact are not considered. An illustration of black-box reuse is checking documentation using only the external information obtained by the "get info" icon on a Macintosh.

The presumption so far in this discussion is that a match of a specified software component and a software artifact from a reuse library can be made using some sort of external documentation. Unfortunately, it is frequently necessary to scan and analyze the contents of a component for additional information. Often, the details of many of the reuse library's software artifacts must be examined. This causes a major degradation in the performance of the search method.

The determination of the semantic difference between different library components and a set of requirements to be searched for using information obtained when scanning or analyzing the components' contents is often called *white-box reuse*. An illustration of white-box reuse is checking documentation using the "sample contents" field in version 6.0 of Microsoft Word on a PC or a Macintosh.

The well-known phenomenon of "creeping featuritis" in later releases of a system often makes artifacts much larger than perhaps they should be. In this case, obtaining exact matches will be even less likely than with artifacts with smaller specifications.

A more serious issue is that the quality of a software system often degrades in subsequent releases even if the system's original design and implementation were extremely good. This can cause major difficulties during integration of later releases into a larger system. It can also have an adverse effect on the maintenance of the resulting product.

The situation is generally even less clear than the muddled picture just described. Most requirements documents are written in a natural language and not in any sort of formal language. Graphics is often a major portion of designs. Inexact matches of software artifacts are much more common than exact ones. The evaluation process often involves fuzzy logic or some other technique for assessing closeness.

There are difficulties with other steps in the process of searching reuse libraries for appropriate software artifacts. It is clear that the knowledge and training of the software engineer will continue to be essential to selecting the proper components for a given use.

Any tool that helps identify appropriate reuse library components is welcome. Most such tools are relatively expensive to purchase and maintain. However, the cost of training software engineers in the efficient use of reuse libraries is likely to be larger than the cost of tools to access reuse libraries, at least for the foreseeable future. We will discuss such a tool, the InQuisiX System, in Chap. 8.

We note that many of the problems mentioned here do not occur when searching a well-defined domain with only a few high-level components in the reuse library. Unfortunately, in most organizations, there is an enormous amount of effort expended to identify these higher-level components.

Unfortunately, there is still a difficulty in obtaining, let alone accessing, higher-level software architectures to provide more leverage of reuse cost savings throughout the life cycle. There are many software components for manipulating simple data structures, such as stacks, heaps, queues, and trees. However, there are few artifacts for using such abstractions as fourth generation languages or complex software to manipulate state machines. We will see this pattern throughout the remainder of this chapter.

3.2 Organizational Issues for Reuse Libraries

As was pointed out earlier in this chapter, very small, mature, well-understood application domains with few software artifacts probably do not need reuse libraries. For slightly larger domains, reuse libraries need not have any special organizational needs other than perhaps the simple one of placing source code for different subsystems in appropriately named directories. For larger application domains, or for those domains for which some degree of horizontal reuse is possible, reuse libraries must be organized. The organization of the reuse library is the responsibility of the reuse librarian.

There are several possible methods that can be used for the initial organization of software artifacts into a reuse library:

- By artifact's life cycle phase (design, code, etc.)
- By functionality of artifact
- By the interface or the standards the artifact meets
- By the tool or utility in which the artifact was created

Each of the methods has several advantages and disadvantages. We will describe the merits of each organizational method in turn. Note that the methods may be combined with, for example, all the artifacts grouped by the life cycle phase in which they occur, or with a second level of the organizational hierarchy done by the functionality of the artifact. We will not discuss combined methods in this book.

The first reuse library organization is by the life cycle phase of the artifact. This approach has several potential advantages:

- Organization by the life cycle phase of the artifact can simplify the search for high-level components.

- Organization by the life cycle phase of the artifact can allow separate storage of artifacts at different life cycle levels.

- Organization by the life cycle phase of the artifact can accommodate components created by different tools or utilities (such as word processors, text editors, or graphical design tools).

There are several disadvantages of library organization by the life cycle phase of software artifacts:

- Configuration management is difficult.

- Maintaining consistent views of components at different life cycle levels is difficult.

- It is often difficult to determine directly the functionality of an artifact.

The next reuse library organizational method we discuss is organization by the functionality of the software artifacts. The advantages of this organization include the following:

- Determining appropriate artifacts is easier than with most other organizations.

- Organization is consistent with domain analysis.

- It is easy to maintain consistent views of different software artifacts belonging to the same system.

There are several disadvantages to reuse library organization by the functionality of the software artifacts:

- It is hard to determine directly the interface or the standards that the artifact adheres to.

- It is not especially easy to determine directly the tool or utility that was used to created the artifact. This can affect the maintainability of future releases of a system that uses a particular reusable artifact.

We now consider reuse library organization based on the interface of the library's artifacts or the standards they meet. We note that this method of reuse library organization requires the services of a reuse asset analyst. The advantages of this organization include the following:

- It is very easy to check that an artifact meets desired interface specifications.

- It is easy to install software artifacts into the reuse library because they have already passed some portion of the certification process. (Certification is a step taken after the software artifact has been tested and actually used. The certification step provides assurance of the quality of the software artifact and the potential costs of interfacing it to other software. Certification will be discussed in detail in Chap. 4.)

- It is easy to keep track of any filter or glueware needed to interface the software artifact to a new application with different interface standards from the one in which the artifact was created. This becomes especially important for reusing higher-level software artifacts such as COTS products.

There are many potential disadvantages to reuse library organization by interface or standards:

- It is hard to determine functionality of artifacts.
- It is difficult to find anything but source code.
- This technique does not encourage life cycle leverage.
- It is moderately hard to maintain consistent views of artifacts in the same system.

The final method we consider is reuse library organization by means of the tool or utility with which the artifact was created. Its advantages are as follows:

- This is the current practice on single-user machines. Most personal computer software encourages the placement of documents, source code, and graphical designs in different directories.

- This organization is consistent with most current software development that uses CASE tools.

- It is easy to install software artifacts.

There are many potential disadvantages to reuse library organization based on the tool or utility used to create the software artifact:

- There are major configuration management problems if the tool or utility used to create the artifact either changes or becomes obsolete.

- It is hard to maintain consistent views of different artifacts belonging to the same system.

- It is hard to determine functionality of artifacts.

- This method does not encourage life cycle leverage.

It is hard to choose one method of reuse library organization as appropriate for all software development environments since each of the library methods has some disadvantages. Organization by functionality of artifacts is the most common in practice and is consistent with domain analysis. Reuse library organization by the tool or utility with which the artifacts were created appears to be the second most common since it is natural for many commonly used tools or utilities.

However, except for software development on personal computers, most development systems are networked and at least share a common server. As such, reuse library organization based on particular tools or utilities may diminish in appeal.

3.3 Managerial Issues for Reuse Libraries

In the last section we discussed some issues in the organization of reuse libraries. Let us now suppose that we have determined an organizational scheme for a reuse library. We still have a management problem: reuse libraries must be managed properly. There must be control over what is entered into a reuse library, what is removed from a reuse library, what is to be upgraded, and what sort of access is to be allowed.

There are lots of management issues related to reuse libraries. Most of them fall into one of the following categories:

- Search methods
- Insertion of components
- Removal of components
- Evaluation of library utility and usage
- Configuration management of components
- Access control and security
- Incorporation of other available reuse libraries

In the remainder of this section, we will address each of these management issues in turn.

3.3.1 Search methods

Determining appropriate search methods is the responsibility of the reuse librarian. Search methods can be as primitive as exact string matches for keywords in either the external description of the software artifact in the case of black-box reuse or in the internal contents of the artifact in the case of white-box reuse. They can be less precise, using a technique such as fuzzy logic to minimize the semantic gap in the case of inexact matches of components.

We note that it is possible to use several different classes of search methods: those integrated with specific reuse library tools, special purpose tools developed just for the purpose of examining specific reuse libraries, or some general purpose library analysis tools. There are many open questions associated with each of these options, as we shall see in Sec. 3.4.

3.3.2 Insertion of components

A formal action must be taken to insert a software artifact into a reuse library. This step will include the placement of the artifact into a classification scheme, assuming that one is available as part of the domain analysis process.

At a minimum, some sort of formal evaluation process must take place before an asset is entered into a reuse library. We strongly recommend the use of the certification process discussed in Chap. 4. We will describe the certification issue in great detail in that chapter, and will content ourselves here with the observation that there must be an independent check of, say, the defect history of any source code module that is placed into the reuse library for use on other systems. This is the primary responsibility of the reuse asset analyst.

3.3.3 Removal of components

Component removal is a somewhat controversial issue. One view is that components should never be removed from a reuse library. The fact that they may not have been used yet need not mean that the components will never be used. The quality of the component should not be a problem because the component would have been certified before it was placed into the reuse library.

The opposing view is that it is often essential to remove unnecessary components from a reuse library. There are more arguments in favor of this position than against it. The business focus of an organization can change, necessitating changes in reuse library organization.

For example, if the component meets the interface standards for an application that has been discontinued for several years, the components are unlikely to be reused in any new system, especially if the interface standards were proprietary. Removing a large component from a reuse library will free up resources and will reduce the number of items to be checked by reuse library search routines. Reuse library components are often replaced by ones with more standard interfaces or better performance.

In addition, if reuse library components were certified using the "certify on demand" approach described in Chap. 4, then the quality of such components is suspect and there is even less reason to keep them in the reuse library.

In any event, the services of a reuse asset analyst are needed before library components are removed.

3.3.4   Evaluation of library utility and usage

Clearly, there are considerable costs associated with systematic reuse programs. It is important for the reuse manager to be able to justify the cost of the reuse program. An important factor in this evaluation is the efficiency and usage of the reuse library. Much of this activity is carried out by the reuse metrician in conjunction with the reuse librarian.

It is easy to keep track of both the number of searches made in a reuse library and the number of successful matches to desired components. This is useful as a global measure of increases in reuse in the organization.

Records also should be kept on usage of individual reuse library components so that the efficiency of the domain analysis scheme and reuse library classification scheme and the utility of particular components can be determined. Such information will be useful when determining if individual library components should be removed.

Additional measures should be made of the number of reuse library components that eventually become part of new software projects. Some of this information will be part of the metrics data for the new project and will be gathered by a software reuse economist.

3.3.5   Configuration management of components

Configuration management is also required in a properly managed reuse library. We must be certain that no component is being "corrected" or "improved" by two different programmers at the same time. In addition, we must be certain that no changes to a component cause damage to systems expecting to use that component.

It is especially important to use configuration management when the underlying technology is changing. For example, any reusable software that uses the GUI of Microsoft Windows version 3.1 may have to be at least partially rewritten to interface with Windows 95. Similar statements apply to software written to interface to X-Windows or Motif. Applications software may undergo considerable changes as well, creating problems for any reusable software that interacts with it. While many new releases of operating systems and GUIs maintain backward compatibility with older releases, the company that developed the software generally phases out its support for the older versions over time. Thus, configuration management becomes especially important.

3.3.6   Access control and security

At first glance, the need for access restrictions may be somewhat less obvious than the need for configuration management. However, companies often have commercial secrets that could leave a company at a disadvantage if the details of the construction of one of their systems were known to a competitor.

Consider also the case of a system where malicious damage could be done if the internal structure of a system were made public. In this case, sensible security measures would preclude indiscriminate access. For example, spacecraft control center software at NASA is developed on a special network that is both physically and electronically isolated from the Internet, and access to source code is severely limited. This limitation is imposed for security reasons, which have as such an impact on reuse libraries.

3.3.7   Incorporation of other available reuse libraries

The remainder of this chapter contains brief descriptions of some commonly available reuse libraries. Note that some of these reuse libraries are in the public domain. Therefore, their components can be included at will in software development projects. This means that these public libraries can be searched and that components can be intermixed with components of the organization's own reuse libraries.

Since external reuse libraries are not under the control of the local reuse librarian, many of the management issues raised earlier in this section do not apply. However, the number of publicly available components used within new systems is an important measurement for management, especially when used in conjunction with the same information for local reuse libraries. Note, however, that the search techniques and library organization may be different for different reuse libraries.

Some of the observations made about publicly available reuse libraries also apply to private, commercial libraries and to other reuse libraries within the same organization.

3.4   Research Issues in Reuse Library Organization

There are many opportunities for high-quality experimental work in reuse libraries. The problem, of course, is that it is difficult to have parallel experiments using alternative methods for the purpose of comparison. Systematic reuse programs have a considerable overhead, and it is difficult to have even more activities that are not directly tied to a particular project. However, there are research possibilities that can be cost effective.

Several of the reuse library organizational approaches suggested in Sec. 3.2 of this chapter can be compared quite easily if there are two or more similar software projects under development. A relatively small reuse library of components (at several life cycle levels) can be used. Ideally, many, but not all, of the library components will have a high potential for reuse in a project. Each of the projects would use a different access method, and the results of searches could be used to assess the efficiency of each organization.

Another research issue is determining the efficiency of different search methods. Particular emphasis should be placed on comparing search engines of three types: integrated with general purpose reuse library tools, special purpose tools developed for specific reuse libraries, and general purpose library analysis tools. These can also be compared using the approach described in the previous paragraph.

Additional data can be collected to support or reject the cost effectiveness of different levels of certification. Certification will be discussed in Chap. 4.

3.5   Reuse Libraries for Ada Software

A guiding feature in the development of the Ada programming language was its support for good software engineering practice. Because of the involvement of the United States Department of Defense in the development of the Ada language, there has been strong governmental activity to provide free information, including educational and software support for Ada software development. The effect of this support has been obvious.

Perhaps equally important for reuse activities is the standardization of the language. An experiment by Michael Feldman of George Washington University illustrates the advantage of standardization.

He encoded an Ada language solution to the famous "Dining Philosophers Problem," which is a well-known example in the theory of concurrent programming and often poses great difficulty for the synchronization of independently executing computations. He used the standard Ada feature of tasking. Communications between tasks were done using the standard Ada rendezvous mechanism. He then ran his solution on many different computers, operating systems, and Ada compilers. The program always ran successfully. His source code was compiled without any modifications, regardless of the operating system or compiler versions used. The incredible portability of this software solution is a tribute to the advantage of standards both for interfaces and for semantics of program behavior.

3.5.1 The Public Ada Library

Perhaps the most convenient grouping of Ada information is what is known as the Public Ada Library, or PAL. This information is available free (for students) on a set of two CD-ROM disks from SIGAda and commercially (at nominal cost) from the Walnut Creek company.

The CD-ROM contains the Ada Software Repository (or ASR, described in Sec. 3.5.2), the ASEET (Ada Software Engineering Education and Technology) educational software, information from the AJPO (Ada Joint Program Office), compilers from the Free Software Foundation's GNAT project based on the familiar GNU system, development tools, documentation tools, courseware guides, the Ada Language Reference Manual, bindings to different operating systems and GUIs, and the ACVC (Ada Compiler Validation Suite).

This invaluable resource, organized by Richard Conn, provides an excellent start toward a reuse library for Ada software.

3.5.2 The Ada Software Repository

The original reuse library for Ada software was called the Ada Repository, or SIMTEL-20 Repository since the software originally resided on a SIMTEL-20 computer. This repository was managed by Richard Conn for many years.

The Ada Repository was organized into several directories. These directories contained a large amount of information about education in Ada software engineering and the activities of different working groups such as ARTWEG, the Ada Run-Time Environments Working Group.

A large amount of software was also included in the ASR. The software included some standard packages for performing utility functions as well as some tools for metrics analysis of Ada source code programs. The metrics produced by these tools include the standard Halstead Software Science and McCabe cyclomatic complexity metrics.

The author has published an analysis of the contents of the repository as of early 1989 [LEAC89]. There was a large variation in the quality of the components, particularly in the number of control flow paths in different components. There was also considerable variation in the appropriateness of educational materials to illustrate concurrent program execution using tasking and the Ada rendezvous mechanism.

Originally, the software was available using one of two mechanisms: on magnetic tape from a single source or electronically from the Advanced Research Project Agency's (ARPA) ARPANET. The single source for magnetic tape was later expanded to multiple sites. The tremendous improvement in data transfer rates and the general availability of Internet connections has made on-line access to this repository easy for many potential users.

However, there is a simpler method of data transfer that is preferred by many people in the Ada community. The ACM SIGAda organization makes the PAL CD available at a nominal cost (free for students). This CD contains the code for the ASR.

3.5.3 The STARS and CARDS programs

The acronym STARS stands for Software Technology for Adaptable Reliable Software. This effort is supported by the U.S. Army.

The demonstration project was conducted on a collection and analysis system within the electronic intelligence domain. A domain engineering process was developed and applied to a subdomain, creating a set of reusable domain assets.

The project has placed particular emphasis on the reuse principles of domain-specific and architecture-centric, taking the approach of developing a domain architecture and assets for reuse ("systematic reuse") as opposed to focusing on the reuse of existing software in a context for which it was not initially intended ("opportunistic reuse").

The project domain engineering process represents a tailoring of the organization domain modeling (ODM) domain analysis method developed under the STARS program. A domain model, domain architecture, and reusable domain assets are being developed for the particular subdomain of emitter location and processing. The domain model is a formal representation of commonality and variability that exists within the ELPA domain. The model is being represented using the Unisys Reuse Library Framework (RLF) tool and the Knowledge Acquisition for Preservation of Trade-offs and Underlying Rationales (KAPTUR) tool. This product was sponsored by ARPA.

The term CARDS is an acronym for the Central Archive for Reusable Defense Software. The CARDS library model is a formal encoding of information produced during domain engineering activities. The formal encoding is then entered into a domain-specific reuse library.

The purpose of a CARDS domain-specific library model is to do the following:

- Determine domain requirements and generic architectures.

- Describe criteria for certification of reusable assets.

- Describe criteria for insertion of reusable assets into the reuse library.

- Catalog reusable assets for search and retrieval applications.

- Provide a basis for constructing other kinds of reuse library applications.

This project has completed several phases. Version 2.0 of the library model is an encoding of the GCC (generic command and control) of the Portable Reusable Integrated Software Modules (PRISM) program, into the RLF, which is both a tool and a formalism for reuse, especially domain engineering and reuse library access.

3.5.4   The ASSET Program

The ASSET program is available on the Internet by anonymous `ftp` from the source `source.asset.com`. It is also available free on disk in IBM PC format from the address given in App. 2.

The most important item on the disk is the catalog of reusable software assets, which occupies nearly all the 720 kbytes available. The catalog is in compressed form so that it can be read by older computers using smaller capacity floppy disk drives.

This catalog includes brief descriptions of the STARS, CARDS, PRISM, and other special purpose programs. For obvious reasons, the details of these programs are restricted to users with proper requirements and access. However, the addresses (electronic and otherwise) of sources for these assets are included in the ASSET catalog.

The catalog also includes information on the following:

- Seminars and training

- Conferences

- Technical publications (including conference proceedings)

- Language bindings (very important for interoperable systems and the inclusion of COTS products)

- Government-sponsored research projects for public use

- Descriptions of successful applications of software reuse

- Reuse library information, including publicly funded libraries, high-quality freeware (such as the Free Software Foundation's GNU software), and commercial sources

- Standards activities, especially those relevant to the Ada environment

- Commercial tools to help in the reuse process

- Specific packages to support lower-level abstractions such as the stack, queue, and related data structures

- Higher levels of potentially reusable software

An important part of the ASSET reuse and standardization effort is a set of guidelines and standards to be used in developing Ada programs and technical documents for delivery to a repository. It provides a proposal for standard prologues for Ada programs which are SGML-processible.

This product was developed as part of the STARS program.

3.5.5 Other sources

Many other sources are available for Ada software. For example, the CAMP (Common Ada Missile Packages) program was very effective in standardizing efforts in this particular application domain. From its inception, this library was designed to serve as a reuse library, and it has clearly served its purpose.

The NASA Repository-Based Software Engineering Project at Johnson Space Flight Center is supported by the University of Houston at Clear Lake through its Research Institute for Computing and Information Systems (RICIS). This repository contains the ELSA system. The acronym stands for "electronic library services and applications." This system is Ada-based and includes software usable for the Space Station project.

This extensive reuse project also includes the reusable objects software environment (ROSE).

The Ada software used on NASA's Space Station project is also available to appropriate users. However, for security reasons, many of these packages will never be part of the public domain. (Obviously, this statement applies even more strongly to the software developed for the CAMP program.)

However, individuals with a demonstrated need to see these systems and the proper security clearances will find them interesting.

3.6 Reuse Libraries for C++ Language Software

A guiding feature in the development of the C++ programming language was its support for object-oriented programming. C++ was considered to be "a better C" because it had stronger support for type checking, especially in I/O operations.

We chose not to group software written in C and C++ together because of the essential differences between the object-oriented and procedurally oriented program design paradigms. This is done despite the close historical relationships between these two languages and the fact that C++ is essentially a superset of ANSI C. Reuse libraries for ANSI C software will be discussed in the next section.

The Internet is one of the best sources for general information about many class libraries. The other readily available sources are the class libraries provided by compiler vendors. The libraries are essentially free because the vendors' libraries come bundled with their compilers.

These class libraries provide a relatively low level of reusable components. We describe the level as being low because the libraries are intended to aid the development of small modules to use certain data types.

We illustrate the level of support for reusable source code modules by considering the class library bundled with the Borland and Turbo C++ compilers for the 80x86 architecture, AT&T C++ for a Sun SPARC Station running Solaris (Sun's version of UNIX) and the GNU C++ compiler from the Free Software Foundation. There is considerable overlap among these libraries in the basic facilities for I/O, standard abstract data types, and mathematical objects such as complex numbers and matrices. These libraries have all moved toward support of the draft ANSI standard for a common C++ library.

The Borland C++ system version 4.0 organizes its many classes into directories and files. It includes an integrated development environment and a simple browser. It works well under both MS-DOS and Microsoft Windows.

A class library is too large to have a simple file structure and is almost certain to be organized hierarchically. The description of an object is likely to be split into at least two files: a header file containing the description of the objects and files that contain the implementation code for the member functions of the objects. (The implementation code is often included in both source code and object code formats.)

The class library will often be organized to reflect the object hierarchy to make it easy to find related objects. Thus, we will be likely to have at least two parallel hierarchical organizations (header files for class descriptions and files containing the code for the member functions).

A class library is often quite complex in its organization. This is a result of three primary factors: the richness of its objects, the need for compatibility with previous versions, and the desire to have the objects in the class library make efficient use of existing objects so they can inherit essential functions from previously developed classes.

For example, the Borland C++ system for computers running MS-DOS or Microsoft Windows includes the following data structures as part of the large set of objects in its class library:

- B-trees
- bags
- deques (like queues, but with insertion or deletion from each end)
- hash tables
- lists (singly linked)
- lists (doubly linked)
- queues (priority)
- queues (regular)
- sets
- stacks
- trees

Some of the data structures just listed may be unfamiliar to you. Don't worry about the unfamiliar ones; we will concentrate on the data structures we discussed earlier in this chapter. For more information about these data structures, consult the references or any good book on data structures.

Let's examine these data structures from the perspective of software reuse. Note that many of the functions that can be applied to lists can also be applied to other data structures. The creation and destruction of a list are simply the common constructor and destructor functions we have seen many times before. The insertion and deletion operations are also included as part of nearly all other data structures. For these reasons, an object such as a stack or a queue is often defined in terms of an abstract list object.

For example, this is precisely the organization of the Borland C++ class library. The fundamental building block for the data structures in this library is the container class.

A C++ container class starts out empty. When objects are placed in the container, by default they are owned by the container. The objects are destroyed when the container is destroyed.

The classes stack, deque, queue, and priority queue have the following properties:

- The order of insertions and deletions is significant.
- Insertions and extractions can occur only at specific points, as defined by the individual class.

In Turbo C++ terminology, these container classes are known collectively as *sequence classes*. Note that a hash table does not fit the description of a sequence class. Neither does the set data structure.

Another class that can be derived from the abstract container class is a collection class. Examples of collection classes are the following unordered collections:

- bag
- hash table
- list (singly or doubly linked)
- abstract array

The collection class has a new feature that the container class did not—it is possible to determine if an object belongs to an object of a collection class by using a member function that tests data for inclusion.

This level of abstraction can be considerably extended. Additional features, such as ordering of the container class, can be used to describe sorted arrays, B-trees, or other structures.

Abstract data types serve as the basis for the organization of the portion of the class library devoted to basic data structures.

The following abstract data types can be implemented in several different ways using the fundamental data structures vector, list, and DoubleList: stacks, queues, deques, bags, sets, and arrays. Thus, all ADTs are implemented as vectors. In addition, stacks are implemented as a list, queues and deques as doubly linked lists.

For a variety of reasons, the data structures are implemented in two ways: with direct access to the structure and with indirect access using pointers. Additional functions are given so that the near and far pointers of different 80x86 architectures can be accommodated. (The terms *near pointer* and *far pointer* refer to the referenced object's being within 64 K memory segments in this architecture.)

For example, there are two implementations of the stack data structure. The functions

```
BI_OStackAsVector()
```

and

```
BI_TCStackAsVector()
```

refer, respectively, to a stack of pointers to a base class named Object and to a polymorphic stack of pointers to the base class Object. In each case, the implementations are done as a vector. The prefix BI indicates that these functions use what is called the "Borland International"; the O indicates that the code is object-based (nonpolymorphic); and the TC indicates that the code is object-based and compatible with earlier versions for the Turbo C++ class library.

The instantiation using typedef statements, such as

```
typedef BI_StackAsVector<int> intStack;
```

and

```
typedef BI_StackAsList<int> intStack;
```

are typical of the fine-tuning allowed for data types in this class library.

Each of the data structures is implemented using templates. Each template must be instantiated with a particular data type, which is the type of the element that the data structure will hold. A linked list of objects of type T will include code that looks something like this:

```
template <class T> class BI_ListImp
{
public:
   void add( T t ) {new BI_ListElement<T>(t, &head );
}
   // Add objects at head of list
   T peekHead() const { return head.next→data; }
};
```

What else should you expect to find in a class library? The proper treatment of strings is slightly delicate and requires careful design of objects. Thus, you are likely to find a string object included in a basic class library. There will usually be a class to describe complex numbers.

Implementations that make heavy use of a target computer's operating system are likely to have objects to represent several operating system functions. These might include access to the system clock, facilities to monitor the performance of running programs, or an interface to the GUI. On an 80x86-based personal computer running Microsoft Windows or on an Apple Macintosh, the class library is likely to include access to pop-up and pull-down menus, as well as the ability to locate and configure windows. The same interface to the GUI is expected on class libraries intended for use in a UNIX environment running X-Windows.

Note that there are many objects declared in typical class libraries and that it is very likely that a large portion of the lower-level programming has already been done for you.

The ready availability of class libraries suggests a natural question—how do we replace portions of an existing class library with some of our own code? Using a name such as list.h for a header file in your program means that you are including the local header file rather than a system-supplied file of the same name. We can reduce confusion in systems by using include statements such as

```
#include <list.h>
```

or similar instead of

```
#include "list.h"
```

to specify the use of a special directory for header files rather than a user-defined directory.

We can also use the C++ preprocessor statements #ifdef, #ifndef, #define, and #endif as in the code fragment

```
#ifndef LIST_NULL
#define LIST_NULL 0
#ifndef LIST_H
#define LIST_H
    // body of the definition goes here.
#endif
```

to make clear precisely which files and constants we wish to use in our program.

This technique is called "conditional compilation" and is especially useful when you are developing programs in a changing software environment. For illustrations of the use of conditional compilation in the rapidly changing area of different implementations of the UNIX operating system, see the UNIX books by myself or Stevens listed in the references section.

There is another view of this sort of configuration management for software library organization. The porting guide for the Solaris 2.x operating system [GOOD93] includes a discussion about library organization and dynamic library linking. These techniques allow programs to continue to work properly without the difficulty of inverting many conditional compilation directives and without having to recompile existing applications to work with new libraries.

The Free Software Foundation's GNU C, C++, and other compilers are readily available from the Internet. However, programs that use their code either as is or modify any of their code must include a statement of its origin and must in turn be made available to the public in source code version. This is termed "copyleft" by the Free Software Foundation.

In any event, we choose not to deal with any of these copyright (or copyleft) issues and will content ourselves with a description of the organization and contents of the class libraries of these systems.

The GNU C++ compiler for UNIX consists of a very large number of classes organized into directories and files. Many software tools are included in the C++ distribution or in other publicly available distribution sources. Their code is probably the most portable, since a goal of the Free Software Foundation (the organizers of the GNU project) is to ensure open access to source code as an aid to portability. The standard development environment does not integrate a language-sensitive editor and compiler. (Such integrated systems are available from vendors such as CenterLine.)

A CD-ROM containing this software library can be obtained easily from Walnut Creek and other sources.

A slightly less expensive collection of source code can be obtained directly from the C/C++ User's Group. The collection is on diskette rather than on CD-ROM, making it cheaper to purchase smaller amounts of software this way. Much of this code is written in C++.

The availability of source code for a compiler's class libraries can be very useful if you wish to port your source code to other environments. Source code is always available to users of the GNU system. In general, vendors' product information guides contain information on availability of source code.

Source code for other class libraries is also available on the Internet. At the time this book was being written, the World Wide Web listed several repository sites that were available. Some of these sources are given in App. 2.

An especially important source is the C++ "virtual library," which can be reached using the Uniform Resource Locator (URL)

```
http://info.desy.de/usr/projects/c++.html/
```

3.7   Reuse Libraries for C Language Software

A guiding feature in the development of the C programming language was its higher level of abstraction relative to what was available via assembly language programming.

The source code available for C includes nearly everything mentioned in the previous section. There is more code available in C than in C++ because C has been a popular programming language for a much longer time. In particular, the Internet sources, compiler vendors, and repackagers such as Walnut Creek provide easy ways to get access to small source code components. (The address for Walnut Creek can be found in App. 2.)

Technical commercial publications such as the *C/C++ Journal* and *C++ Report* also make software available at very low prices. This software ranges from libraries to complete applications.

Since successful programs of systematic software reuse must eventually focus on higher levels than source code, and there is a great danger of simply hacking code when programming in C, we will not describe specific C language source code reuse libraries in any more detail.

Instead, we will note that there are many higher-level software artifacts that are readily available and can greatly simplify reuse programs. For example, there are complete grammars and lexical descriptions of the ANSI version of the C programming language available on the Internet. Since these are in the correct format for use by the UNIX `lex` and `yacc` utilities, it is easy to write lexical and semantic analysis tools for evaluating C programs. This is a much higher level of reuse than developing such analyzers from scratch.

You should note however that such high-level software artifacts as formal grammars and lexical descriptions and the appropriate tools (in this case `lex` and `yacc`) are not a panacea for solving all software problems. For example, a study of certain NASA systems indicated that 44 percent of software errors for which a single source for the error was determined arose from a parsing routine. The parser had been generated using a formal grammar employing `lex` and `yacc`. However, the innate complexity of the command language being analyzed caused great difficulty, even for good programmers using advanced tools. (The command language had evolved over a period of more than 30 years.)

Another issue to be considered with reuse of source code written in C is the version of the language used. Some of the differences between different language versions are subtle, and their effects are difficult to trace, especially when used with operating systems different from the one for which they were first developed. The conditional compilation technique is likely to be required when using C libraries, especially with different operating systems than the one originally used.

There are other problems associated with reusing software written in the C language that are due to the language's treatment of pointers and arrays. The C statement

```
float *p;
```

declares p to be a pointer to an address that contains a floating point number. The C statement

```
float a[];
```

declares that a is an array of floating point numbers, with the address to be used as the starting address for the storage of elements, if any, of the array a. Nothing is stated about the amount of storage necessary for the array named a.

There is no conceptual difference between the two declarations just given. They each indicate a single address, and a C compiler has no way of distinguishing between a pointer and an array declaration. Indeed, the meanings of the two notations

```
a[0];
```

and

```
*a;
```

are identical, as are the two declarations

```
a[n];
```

and

```
*(a + n);
```

for any integer n. This is the basis for the use of pointer arithmetic in C (and C++).

Thus, it is impossible for either a human reader of source code or a compiler attempting to translate the source code to determine if the statement

```
char *a;
```

refers to the address of storage for a single character or if it refers to the address where the initial element of an array of characters (with the array possibly being terminated by a null byte ('\0') is stored.

The C function malloc() does not provide an easy way to check for memory errors. Consider the two C statements

```
char *str;
str = (char*) malloc (5*size of (char));
```

that allocate space for storage of five characters and return a pointer to this space.

A later C statement of

```
str = "Hello"
```

causes great difficulties in programs because the string `"Hello"` requires *six* characters for storage, since there is a final "\0" that terminates the string.

The difficulty here is a fundamental one. The C language treats pointers and arrays as identical concepts and cannot distinguish between the notations

```
char *p; /* a pointer to a single char*/
```

and

```
char *s; /* a pointer to a string of char*/
```

Some very good C software development environments include the ability to find errors such as the one indicated here. However, most C compilers would provide little help in this situation.

These memory allocation and pointer problems can cause major difficulties when such software is reused. Many programs that do not allocate memory properly will work forever on one computer but will crash the system when ported to another computer. A more difficult situation is when a subtle error occurs. Such errors are difficult to trace.

Other problems can occur because of the weak type checking in C. Passing a floating point number to a library function that expects a double precision argument is frequently ignored by C compilers.

We strongly recommend using the `lint` utility for C programs written on the UNIX operating system. There are also PC versions of `lint`. This utility can help locate several problems that many C compilers ignore. It is essential for reusable software written in C.

A slightly different approach to identifying type mismatches in C is to use a C++ compiler to test the C code. The system may not compile correctly because of differences in certain header files. However, all C++ compilers provide additional information about the number and type of arguments to a function and the function's return type. This is very useful information for software that is to be ported to other environments.

A formal certification process is essential for software written in C before the software is inserted into a reuse library. Certification of source code will be discussed in Chap. 4.

3.8   Reuse Libraries for Higher-Level Language Software

In this section we discuss some reusable components in languages that are higher level than Ada, C, C++, or FORTRAN. Specifically, we consider the effect of a fourth generation language (4GL) and higher level architectures.

Our view of what constitutes a high-level language is best illustrated by some work of Behrens on the Albrecht function point metric [BEHR87]. On the basis of an examination of several software systems, it was estimated that one function point corresponded to 320 lines of code in assembly language, 150 in C, 106 in COBOL, 16 in a query language, and 6 in a spreadsheet language.

While the absolute numbers might be controversial, there is little disagreement about the relative power of query and spreadsheet languages. In view of the cost savings possible with reuse of higher-level artifacts, it is reasonable to ask for libraries of such higher-level languages.

Unfortunately, we found little to be available, at least from inexpensive Internet sources. However, the potential for cost savings with reuse of such software artifacts is so great that commercial sources should be considered.

The ASSET catalog indicates the availability of bindings from Ada to SQL, thereby allowing the leveraging of database operations. (The original version of Ada, Ada83, had no special support for database operations.) This allows interoperability with commercial database packages and is a very encouraging prospect.

The ASSET catalog also indicates the availability of packages that can manipulate finite state machines. State machines offer greater opportunity for cost savings than does source code for abstract data types because the state machine paradigm fits so many programming situations.

The most common program paradigms seem to be state machines, database operations, parsing and other lexical analysis operations such as in a compiler, and GUIs.

The use of parser generator tools such as `lex`, `yacc`, `flex`, `bison`, `Alex`, and `Ayacc` greatly speed up the development process for standard grammars written in formats related to Backus-Naur form. Such tools have been used for many years.

Tools and languages to develop GUIs, such as the X Toolkit, UIL (User Interface Language), and others greatly accelerate the software development process. Languages such as Visual BASIC, Visual C, and Visual C++ are becoming increasingly useful in developing GUIs.

Thus, the availability of state machine manipulation software now means that there are existing software artifacts for most of the common program design paradigms.

The state machine package is written in Ada and has a simple interface. It lists the types and operations needed to manipulate a state machine over the exported state table. The package abstracts the type State_Machine. The generic formal parameters are as follows:

State $\rightarrow$ A discrete type that enumerates the possible states for a state machine.

Input $\rightarrow$ A discrete type that enumerates the possible inputs to a state machine.

Action $\rightarrow$ A discrete type that enumerates the possible actions that may be taken after a state machine makes a transition from one state to another.

This is a powerful package. It is written in Ada to make use of the facility for Ada generics. It would probably be a good idea to have this same facility available in C++ using templates.

Summary

There are many issues that must be considered when creating, modifying, using, or managing reuse libraries.

There are many places to look for general purpose reuse libraries of source code modules in particular computer languages such as Ada, C, C++, and FORTRAN.

Perhaps the most readily available source for Ada reusable software artifacts is the Public Ada Library (PAL), which is available on CD and contains many Ada packages and tools. The ASSET program also contains a catalog of reusable software assets and is available electronically and in printed form.

Before placing source code written in C into a reuse library, the code should be checked for memory allocation and pointer access problems. The lint utility should be used if available. Running the C source code through a C++ compiler can provide information about mismatches in the number and type of arguments or in the return type of a function.

There are few readily available sources for software artifacts developed using fourth generation languages. However, the potential for cost savings with reuse of such artifacts is so great that commercial sources should be considered.

Perhaps the most useful tool when managing a reuse library is configuration management.

Further Reading

There are few references on the proper management of reuse libraries. It is probably more useful to attend technical conferences, listening to the speakers and talking to practitioners and vendors of tools and libraries. The "lessons learned" papers are often extremely helpful.

The tutorial guides to the different publicly available resource libraries are excellent starting places.

Exercises

1. Choose one of the commonly available reuse libraries and estimate the number of directories, functions, and data types. Compute the average number of functions and data types per directory. For object-oriented libraries, compute the average number of abstract data types, objects, and methods (member functions).

2. Choose one of the commonly available reuse libraries and select two directories. Apply domain analysis to the contents, and see if your analysis agrees with the organization of the library into directories. Explain any major differences.

3. Select a module in a completed project and a reuse library that is available to you. Determine an appropriate set of specifications for matching components of a reuse library to queries. Apply the algorithm of Sec. 3.1 to determine if there is a match. Describe any difficulties you encounter.

4. Examine a collection of software written in C. Determine if any of the problems with pointer access and memory allocation that we have discussed in this chapter occur. If so, tell how you would modify the code. If you have access to the lint utility, apply it to the code.

5. Obtain the state machine software from the ASSET library. Rewrite the software in C++ using templates.

Chapter

4

Certification of Reusable Software Components

Suppose that, as a software developer, you are given a source code module and are allowed to reuse it as a component in a system that must be 100 percent failure-free. Suppose also that you know that this source code module is fault-free. Without examining the contents of the source code module could you assume that using it could not possibly affect the probability of a failure of the resulting system? Probably not. You might have to produce a considerable amount of preventive code for the module to be sure that the module could not cause the system to fail.

We recently had an experience that emphasized the difficulty of perfecting software. We had just had a conversation with a software engineer about a decision to base a fairly large software system entirely on COTS. While writing a report on a computer with a CPU from a well-known and respected company, using a well-known and respected word processor and spreadsheet for data analysis from a well-known and respected software house, the computer crashed several times performing simple tasks. Needless to say, we was not convinced that one could always depend on COTS to be error-free.

In this chapter we discuss the issue of certification of reusable software components. The testing, evaluation, and documentation of software artifacts is called *certification*. Certification is a process that must be performed after the software is placed in service but before the software artifact is entered into a reuse library. It must be a cornerstone of any successful software reuse effort if such an effort is to work over a reasonable interval of time. Certification is especially important if the software component is to be used in a different environment or in a different organization from the one in which it was originally developed.

We will use the standard terminology that a software *fault* is some deviation, however small, from the requirements of a system, and a software failure is the inability of a system to perform its essential duties. In an ideal world, software artifacts that are intended to be reused will be 100 percent fault-free. However, very few individuals with experience in the software industry believe that many systems of any significant complexity are perfect, and thus some degree of faults is unavoidable. Certification is intended to improve the chances that a reused artifact will work properly in a new environment.

The first two sections of this chapter describe the need for certification and the difference between certification and testing. Section 4.3 is devoted to procedures for certification and is divided into subsections that describe certification procedures for different types of software artifacts such as requirements, designs, source code modules, and the like. Section 4.4 describes some metrics that are helpful in a systematic program of software reuse.

Section 4.5 contains a brief description of software reliability. This section can be skipped by readers already familiar with the topic. Section 4.6 describes the relationship between certification, reliability, and testing.

In Sec. 4.7 we provide a different viewpoint on certification. In this last section we will present a scenario in which certification of a potentially reusable software artifact is delayed until the artifact is to be reused. The motivation for this approach is potential cost savings.

4.1   The Need for Certification

Suppose that a preliminary set of requirements has been developed for a new software system. At first glance, the two techniques of domain analysis and library or repository assessment (whether locally developed or not) might seem sufficient to develop a successful program of software reuse, at least for this new system. Domain analysis would let the software engineer or manager determine the appropriate reusable assets his or her ideal systems would need. An assessment of available repositories would then allow the software engineer to determine if the desired reusable asset were available. If it were, the component could then be included in the new system.

Unfortunately, much more is needed if the system is of any size or complexity. The reality is that domain analysis is an abstraction and must allow for inexact, approximate matches between different terms when searching for descriptions of appropriate library modules to perform certain functions.

In addition, as we have pointed out several times previously, the library search algorithms themselves are not perfect and must rely on inexact approximations.

Finally, and perhaps more important given the current state of software reuse practice and the flexibility of existing reuse libraries, an artifact in a reuse library may undergo some degree of modification before it is placed into service in a new system. The degree to which the artifact is reused should be reflected in the cost estimate for the new system.

For example, a source code module that has 90 percent of its code unchanged from the original component in the reuse library might have its testing requirements considerably reduced from those required to test a new source code component of the same size and complexity. The amount of testing would depend upon the nature of the code changed. For simple straight line code that prints a series of menu times, there is very little need for additional testing. For a few lines of code that change the logic of a real-time, embedded control system, a large amount of new testing might be necessary.

The reduction is clearest if the test plan for the module involves only examination of the logical predicates, or branches, in the module. If only one of ten branches is changed in a source code module taken from a reuse library then it is possible that only 10 percent of the original amount of module testing is required for this new module.

In the absence of information to the contrary, we will use the percentage of reused material in a software artifact as a first approximation of the cost savings associated with reuse in our cost models in Chap. 5. We will note for now that other savings are possible, depending upon the place of the artifact in the software life cycle.

Additional analysis of a software artifact before it is placed into a reuse library can produce considerable savings over the life cycle of the artifact, particularly if it is reused many times. Therefore, a reusable component obtained by the combination of domain analysis and reuse library assessment will need to be examined further before it is included in a system. This additional examination will result in the certification of a reusable component before it is placed into the reuse library.

Certification of reusable software components is thus a logical step in the reuse process. It involves a description of the component. This description will often be more complete than a description used for a normally documented component developed without reuse in mind because of the need for documentation of both the standards used and the performance characteristics of the algorithm used.

Let us consider the case of a source code module that is a candidate for inclusion in a reuse library. Good software engineering practice requires that a description of the module's interface, number and type of arguments, return type, purpose, and algorithm be included in the documentation of the module. However, this documentation is not adequate for a reusable component for several reasons.

It is easiest to illustrate this with an example. Many organizations have software development practices that require that each delivered source code module be tested according to organizational standards. This might mean that each decision path within the module is to be executed by some test data during the testing phase. If no errors occur, then the module is assumed to be correct.

Suppose now that the same module is reused in an application other than the one for which it was ordinarily created. If the new application system has a real-time requirement, then it is not immediately clear that the module can be used in the new system because of the new, real-time constraint.

However, suppose that the documentation for the module included an estimate for the upper bound of the running time of the module. This estimate could be given in terms of the size of the data (such as the number of elements in an array to be sorted), the number of arithmetic operations (for some computation), the testing that the module was given, test results, or the actual running time on some particular computer in a certain operating environment (CPU speed, memory size, time for context switches by the operating system, etc.). This type of documentation can make the module a much more attractive candidate for reuse than an equivalent module without this additional documentation.

Clearly, additional testing, evaluation, and documentation are required before we can be confident about the reuse of a module. This is true regardless of the fact that the module was included in a reuse library.

4.2 The Difference between Certification and Testing

Certification is an attempt to circumvent the limitations of software testing. These limitations include the practical impossibility of testing all possible execution paths through software, all possible module boundary conditions, all possible inputs in an interactive system, and all possible event sequences in a concurrent system. The limitations apply to nearly all systems of more than a few thousand lines of code. The number of program execution paths, boundary conditions, inputs, or event sequences may be a huge number or may in fact be infinite. This makes it impossible to completely test any nontrivial software.

In any event, exhaustive testing is usually impossible, and so some compromise is always necessary. This is usually described in a software testing strategy. Most software development organizations have detailed procedures describing their strategy for software testing. Similar statements apply to the regression testing that is necessary during software maintenance.

Thus, it is clear that there are levels of software testing. Software that has had each branch of a conditional statement tested (branch testing) is more likely to be correct than software that has not undergone these branch tests. A similar statement applies to software that has had every loop exercised at least once. This software in turn is less likely to be correct than software in which each nested loop has been tested at least once, and so on.

Certification is not a replacement for the testing process but is an additional step in the reuse-based software development process. It requires an additional examination of potentially reusable source code modules to determine errors that have not been observed previously.

Let us consider a typical testing process for a source code module. We will first consider modules that were developed using the procedural paradigm, which was the major development strategy before object-oriented techniques became common. As we suggested previously, this might include exercising each possible branch for each decision statement within the module. Other testing practices might include path testing (in which each logical path through the module is tested), loop parameter testing (each of the cases of zero, one, or many iterations of the loop is exercised), or other similar methods of white-box testing. The term white-box testing refers to testing based on the observed structure of the code and is different from black-box testing, which is based only on the interface and specifications of the module being tested.

The test process for object-oriented systems is considerably different from the process for procedurally developed ones. The notion of a driver module is not especially relevant to objects because of the primary nature of objects. In many common object-oriented programming languages, an object contains its own methods and data. The term *method* is often called "member function" and refers to the functions that are encoded as part of the object. The object responds to a "message" from an external source and reacts by acting on some combination of its private (only visible to the object) and public (visible to other objects as well as to the object itself) data. Most other object-oriented languages have similar features and definitions.

The theory of testing objects in object-oriented programs is in its infancy compared to the much older theory of testing modules in procedural programs. In general, the preferred test process involves a higher degree of code reading and either formal or informal reasoning about the correctness of the methods than is common in procedurally based modules. Special treatment is necessary for inheritance and the potential overloading of operators in object-oriented languages. For more information on the testing of objects, consult my book *Object-Oriented and Programming in C++* [LEAC95A] or the September 1994 special issue of the *Communications of the ACM,* which contains many articles on testing object-oriented programs.

We now return to the subject of software reuse. From this point on, we will assume that the organization that produced the software is satisfied with its software products in general as well as its testing process. (Without this assumption being correct, there is not much hope of a successful reuse program. Thus, you have to be careful when buying COTS products. Either you should know and trust the vendor, or else you should be willing to live with the problems that poor software creates.)

The fundamental reason to certify code is that a software module developed for one system might meet the specifications for that system but not the requirements of another.

As we indicated previously, we must know something about the performance of the module before we can allow it to be used in environments other than the one for which it was originally intended. Consider the case of a source code module that has had each possible Boolean decision executed during the testing process. Suppose now that the module is reused in a new setting and that during the course of the execution of the newly created software, a sequence of decisions is made that changes the internal "state" of the module from the one that existed when a particular logical branch of the program was chosen. That is, the software follows a different execution path in the new application that was not tested previously.

Suppose also that an error occurs because of this previously uncovered fault. Let us assume that the postmortem determines that the failure was caused by the reused source code module. Suppose further that the error causes severe hardship to a business because some essential customer data are lost. More critical problems would occur if the software is used to monitor a life support system in a hospital or control the flight path of an airplane.

There are many legal questions that will be raised because of the failure of this reused component. A statement such as "we used this software on another system and it worked fine" would not be very satisfactory.

A certification process is what is needed here. It goes beyond the normal testing procedures of the software-producing organization and determines either the correctness of the source code module or the relative risk of using the module in situations other than the one for which the software was originally designed. A risk-based approach is probably more appropriate in many applications because of the difficulty of proving the correctness of anything but the most simple programs.

Correctness is used here in the sense that the software being implemented is a perfect match to the design, which will be assumed to be correct. For a source code module, the design may be available in the form of internal documentation of the module using some pseudocode or program design language (PDL). The other sense in which the term *correctness* can be used is the fidelity of the code to the requirements for the software.

Unfortunately, the requirements used for many reusable source code modules are not readily available, and thus we would only be able to assume correctness of a match to design, not requirements. Any errors, omissions, or ambiguities in the original requirements can cause a system to fail, even if the system's design faithfully satisfies the requirements and the source code faithfully implements the design.

The issue of correctness for COTS products is more complicated. In most cases, the designs are not made available to purchasers without considerable extra cost. The detailed requirements for COTS systems available are frequently only at the highest levels. The best approach is to know the COTS vendor, know the reputation of the vendor's products, and attempt to match the declared interfaces of the COTS product with the functionality needs of the system you are developing.

Note that complete testing of many modules is impossible because there are an infinite number of possible execution paths in the module. Interactive systems and systems with multiple processes running (either on the same or different CPUs) are notorious for making the testing of all possible combinations and sequences of inputs impossible.

Potentially reusable software artifacts other than source code should be certified before they are placed into a reuse library. For example, any documentation should be read by an independent team before it is placed in a reuse library for use in a new system. The purpose of this is to provide an independent view of the documentation and avoid major inaccuracies.

Certification of a reusable software artifact should be based on at least two factors: the perceived correctness of the artifact and the values of some metrics that describe the potential for reuse of the artifact. The metrics should indicate the number of other software systems that might be expected to use the artifact, the difficulty of incorporating the artifact into other software systems, and some sort of quality assessment of the artifact.

Requirements and designs intended for reuse can also benefit from a certification process. Perhaps the simplest method is to enter the design or requirements into a CASE tool. The benefit of this activity is that the potential reusable software artifact is tested for consistency using the internal checks provided in the CASE tool. In this case, the perceived correctness and the values of some relevant metrics are also important.

The same two factors of perceived correctness and the values of some relevant metrics are also applicable to reusable documentation and test data, as we shall see in the next section.

4.3 Suggested Standards and Practices for Certification of Software Artifacts

In this section we will recommend some development practices that will improve the utility and reliability of potentially reusable components. Suggested standards will be given for several different types of software artifacts.

Following the analogy with software testing, it is not surprising that there are potentially several levels of certification. For simplicity, we will only describe two levels, which we call basic and complete. Unfortunately, this terminology is not standard.

You should note that most researchers in the area of software reuse believe that there is nothing resembling a formal standard for certification of reusable software components either now or on the foreseeable horizon because of proprietary concerns and time pressures. We subscribe to these beliefs. Therefore, we will restrict ourselves with some appropriate practices before a software artifact is placed into a reuse library.

The suggested standards and practices presented here are guidelines. They should be integrated into the organization's software development methodology whenever possible. To help with this process, we will separate the guidelines into two parts: a minimal set of activities that can be performed in nearly all software development environments at low cost and a more elaborate set of activities that will provide more robust and reliable software components as part of a reuse effort in organizations with more advanced software programs. (The term *advanced* is used in the sense of adhering to the list of higher-level software engineering practices given either in the Software Engineering Institute's Capability Maturity Model [CMM] or NASA's/Goddard Software Engineering Laboratory's Process Improvement Model.)

Most of the guidelines require the computation of certain metrics. We will mention some relevant metrics briefly in this section and discuss them in more detail in Sec. 4.4.

There may be some reluctance to collect and analyze data at even the minimal level suggested here. Note that it is unlikely that even the more elaborate model is likely to add less than 10 percent to total software development costs, but that the advanced practices should help prevent canceled projects and major cost overruns. The 10 percent figure is taken from experience on several projects at NASA/Goddard and is an upper bound. The Software Engineering Laboratory reports many projects with data collection costs closer to 5 percent [SEL95]. Your organization will probably be in this range.

The 5 or 10 percent figure mentioned in the previous paragraph seems like a large amount of overhead for projects. However, the costs of not collecting this data may in fact be much larger because of the loss of early warning about potential disasters in project development. Software models such as the CMM or Process Improvement Model have shown their effectiveness in a variety of situations. The most advanced of these models require that metrics be collected, analyzed, and used to control the software development process. Most organizations that score high in the assessments of their software development process according to the CMM or Process Improvement Model believe the extra overhead investment pays for itself.

We have chosen to present certification procedures for source code first since this is likely to be the first place where a certification process for reusable software artifacts is implemented in an organization.

4.3.1 Code certification

Certification of source code is the most common form of additional assessment performed on software artifacts before they are placed into reuse libraries. We assume that the source code has been tested to the satisfaction of the development organization and is now considered a candidate for reuse.

The next step is to compute the values of some relevant metrics. The metrics should address testability, ease of interconnection with other modules, and the probability that the source code module is complete at the time of placement into the reuse library.

We suggest the following practices be followed as part of a minimum cost program for certification of source code components:

- Domain analysis
  The module should be subjected to domain analysis. This will aid in the proper classification when the module is placed into a reuse library and will help with library access.

- Metrics
  The goals of measuring source code modules in a reuse library are to determine any potential problems when interfacing the module to

other software. Potential problems include the size and quality of the interface and the likelihood of any untested errors remaining in the module. The module should be evaluated for at least three things:

1. Size of the interconnection to other modules
   Modules with too large an interface are poor candidates for inclusion into a reuse library because of projected costs in system integration.
2. Number of logical predicates in the module
   An overly large number of predicates suggests difficulty in testing. McCabe [MCCA76] suggests the use of the number 10 as a warning flag. Many organizations use a higher number, based on their experience.
3. Stability of the module
   This metric should indicate a range of values for the number of changes to a module. Fewer modification requests for the code than normal for a module of the same size for the organization suggest that the code is mature and correct. Conversely, a larger than average number of modification requests for the code suggests that either there have been several design changes (perhaps due to requirements changes) or else the code has many residual errors. In either case, the code should be examined again.

- Coding problems
  The code should be examined for memory allocation and pointer access problems. If a form of the lint utility is available, it should be used to examine C source code. C source code should also be run through a C++ compiler to obtain more information about inconsistencies in the number and type of arguments to a function or in a function's return type.

- Atomic operations
  Any source code that makes use of a shared system resource must be atomic. This means that the operation, once started, is either uninterruptible or else has essential data rolled back to a previous state if the CPU is interrupted. Operating system calls can usually be assumed to be atomic. However, using the return values of user-defined functions that contain system calls within their code, rather than using the system calls directly, may leave essential data in an inconsistent state if there is a context switch during that function's execution.

- Test plan
  A test plan and the set of test results should be available and linked to the module when both are placed into the reuse library.

- Untested logic
  Any untested logic in the module should be indicated in the module's documentation so the probability of an untested logical error in the module when used in a new environment can be estimated.

- Documentation
  The documentation should indicate the performance of the module in a real-time environment. It should also indicate the system resources needed for the module. The documentation should be read by a person not familiar with the module in its original setting.

- Standards
  The source code module should be evaluated to make sure it meets the organization's coding standards.

A more elaborate certification process for source code modules would include all of the foregoing and in addition would include

- Entry of the source code module into a CASE tool for a consistency check.

4.3.2 Requirements certification

Requirements certification is intended to allow a high level of leverage of life cycle costs in the event of future reuse.

We suggest the following practices be followed as part of a minimum cost program for certification of requirements:

- Domain analysis
  The requirements should be subjected to domain analysis. Each entry in the requirements traceability matrix should also be included in the domain analysis.

- Metrics
  Some metrics should be computed for the system's requirements. The goals of these metrics are to determine the size of the requirements and the resulting system. The Albrecht function point metric [ALBR83] is perhaps the best-known metric for requirements. The cost estimates for the previous systems built using the requirements that are to be reused should be compared to the actual costs, and any unusual deviations should be noted and explained. As a minimum, any requirements metrics collected should be entered into a database. Since reuse of a set of system requirements is similar to reuse of an off-the-shelf product (whether COTS or privately produced), size metrics will help predict costs if the system is employed in future projects. This metrics data will be important for estimating size of

systems where the number of lines of code provides little relevant information.

- Documentation
  The documentation should be read by a person not familiar with the module in its original setting.

A more elaborate certification process for requirements would include all of the above and in addition would include

- Entry of the source code module into a CASE tool for a consistency check.

4.3.3 Design certification

Certification of a system's design is somewhat simpler than certification of its requirements. Many of the issues involved in requirements reuse will also appear here.

We suggest the following practices be followed as part of a minimum cost program for certification of designs:

- Domain analysis
  The design should be subjected to domain analysis.

- Metrics
  Here the goal of the metrics is to produce as simple a design as possible, with the coupling between subsystems minimized. Metrics that compute the degree of interconnection among different subsystems or modules should be collected. System designs with broad interfaces should be reviewed to reduce integration and testing costs. The cost estimates for the previous systems built using the design that is to be reused should be compared to the actual costs for implementation of the design, and any unusual deviations should be noted and explained.

- Documentation
  The documentation should be read by a person not familiar with the module in its original setting.

- Test plan
  The test plan should be read by a person not familiar with the module in its original setting.

A more elaborate certification process for software designs would include all the foregoing and in addition would include a

- CASE tool
  The design should be entered into a CASE tool for a consistency check.

4.3.4 Test plan and test results certification

We suggest the following practices be followed as part of a minimum cost program for certification of test plans:

- Metrics
  The goals here are to improve the testing process and improve quality. The number of test cases, number of untested paths, and error pattern (number of errors detected at each phase of the life cycle) should be counted. Here the term *error* includes both software faults and software failures.

- Untested logic
  This is related to the metrics collected in the previous items.

- Documentation
  The documentation should be read by a person not familiar with the module in its original setting.

A more elaborate certification process for test plans would include all the preceding practices and in addition would include

- Domain analysis
  There is no reason to apply domain analysis to test plans or test results. However, the module associated with a particular test plan or test results should be subjected to domain analysis.

- CASE tool
  If the CASE tool supports the capabilities for inclusion of test plans and test results, they should be entered into a CASE tool for a consistency check.

- Reliability modeling
  Ideally, the error data should be entered into a reliability model. One of the purposes of a reliability model is to determine the number of residual errors remaining in the software at each step in testing. See Sec. 4.5 for a brief discussion of software reliability.

4.3.5 Documentation certification

We suggest the following practices be followed as part of a minimum cost program for certification of documentation:

- Domain analysis
  The documentation should be subjected to domain analysis.

- Metrics
  The goals here are to measure the size and utility of the documentation. The number of new, reused, and total pages should be recorded.

The reading level should also be obtained. (See Sec. 4.4 for a discussion of measurements of reading levels.)

A more elaborate certification process for documentation would include the preceding practice as well as a

- CASE tool
  The documentation should be entered into the same CASE tool as the design, source code, or requirements.

4.3.6   System certification

We suggest the following practices be followed as part of a minimum cost program for certification of systems:

- Domain analysis
  The system should be subjected to domain analysis.
- Metrics
  The metrics collected should include those collected for the individual source code modules in the system and the Albrecht function point metric such as those collected for the requirements or design. The size of the interface should also be measured.
- Documentation
  The documentation should be read by a person not familiar with the module in its original setting.

A more elaborate certification process for systems would include the preceding practices as well as the following:

- CASE tool
  As much of the system as possible should be entered into a CASE tool for a consistency check.
- Test plan and test results
  These should be kept and entered into a reliability model for the system.

4.4   The Role of Metrics

Metrics are used to provide feedback about the efficiency of the software development process and the quality of the software produced. The values of a metric can indicate that certain attributes of a software artifact fall within generally accepted standards for software engineering processes and products, thereby suggesting a degree of confidence in the process or product.

For example, the commonly used lines-of-code metric can be used to determine if source code modules are excessively long. Source code modules with fewer than, say, 10 lines of code are probably much easier to understand and modify than modules that are 1000 lines long. The Halstead length, volume, and effort metrics provide additional assessment of the size of a source code module [HALS77]. Unfortunately, these metrics ignore the control flow or data complexity of the source code. The primary goal of the lines of code and Halstead metrics is to measure the size of a source code unit.

Alternatively, a software artifact for which the value of some metric exceeds certain standards is much less likely to inspire confidence in its quality. What we have in mind is the approach of organizations such as Hewlett-Packard, in which source code modules with a McCabe cyclomatic complexity greater than 10 must be returned to the software developer for further analysis and test plan design. (The McCabe cyclomatic complexity indicates the complexity of the logic of the program. It is based on an analysis of the control flow graph. It will be discussed in App. 1, along with other relevant source code metrics.)

There is nothing magic about the use of the number 10. Many organizations will use a very different number because of the nature of their typical software application. It is generally dangerous to arbitrarily use a single number without considering its validity in a particular setting. The goal of the McCabe metric is to determine the complexity of the execution paths within a source code unit.

One major concern regarding source code modules concerns the nature of their interface to other modules. Neither the Halstead or McCabe metrics attempt to measure the interconnection to other modules. Thus, neither of them meets the goal of the interconnection metrics: to determine the size of the interface between modules or program subsystems.

The size of the interface between source code modules can be measured in several ways.

One metric, popularized by Kafura and Henry, is called the *fan-in-fan-out metric* [KAFU81]. This metric involves a count of the difference between the number of inputs to modules and the number of outputs from modules. This metric is recommended by the REBOOT project [KARL95]. This is an interconnection metric.

A recently developed metric, called the *BVA metric* because of its theoretical origins in the testing of source code by boundary value analysis, counts the inputs and includes estimates of the number of test cases needed for complete white-box testing using boundary value analysis [LEAC96B]. A different metric for estimating coupling and cohesion of source code modules is described in [DHAM95]. These interconnection metrics are also described in App. 1.

Another measurement of a source code module is its stability. An unstable module (one that has undergone many modification requests) is not very promising as a candidate for reuse. Stability is easy to estimate if the module was developed under revision control. It is simply a weighted sum of the product of the number of modifications and the size of each change. The sum should be computed for equal-length periods, such as for a year. High numbers suggest poor candidates for reuse.

Some of the metrics used for source code can be applied to software artifacts at other phases of the life cycle. For example, the McCabe cyclomatic complexity can be computed from PDL (program design language) or from a detailed design. The interconnection metrics can also be estimated from a detailed design.

We now consider metrics that can be applied to the requirements and high-level design phases of the life cycle. The earlier we can estimate some aspect of software, the earlier we can plan for its effective use.

The most commonly used metrics are the simple ones of counting the number of bulleted items and the Albrecht function point metric. The number of bulleted items indicates the size of the requirements traceability matrix. While a single number can be very misleading, it does provide a rough measure of the difference between different systems for which the requirements are written by the same person or organization.

We will illustrate these measurements with a simple example: a simulation for a disk operating system that was written as a teaching aid for an undergraduate operating systems course taught at Howard University. For demonstration purposes, the simulation allowed interaction with a user to do several things, including:

- Select blocks of data to be loaded directly into the simulated memory.
- Select blocks of data to be moved from simulated memory to a simulated disk.
- Select blocks of data to be moved from the simulated disk to simulated memory.
- Print the contents of the simulated memory.
- Print the contents of the simulated disk.
- Simulate the action of a virtual memory paging system using a set of commands from an external file.
- Install a tiny, UNIX-like file system using details on file contents and locations to be read from an external file.

There are seven bulleted items listed in the preceding set of high-level requirements. Expanding the high-level requirement for the selection of blocks of data to be loaded directly into the simulated memory would include specification of requirements for the user interface, error checking, and actions to handle boundary situations such as the simulated memory being full when an attempt is made to load data directly. This expansion of requirement details would add three to the count of the number of bulleted requirements.

The Albrecht function point metric provides an assessment of the functional complexity of a system based on its use of external entities such as the human-computer interface and interaction with external files and databases. This metric does not require any source code to be computed. As such, it is suitable for evaluating the functionality of systems and their interfaces.

For our simple example, there are two types of interfaces: with a user and with external files. The user is asked to select options from a main menu. Hard-coded interactions occur with the two external data files. Each of these types of interaction can cause different problems for a system. Potential software problems include incorrect user response to a request for input or incorrectly formatted data fields within a file. The Albrecht function point metric is primarily a weighted sum of the number of interactions multiplied by a subjective assessment of the importance of the interactions as well as their complexity. The weights would be different for the user responses to a menu and the number of external file interactions. Other factors are used to make a final adjustment to the value of this metric.

The Albrecht function point metric is discussed in App. 1. For more information on this metric, consult Albrecht and Gaffney [ALBR83].

Test plans and test cases should also be evaluated quantitatively. Measurements of the percentage of branches or execution paths covered by a test plan provide useful information. Unfortunately, there are few commonly agreed upon metrics for these software artifacts.

We will be content with a combination of quantitative and qualitative metrics to be kept for test plans. We recommend the following metrics: organization of test plan (branch testing, path testing, white-box, black-box, object-oriented, etc.), completeness of test coverage, and the use of operational profiles (if any).

For test cases, the metrics are more quantitative. In addition to the results of individual test cases, the results of any regression testing analysis should be given to measure stability. The time and effort expended fixing any known errors should also be given so they may be incorporated into reliability models.

The reading level is a good metric to use for documentation. Generally speaking, lower reading levels are better, especially if the documentation will be read by nondevelopers. The reading level is probably sufficient for documentation of a system's user interface. Knowledge of the application domain is generally required to understand more technical details of a potentially reusable system.

The Kincaid and other reading level tests are useful in this context. They are available from many sources and are included in the wwb (writer's workbench) package commonly available on AT&T System V UNIX. The wwb tool does what every modern, complete word processing system does: it indicates incorrectly spelled words, double words, missing punctuation, and other ungrammatical constructions.

This software has many features not commonly available in commercial word processing systems. The metrics computed by the wwb tool generally include the document's reading level and its ranking compared to some documents deemed to be examples of clear writing. The wwb tool indicates unusual sentence complexity, such as too many compound-complex sentences, or the other extreme, too many simple declarative sentences, which make the document seem choppy. The wwb tool also flags documents that use the passive voice too much.

4.5   An Overview of Software Reliability

Electrical and mechanical equipment is well known to follow a "bathtub" curve during its useful life. That is, the equipment is most likely to fail at the beginning of its placement into service because of poor installation, faulty design, or one bad component. After the equipment has been "burned in," it typically works well for some interval of time and then begins to have more and more need of repair as different components wear out. Eventually, the cost to repair the equipment becomes too high, and it is taken out of service.

This situation is shown in Fig. 4.1. In this figure as well as in Fig. 4.2, the vertical axis represents the number of faults, and the horizontal axis represents time.

The term *software reliability* appears confusing at first glance. Software doesn't wear out (although the medium on which the software resides may). Thus, software reliability would not seem to be measurable. However, software errors and the lengths of intervals of correct operation *are* measurable quantities.

Software reliability models are based on statistical estimates of the failures that remain in software after each checkpoint in the development life cycle. In this context, the term *checkpoint* can refer to the correction of an error in the software at some phase of the testing process, in some release of the software, or at the time of some external event.

faults

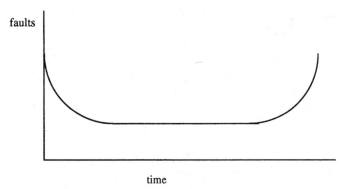

time

Figure 4.1 The typical "bathtub curve" for malfunctions of electrical and mechanical equipment.

faults

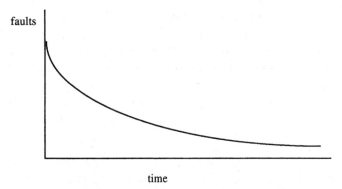

time

Figure 4.2 A typical probability distribution for software reliability.

Software reliability models such as those of Musa, Iannino, and Okumoto [MUSA87] or Musa [MUSA93] are the basis for the estimates, which are frequently measured as the *mean time between failures* or MTBF.

The basic premise of software reliability is that faults that can cause failures will remain in the software regardless of the efforts made to detect and correct them. Reliability theory estimates the remaining failures, the so-called residual faults, by using existing fault data collected at the checkpoints to develop a probability model of the distribution of the software's errors.

It is important to note that the data used in the reliability model are collected before the software is released. The data collected are placed into an appropriate probability distribution model that is then used to predict the behavior of the software after delivery.

The organization used for the reliability model in this type of situation is shown in Fig. 4.2.

The reason for applying a software reliability model to a software system is to determine the probability distribution of software faults over time. The key variable is the time between distinct software faults, the so-called interfailure time.

This means that the number and timing of faults occurring at each checkpoint in the development process is obtained, and the data are then analyzed. The checkpoints can be continually updated during the testing process, at regular time intervals, or at milestones in the development of the source code. A commonly used milestone is the completion of an internal release for the software. Ideally, the information is collected on a per-system or, better yet, on a per-module basis. For simplicity's sake, we restrict our attention to a single reliability test of an entire system.

The method of data collection is interesting. The objective is to count the number of failures at each checkpoint in a way that is consistent with the way the software will actually behave when it is placed into service. In practice, this means that an operational profile must be obtained.

An operational profile is a set of inputs to the software based on an assessment of how the software will be used in practice. Thus, for the disk simulation software briefly given as an example when we discussed the function point metric in Sec. 4.4, an operational profile would include a stream of inputs of menu selections interspersed with data to be placed in the simulated memory or disk. Different external data files to represent file systems to be simulated would also be included.

The selection of items in the input stream used for the operational profile is guided by how the software is actually used. Often a profiler is used to determine precisely which functions in the software are exercised in "typical" uses. Many of the choices of inputs are randomly generated. For more details on this process, see Musa, Iannino, and Okumoto [MUSA87] and Fenton and Pfleeger [FENT96].

Once the data are collected, they must be analyzed. The idea is to fit a probability distribution to the data so that errors that will occur in the future can be predicted. The most commonly used probability distributions are the Poisson and exponential distributions. See Box et al. [BOX78] and Montgomery [MONT91] or any good book on applied probability and statistics for more information about estimating probability distributions.

If your organization does not collect reliability data, it should begin to do so immediately using any internal data about errors as well as modification requests to fix errors after release of the system. The data should be entered into a database, and the error-prone modules should be checked. This data will help to flag modules that are likely to cause problems in a reuse situation. They will often help in flagging modules and systems that are so complex and difficult to modify and test that they should not be modified unless the change provides extremely large benefits for the organization producing or using the software.

Several issues need to be addressed in reliability modeling. For example, we must be certain that the data are accurate and pertinent. Using only fault data forms, in which all information is filled out, is not accurate because it may give a biased sample. Test data are not relevant if they attempt to predict failure under operational loads that are different from testing loads.

The recommended practice for reliability is [IEEE88] as follows:

1. Estimate size of source code.

2. Estimate fault density (faults per KLOC). This is best done by reusing the fault density from projects that are similar in their requirements, in the development methodology, and in the programming environment. If no estimate is available, then a number in the range 10 (for routine programs) to 1 (in a disciplined environment, with programmers experienced in the application domain) should be assumed.

3. Multiply the two numbers from steps 1 and 2 to get the expected number of faults at the beginning of formal testing.

4. Select a model for the probability distribution of the reliability data, generally the Musa Basic Model or the Jelinski-Moranda Model. Several other models, including the Keiller-Littlewood Model, could also be used.

5. Determine the key values:

   - Initial number of faults
   - Probability of executing a specific fault during a single execution (the *fault exposure ratio*). A good default value is 5×10^{-7}. This allows us to model the expected time interval between successive software faults.
   - Time for which prediction is to be valid
   - Failure probability per fault and unit time
   - Initial failure rate [IEEE88]

The most important use of reliability measures is for a general assessment of the system's quality and as an indication of when to stop testing (when the expected number of errors remaining meets the objective error rate).

This information can indicate where the testing process should be stopped, depending upon the ultimate reliability goal of the number of defects remaining per KLOC.

A typical situation is shown in Fig. 4.3. The curved line in this figure represents the probability that a particular number of faults (as measured on the vertical axis) remains in the code at the time indicated by the horizontal axis.

Note that detailed reliability information is not likely to be readily available for software that is not developed in house. It may not even be available for locally developed software if the organization's software development standards do not require it to keep reliability data.

However, some software fault information is almost always available for software developed in house. The fault ratio (number of software faults per KLOC) is probably well known and readily available. If not, it can be deduced easily from known size information and testing data. Clearly, any potentially reusable software artifact should undergo a severe test of its fault ratio.

Fault information can often be obtained from other groups within the same organization if sufficient effort is applied and the organization is supportive.

The situation with COTS is somewhat different. Very few commercial organizations release fault information. In fact, they often claim that there are no known faults. This is often supported by licensing agreements stating that there is no guarantee the software will work. No software manufacturer that we are aware of makes a blatant attempt to defraud the buyer. Instead, there are often subtle errors that are hard to detect during the products' development and testing.

If the COTS vendor is likely to stay in business, purchasing a maintenance agreement is generally the only way to go. If you cannot be sure the COTS vendor will stay in business, it may still make sense to purchase the product, depending on your needs. In this case, you will need to make alternative arrangements about maintenance.

Of course you will need source code to perform your own maintenance. (It is a good idea to always purchase source code for any nonstandard COTS product. It is not always necessary to purchase source code for a standard word processor or database manager.) You should note that much of the time spent in software maintenance is devoted to code reading. Therefore, this time, and hence maintenance costs, will be larger if your organization has to maintain a COTS product developed elsewhere. The potential increase in maintenance costs will be reflected in several cost estimation models that we will discuss in Chap. 5.

In the absence of any information about the reliability of the software, it is probably appropriate to assume that it is of the same quality as most other software used for a project. That is, you should assume

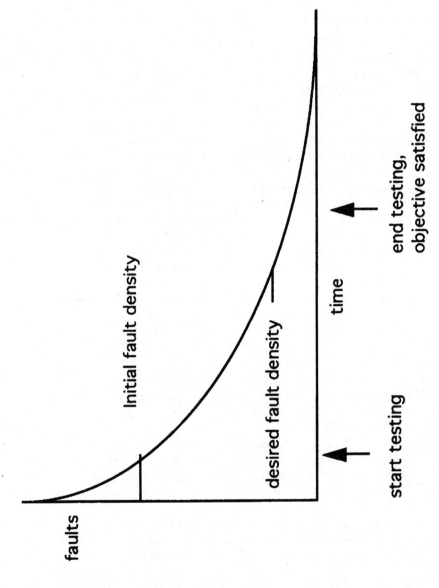

Figure 4.3 The use of reliability models.

that its fault ratio is the average of your other systems' ratios for similar applications. Be careful of comparing fault ratios between different application domains. There is considerable variation.

4.6   Certification, Testing, and Reliability Modeling

In this section, we discuss the relationship between certification of reusable source code modules, testing, and reliability measurements.

Suppose that a source code module is certified for reuse in an application domain that is different from the application domain in which the software was originally developed. Our view previously has been that proper certification of a source code module is necessary and sufficient to allow other modules to use this module at will.

However, there are some researchers who believe that certification is a dynamic activity. One of the most readily available expositions of this viewpoint was presented in an article by Wohlin and Runeson in the *IEEE Transactions on Software Engineering* in 1994 [WOHL94]. Their view is that the certification of a source code module must include software reliability information for use in further statistical analysis.

The simplest way to illustrate this point is to consider the way in which the potentially reusable source code module was tested. In a traditional, procedurally based environment, the module was (presumably) extensively tested according to certain preset testing criteria. These criteria may have consisted of white-box testing, black-box testing, or some combination of the two. If the software being tested was object-oriented, then presumably some other appropriate testing method was used. There was generally no particular use made of the operational profile of the system of which the module was a component.

Now consider the case where the potentially reusable module is to be used in another system, whether in the same or a different application domain. The same testing standards, using the same testing criteria, will produce the same results. This is expected, since we would expect to be able to reuse the test plans, test results, and documentation for any reused source code module. Indeed, this is a primary reason why the life cycle cost of reusable software should be less than that of newly created code.

However, it is unlikely that the testing process used for this module made any use of the operational profile of the system in which it was used. We are therefore faced with two alternatives:

- The correctness of the module is independent of the operational profile of the system in which it is embedded.

- The correctness of the module is dependent on the operational profile of the system in which it is embedded.

Our view of the certification process is that the first alternative applies; the view of Wohlin and Runeson is that the second is the appropriate viewpoint.

Another phrasing of the dilemma suggested by these two alternatives is the following question:

Is certification permanent or is it either application- or domain-dependent?

Consider the consequences of these two alternatives for software reuse methodologies. In the first alternative, once the module is entered into the reuse library, the prospective user can be relatively confident that the module is correct and has satisfactory performance. We have slightly qualified our confidence in the module's correctness, indicating that we are "relatively confident" because we believe the testing and certification processes are sufficient.

This form of reuse is the least expensive, at least initially, because there are few, if any, changes to the source code module. Thus, the system can be developed more quickly than if new code were developed to replace the module that is already in the reuse library. However, there may be considerable costs later in the new system's life cycle if this strategy is employed.

The second alternative incorporates information about the reliability of the module in question into the reuse library. That is, in addition to the source code, documentation, test plans, test suites, and test results, some sort of reliability measurement is incorporated into the reuse library entry for this module. The intent of the second alternative is to use this information to develop a reliability estimate for the module and the new system in which it is placed.

In the second alternative, the operational profile is used as a major factor in testing the system. Since the operational profile is almost certain to change in the new application, the assumption here is that the existing test data for the source code module are not completely relevant to the behavior of the module in the new system. Therefore, the module must be recertified before it is reused, at least according to this viewpoint.

Which of these alternatives is the correct approach to the reuse of source code modules in different application domains or at least in applications where the operational profile is different from the one in which the modules were originally used?

The answer is far from obvious, at least from a theoretical perspective. However, an informal assessment of the state of the practice of software reuse will provide some guidance.

Many software-producing organizations have been concerned with reuse for many years but practice only some form of ad hoc reuse. The movement toward systematic reuse has been slow, to a large extent because of problems in domain analysis, reuse library maintenance, and component selection.

These realities are not going to disappear in the near future, and thus the first alternative appears more promising, at least in the short term. We will emphasize the use of this first alternative of a single certification action, with only occasional reference to the notion of application-specific certification.

A stronger argument can be made in favor of permanently certifying source code components for those components that are to be reused in safety-critical applications. For such applications, this is the only alternative consistent with the goal of software reuse—to be able to recover the original investment in the software component and to be able to trust that any new system built using this component will not fail because of the component. Thus, for safety-critical applications, we favor a single, absolute certification of source code modules before they are placed as components into a reuse library. Of course, this certification should be updated as more information, particularly negative information, becomes available for a module.

For other types of applications not involving safety-critical uses, deciding the level of certification is not as straightforward. Thus, another approach to certification is described in the next section.

It should be noted that Wohlin and Runeson based their research on object-oriented systems, for which the problems associated with software reuse *appear* to be much more tractable because of the higher degree of information hiding. Their approach may be better suited to reuse in object-oriented systems than in the legacy systems that many people wish to reuse, at least in part. In any event, the experience with object-oriented systems is so new that little data are available on the ease of maintenance of object-oriented systems.

A final observation is in order concerning the reliability of software components. The goal of course is the same as for all software reuse efforts and much of the work in object-oriented technology: to develop a system of interchangeable components with specific interfaces so that systems can be developed at higher levels more cheaply, quickly, and reliably. However, we often use somewhat subjective factors in our decision making.

Consider for example, the problem a consumer is faced with when purchasing a personal computer. The general information about the speed of the microprocessor; the amount of physical memory, cache memory, or disk capacity; the speed of available CD-ROM drives; the size of the power supply; and the software that is available is easy to determine from manufacturer's advertising or sales information. However, the consumer will have a great deal of difficulty determining which system is most reliable, unless he or she consults a different source, such as a consumer product evaluation magazine or a computer magazine that performs tests or conducts surveys. In many cases, the marketplace eventually drives out inferior products (we hope). However, the purchaser of an inferior system is probably not happy knowing that he or she participated in a market experiment and probably would have preferred to have had the reliability data available to make a more informed decision about the (presumed) trade-off between price and quality.

4.7   Certification of Potentially Reusable Software Components Is Not Always Necessary

The discussion so far indicates that it is expensive to certify potentially reusable software components. One way to reduce the overall cost of a systematic program of software reuse is to use a *certify-on-demand* *approach*. This can avoid the costs of certifying software artifacts that are not likely to be reused, even though these artifacts have been placed into a reuse library.

When the certify-on-demand approach is used, all potentially reusable components are placed in a reuse library, but those components that are not certified are identified with a special symbol or flag. The domain analysis process and the implementation of an algorithm to determine appropriate matches between reuse library components and desired features are the same as before. Reuse library searches may be slower than with precertification because we have not considered potential for later reuse, and thus our libraries may be considerably larger than otherwise.

The special symbols or flags associated with the selected reuse library component are then examined to determine if the component has been certified. If the component is marked as certified, the component is used as desired, either as is or with necessary modifications. This is exactly the same procedure we would follow in a software development environment in which all reuse library components have been certified prior to their placement into a reuse library.

If the reuse library component has not already been certified, it should be subjected to additional testing because it may not yet have been tested in the new environment for which it is intended.

Techniques analogous to the certify-on-demand approach are used frequently in computer science. These techniques are called by many different names. For example, the techniques of deferred evaluation of operands in an expression, late binding in Lisp programs, and lazy look-ahead in Pascal use similar ideas. As with these alternate techniques, the efficiency of the certify-on-demand technique depends on the relative frequency with which previously uncertified reuse library components are requested relative to the total number of requests for reuse library components.

Of course, the certify-on-demand approach has a considerable time penalty in that location of a potentially reusable component is not the end of the reuse process. The time needed for additional testing of any uncertified components must be added to the overall cost of software development. Therefore, this time penalty can occur at the most inopportune time and can delay the release of new systems.

There is an additional problem if the certification of the module is dependent on the application domain, as Wohlin and Runeson suggest. This time penalty can be even greater if the reusable software component has a high reliability requirement that is different from the reliability requirement in the original application domain.

Of course, the benefit of the certify-on-demand approach is the potential reduction in the costs of setting up and maintaining the reuse library.

There is a compromise position that is based on a rule of thumb offered by Biggerstaff and Perlis [BIGG89]: "Don't attempt to reuse something unless you intend to use it at least three times." Applying this rule of thumb, an uncertified component in a reuse library may be subjected to this ad hoc testing selected for reuse only two times before the component undergoes a formal certification process.

This compromise approach expends little effort on additional testing and certification for those software components that will not be reused frequently. The additional overhead of the compromise approach is simply an external counter for the number of times that a software component has been reused.

We note that Biggerstaff and Perlis have another rule of thumb about reuse based on the concept that multiple successful use of a software component provides reasonably good assurance that the component was relatively error-free: "Don't attempt to reuse something unless you have already used it at least three times." These two so-called *three-times rules* provide good guidelines for estimating cost-benefit ratios involving the reuse of software artifacts.

Note that there are other possibilities for certification of reuse library components. At the time of placement of a software artifact into a reuse library a domain expert can be asked to estimate the number of times that this artifact will be accessed. This estimate can be used as a guideline when determining if the software artifact warrants the added cost of the certification process.

Alternatively, the certification of a reuse library component can be based on the values of appropriate metrics, the amount and quality of test information, and any formal evaluation of the component. The resulting certification could be based on a scale ranging from relatively untested to guaranteed for safety-critical applications.

In general, we recommend a formal certification process instead of these usage-based methods. However, a usage-based certification method may be appropriate for reusable software components that have been used millions of times, such as operating systems modules or popular applications software for personal computers.

Unfortunately, there are no careful comparative studies of the effectiveness of these alternative approaches to certification. We have chosen to present the most detailed certification process. You should use a less rigorous certification process only if you suspect that most components in your reuse library will rarely be used or else you have strong external indications of the correctness of potentially reusable software components. If you believe that a software component will never be reused, it should not be in the reuse library. (Recall that one part of the domain analysis process is to determine the reusability potential of software artifacts.)

Summary

Software artifacts need additional certification before they are considered for reuse and placed in a reuse library. Certification should be done in addition to an organization's normal software development process. In particular, certification of potentially reusable software components is a separate activity from software testing. Certification will involve both informal assessment and formal metrics.

Certification activities can take many forms. For example, a source code module should have documentation indicating any logical predicates or program execution paths that have not been tested. Metrics should be collected to indicate any unstable modules, which have been subjected to so many modification requests (MRs) that they may not be reliable.

Requirements and designs selected for reuse should be tested in a CASE tool whenever possible to provide an independent consistency check.

Nearly every certification of a potentially reusable software artifact will involve domain analysis.

Metrics will be the central focus of any certification effort. Metrics should be applied to each type of software artifact. Useful metrics include those based on size and on the extent of interconnection between program modules.

One approach to certification of potentially reusable software artifacts is to delay the certification process until the software artifact is actually reused. This avoids some up-front costs but can slow down the software development process at a critical stage. Two general rules of Biggerstaff and Perlis are useful in this context:

> Don't attempt to reuse something unless you intend to use it at least three times.

> Don't attempt to reuse something unless you have already used it at least three times.

Further Reading

There are several excellent classic references on software testing. Two editions of Beizer's book [BEIZ83, BEIZ90]; the book by DeMillo McCraken, Martin, and Passafiume [DEMI87]; and a book by Myers [MYER79] are perhaps the most well known. Miller and Howden's IEEE tutorial books [MILL78, MILL83] provide an excellent introduction to the research literature in the area of software testing.

General information on testing can be found in any good reference on software engineering. Perhaps the most accessible general software engineering books are those by Pressman [PRES92] and Pfleeger [PFLE89]. These references also contain some general material on software metrics.

Humphrey's recent book *A Discipline for Software Engineering* [HUMP95] incorporates reuse and metrics into what he calls a "personal software process." It is likely that this book will have a major impact on software engineering education because of the scientific basis for software engineering that it provides. It is essential reading for educators and practitioners of software engineering.

Useful research articles on software testing include Barbey and Strohmeier [BARB94], Harrold, McGregor, and Fitzpatrick [HARR92], and Weyuker [WEYU86].

Software reliability is most easily learned by reading several standard books before examining the journal literature. The books by Musa, Iannino, and Okumoto [MUSA87] and Myers [MYER76] are the most frequently used. Musa's paper on the use of operational profiles in reliability theory is also essential reading on this topic [MUSA93].

There is little information on certification (for the purpose of reuse) in book form. Some relevant papers include Wohlin and Runeson

[WOHL94] and several articles in the various proceedings of the international conferences on software reuse; see Frakes [FRAK93B, FRAK94C].

General information about software metrics and reliability can be found in the book by Conte, Dunsmore, and Shen [CONT86] and in the newer reference by Fenton [FENT91]. (The book by Conte et al. is out of print but should be available in many university libraries.) A new edition of Fenton [FENT91], coauthored by Pfleeger, is now available [FENT96].

The older book on software metrics by Halstead [HALS77] is also instructive. Unfortunately, some of the conclusions presented in Halstead's book cannot be generalized to larger systems without very careful treatment of data statements.

McCabe's seminal paper [McCA76] on the control flow-oriented cyclomatic complexity metric is still very much worth reading. The experiences described in Grady and Caswell's book *Software Metrics* [GRAD87] and the recent IEEE standard for software productivity metrics, IEEE Standard 1045-1992 [IEEE92A] are also essential background reading for systematic applications of software metrics.

Exercises

1. This exercise is intended for those organizations with systematic reuse programs. Determine if your organization has a certification plan for reusable software artifacts. If so, what type of software artifacts are certified?

2. This is a fundamental question about your organization's software products. What is the average defect ratio for software? If there is any variation between systems, what is the degree of reuse in the systems with the lowest defect ratio?

3. Examine the number of software defects found in each release or milestone of some system. Plot the number of errors over time, and determine an appropriate probability distribution for use in a reliability model.

4. Select some portion of one of the publicly available reuse libraries discussed in Chap. 3 and review it from the perspective of certification. Which certification steps appear to have been followed? Compute the values of the appropriate metrics for each artifact considered.

5. List some of the potential benefits of delaying certification until a software artifact is actually reused. List some of the disadvantages of this approach. After describing some general advantages and disadvantages, consider your organization's reuse practices to determine if this technique has potential benefits for you.

5

The Economics of Software Reuse

We should expect some cost savings from the reuse of software. After all, we are reusing some portion of a system rather than developing the particular component from scratch. The initial reaction of many people, especially budget officers, is that all the cost of the software artifact being reused can be saved. However, as with many things in the field of software engineering, the actual cost savings are sometimes illusory. There are costs involved in selecting a reusable software artifact that is appropriate for a particular application. After a reusable software artifact has been selected, there are additional costs associated with understanding, modifying, certifying, and maintaining it. Barnes and Bollinger [BARN91] discuss some issues in a paper appropriately titled "Making Reuse Cost Effective."

There are several reasons for the discrepancy between real and apparent cost savings. The amount saved depends upon many factors. The most important factors are the following:

- The life cycle model used in the software development process

- The development history of the software system, of which the artifact is a substantial portion

- The cost of beginning a policy of software reuse

- The cost of creating and maintaining a reuse library of software artifacts

- The percentage of the system that is created using existing software artifacts

- The percentage of change in each software artifact being reused

- The different goals for reuse programs of the different levels of an organization

Some of these factors are fairly obvious. Others appear at first glance to have little to do with the process of estimating cost savings from a policy of software reuse. The last factor—differing goals—is often overlooked when considering reuse savings. Pfleeger's recent paper [PFLE96] describes this situation well.

In her scenario, a project team may have the primary goal of developing software within scheduling constraints. Thus, a major goal for a project-level reuse program might be to locate and employ reusable components whenever possible. The project-level reuse program would not attempt to apply extra effort to certify potentially reusable software artifacts created by the project team.

However, a division-level reuse program would also be interested in improving productivity at the division level. Thus, division managers probably would be willing to invest extra resources into certification of those software components with a high likelihood of being reused by the division. This division-level objective may or may not be reflected in additional resources for a particular project.

In the next three sections we will illustrate the effect of the life cycle model of the software development process on the cost of reuse and the potential savings. In view of the scenario just described, we will not limit the costs of a systematic program of software reuse to those that may be charged against a particular project's budget. As Pfleeger [PFLE96] has pointed out, properly attributing the costs of systematic software reuse programs is not simply a technical issue.

Before we begin our study of reuse costs, we present some terminology. There is no reason to attach a rigid yes-or-no approach to reuse. It is certainly reasonable to consider the use of a portion of a software artifact as reuse, even if modification is necessary.

A common standard in the reuse community is to distinguish four levels of reuse.

1. The software artifact is used as is. This is the highest level of reuse. In one standard terminology, the software artifact is called *transportable,* and the software artifact is often said to be used *verbatim.*

2. The software artifact has minor changes totaling less than 25 percent for all insertions, deletions, or modifications. In one standard terminology, the software artifact is called *adaptable* or is said to have *few changes.*

3. The software artifact has more than 25 percent but less than 50 percent changes, including additions, deletions, and modifications. In one standard terminology, the software artifact is called *changed* or is said to have *substantial changes.*

4. The software artifact has more than 50 percent changes or is so inappropriate to the problem at hand that it must be completely

rewritten as new code. In one standard terminology, the software artifact is called *new*.

The terms *verbatim* and *transportable* refer to a slightly different concept than the term *black-box reuse* discussed in Chap. 3. The latter term refers to making a decision about reusing some software artifact by using some external documentation or other information rather than by the artifact's internal organization. Even if the artifact is used as is, with no changes, black-box reuse occurs only if the initial decision to reuse uses only external information. Conversely, any changes in the artifact imply that black-box reuse did not occur.

The use of 25 percent as the dividing line between "few changes" and "substantial changes" is fairly common in the software reuse literature. Another approach is to distinguish the four categories of no changes, fewer than 10 percent changes, 10 to 25 percent changes, and more than 25 percent changes. Of course, you should follow a locally developed terminology and set of numerical break points if your organization's reuse plan is sufficiently advanced to have one. For comparison purposes, it is essential to use the same terminology throughout an organization.

Note that these percentages do not offer any help in estimating costs. We will develop some guidelines that will help estimate the potential total life cycle cost savings of reusable software artifacts at the four levels just indicated.

This is not the place to duplicate the cost estimation methods in Boehm's classic *Software Engineering Economics* [BOEH81]. To do so would make this book prohibitively large. Any organization involved in software development will have its own methods for software cost estimation and is unlikely to stop using them to follow some new theoretical (and probably unproven) model that purports to address the effect of software reuse. Thus, we will place primary emphasis on those reuse-based software cost models that can be incorporated easily into a development organization's existing cost models.

We will develop several cost models in this chapter. Each of them will be a linear model that (hopefully) contains all relevant factors. Linear models seem appropriate as a first approximation since the development of reuse-based cost models (and reuse itself) is relatively new, at least on a systematic basis.

Each of the models presented in Secs. 5.1 through 5.5 of this chapter will build on cost models that presumably already exist in your organization. As stated before, the intention is to enable a software organization to incorporate reuse factors in an appropriate way into its existing cost modeling activities, not to write a book on software engineering economics.

The range of software cost estimation models is often very large, even within a single organization [SEAT95]. Clearly, no single global reuse-based cost model is workable across many projects if there are too many existing cost classification methods for different models. Thus, for many organizations beginning systematic programs of software reuse, the simple, first-order cost approximations given here are appropriate.

The models presented here are based on discussions with a variety of project managers and do not necessarily reflect the conflict between project goals and division goals that were discussed earlier. They should be of use to division managers wishing to implement division-wide systematic reuse programs. Part of the job of project managers employing software reuse is to educate their division managers about the true costs of systematic software reuse programs.

In Sec. 5.6 we will describe a typical sophisticated cost model in some detail. The model presented there is based on some work by Bollinger and Pfleeger [BOLL90, BOLL95], Frakes and Fox [FRAK95A], and Lim [LIM94].

Estimates for resources other than cost are discussed briefly in Sec. 5.7. The chapter closes with a discussion of the optimal size of reusable software components (Sec. 5.8).

The following quotation from a report on the reuse experience of NASA/Goddard Space Flight Center's Flight Dynamics Division [SEL95] illustrates some problems associated with cost modeling:

> However, the reuse factor, which represents the amount of work required to reuse the code, should be higher for Ada systems (0.3) than for FOR-TRAN (0.2). The study was unable to explain the cause of this difference (p. 20).

The result of this study should be taken as a comment on the difficulty of cost modeling, especially in a reuse situation, rather than as a critique of the Ada language or its support for software reuse. In the analysis described in Software Engineering Laboratory [SEL95], Ada performed better than FORTRAN as a reuse environment in several other parameters.

5.1   Life Cycle Leverage

To drive down the cost of software development, a principle that software theorists have known for years should be applied: "the best programmers aren't just a little better than average programmers; they're shockingly better—10 times, maybe 100 times more productive" [UDELL94]. Of course, many interpretations of the terms *better* and *more productive* are possible. *Productive,* for example, is not the same as *high quality.*

The systems and subsystems built by the best people are most likely to be reused because of their high quality and flexibility of design. Thus, we should expect that their reusable architectures, designs, source code, data, and the like will be of high quality and will not cause any special problems for the remaining software development activities.

Richard Probst, SunSoft's business development manager, notes that "the way you work is about the same no matter what kind of software you work on, and that's a sure sign of an immature industry" [UDEL94]. This would suggest that software reuse should improve quality, regardless of the application domain. The reason for this is that the effect of the work of the "best" software engineers appears to be more likely to be leveraged than the work of "below average" people.

Because of reuse, the time needed for the software development cycle can be reduced [LILL93]. In many cases, development estimates have been reduced by one to two weeks per feature from the average feature development times of three to six months. Much of the cost savings can be linked to the reuse of existing designs and classes.

Reuse practices in the testing and integration phase also show significant savings. This is the phase in which features naturally fall together. The cost savings at these phases occur primarily because the underlying classes are shared between interfacing processes, and classes have been extensively tested before reaching the integration phase.

In general, reuse applied early in the software development life cycle has the potential to reduce costs tremendously because many subsequent, lower-level software life cycle activities can be either eliminated or at least performed more efficiently. The decrease in total software life cycle costs due to reuse of higher-level software artifacts is called *life cycle leverage*.

The cost savings from reuse can be realized at any phase of the life cycle after the code module is reused. For example, if a code component is taken from a reuse library consisting of software components and is used without change, then the component need not be tested as a module. Instead, the source code module in which the reusable component is to be placed need only be given unit and integration testing. No additional test cases, test plans, or documentation need to be given for this reused module since we can use any existing documentation for the module.

The amount of cost savings is leveraged if we can reuse a system earlier in the life cycle. That is, if we can detect that a portion of the requirements specification is repeated over several systems, and we note that this portion of the requirements corresponds to a well-defined set of modules, then we can reasonably expect to be able to do the following: use the design of the existing subsystem as the design of the new subsystem, use the code of the existing subsystem as the code of the new subsystem, use the test plans for the existing subsystem as the test plans of the new subsystem, and use the documentation of the existing subsystem as the documentation of the new subsystem.

In the next few sections, we will present cost models to describe the effect of reusable software artifacts at different phases of the life cycle. There will be different cost models for different software life cycle development models. Note that the important effect on cost are the actual activities that occur in a software system's software development and not the precise point in an elaborate time schedule at which these activities occur.

5.2 Cost Models for Reuse Using the Classic Waterfall Life Cycle

One version of the classic waterfall life cycle has the distinct phases shown in Fig. 5.1. Other versions of the waterfall life cycle are similar. The two-directional arrows in Fig. 5.1 indicate the possible flow of communication between phases.

There are several different cost models that can be applied to software development in a reuse-based environment depending on the life cycle phase in which reuse is applied. This is necessary because of the effect of life cycle leverage on total system costs.

Because the classic waterfall life cycle has such distinct phases, our cost models will have the advantage of separating the costs of the system into three separate parts:

- Activities before any reuse occurs

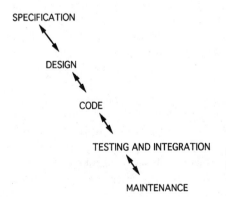

Figure 5.1 The classic waterfall life cycle model

- Identification of the reusable artifact itself
- Activities after the reusable artifact has been created and identified

In each of these models, we assume that the software artifact has been certified using the (minimal) recommended procedures given in Chap. 4. This level of certification allows us to have considerable confidence that the software artifact adheres to appropriate standards.

Clearly, the additional certification using CASE tools will provide more confidence. However, there is no easy way to measure the effect of added reliability of the system to be reused against the cost that this additional certification would require.

Of course, the cost of analyzing software artifacts for potential reuse; cataloging them using domain analysis; incorporating them into a reuse library; accessing and maintaining the reuse library; and collecting, analyzing, and reporting the values of appropriate metrics and other data about reuse costs is not free. For lack of any better estimates, we will assume the accuracy of the commonly reported estimates [SEL91] that 5 to 10 percent of total development costs are devoted to metrics collection and data analysis.

It seems likely that with a systematic reuse program already in place in an organization the cost to reuse *anything* is slightly higher than if the same software artifact were located by fortuitous coincidence. (Of course, the chances of locating appropriate reusable software components is not very high in nonsystematic, ad hoc reuse.) Thus, we estimate that there is an additional 5 percent overhead for reuse activities, including analysis, data gathering, and reporting. (The costs to begin a systematic reuse program will be higher, as will the true costs of not having an adequate metrics process.) Thus, the total cost of a mature software development process with systematic reuse will incur from 10 to 15 percent overhead. We view this as part of the normal overhead of doing business.

The cost to identify a reusable software artifact will be part of the general costs of a systematic reuse program, whose cost is amortized throughout the organization's software development costs.

5.2.1 Reuse in the requirements or specification phase

Reuse at this phase presents the greatest opportunity for total life cycle cost savings.

Ideally, all the remaining phases of the life cycle can be greatly simplified because of the ability to "plug in" a previously developed system into a new situation. The assumption in this case is that all the design, code, test plans, test data, test results, and documentation can be used as is. It is also assumed in this rosy scenario that integration with other systems will be relatively straightforward and certainly no more difficult than an ordinary systems integration process. This ideal situation occurs very rarely. It almost never happens with systems that are to be used as components of a larger system.

A realistic cost model for reuse of a set of requirements would include the cost of integration as the primary new cost. The rationale is that the design, code, and testing for the system being reused can be placed into service with few changes. The same is assumed to be true for the documentation to be reused.

The basis for cost models of reuse in the requirements phase is presented in Eq. 5.1. The cost to reuse the system includes the cost to match the system's requirements from a set of reusable requirements.

Equation 5.1   The basic model for reuse of requirements for the classic waterfall development process

```
cost = cost to reuse system +
       cost to integrate system +
       cost to maintain system
```

This is the simplest model because there are essentially no life cycle activities listed before the cost of reusing a system other than determining if existing reusable software systems are appropriate for the new software system to be developed. This is very unrealistic. Since we have previously suggested an overhead of 10 to 15 percent as the typical cost to reuse a software artifact, we need to focus only on the costs of integrating the system.

We now consider the effects of the reuse factors of the requirements being transportable (used as is), adaptable (minor changes, less than 25 percent for all modifications), changed (more than 25 percent but less than 50 percent modifications), or new (essentially rewritten).

The costs to integrate the reusable artifact into a new system obviously depend to a great degree upon the relative size of the interface. This is where the assumption that the potentially reusable artifact has been certified becomes important. We will assume certification of all reuse library components in each of the cost models given in this chapter.

The lowest cost will occur when the requirements are transportable. In this case, there is reasonable assurance that the resulting system meets its requirements, has a modular design, and adheres to standards. Thus, we should expect minimal integration costs, consistent with standard costs for systems integration.

The maintenance costs should also be predictable since we have the additional information available from the maintenance history of the system being reused.

The effect of reuse of transportable requirements is thus

```
cost = cost to reuse system
       +
       integration and maintenance costs of
       a nonreuse-based system
```

We should expect enormous savings in this case. Using the estimate that the amortized cost of a systematic reuse program is between 10 and 15 percent of the cost of software development, for a transportable (no changes) set of requirements, the cost will be the expression given in the right-hand side of Eq. 5.2. The term *amortized cost* means that certain fixed costs, such as the salary of a reuse librarian to manage one or more reuse libraries, are divided proportionally among all projects using these libraries.

Equation 5.2   The cost model for transportable reuse of requirements for the classic waterfall development process

```
cost = .125 * (nonreuse costs to develop)
       +
       integration and maintenance costs of
       a nonreuse-based system
```

In Eq. 5.2 we have taken the average (12.5 percent) as the amortized cost of a systematic reuse program. Note that these costs may be even lower if properly certified reusable requirements lead to subsystems that are easier to maintain than other subsystems not explicitly intended for reuse.

Most software managers expect that the maintenance costs will be lower on reused systems. This seems plausible, especially since the maintenance costs might be amortized across the original project and the one in which the existing system is reused. However, we are not aware of any data to support this claim. The maintenance costs must be accounted for, regardless of whether the producer or consumer of the reused component is responsible for its maintenance.

The next reuse situation we consider is when the requirements are adaptable, that is, have fewer than 25 percent changes.

At first glance, we should separate the reuse and nonreuse portions of the system. We should then multiply those costs in our simple model by the appropriate percentage and add them up. However, this ignores the often stated *70-30 rule,* in which 70 percent of the effort is devoted to 30 percent of the requirements, and conversely. (The rule is sometimes stated as 75-25, 80-20, or even 90-10. The same principle applies, regardless of the specifics.)

The easiest way to estimate costs is by the percentage of the requirements that are being reused as is. If, for example, only 10 percent of the requirements are changed, we should then expect 10 percent of the system to be created from scratch, with the remaining 90 percent arising from the reused requirements.

```
cost = .125 * (nonreuse costs to develop)
       +
       .1 * (nonreuse costs to develop)
       +
       integration and maintenance costs of
       a nonreuse-based system
```

A better way to model the costs is to use the Albrecht function point metrics [ALBR83] to compare the new and reusable requirements. In this approach, the relevant percentage is computed from the ratio of function point metrics instead of just counting the numbers of new and unchanged requirements.

The remaining factor to be considered is the "hit ratio," which reflects the degree to which the problem 25 percent of the requirements are included in the reused portion. We will assume that the 75-25 rule is a good description of the efforts needed to create the existing reusable requirements.

We suggest a conservative estimate of the hit ratio, based on the observation that many reuse programs fail because they promise too much and deliver too little. We thus suggest a value of 0.25 for the case of adaptable requirements. This is illustrated in Eq. 5.3, where the second term (line 3) represents the cost of new development.

Equation 5.3   The cost model for adaptable reuse of requirements for the classic waterfall development process

```
cost = .125 * (nonreuse costs to develop)
       +
       .25 * (nonreuse costs to develop)
       +
       integration and maintenance costs of
       a nonreuse-based system
```

A similar situation occurs in the case of changed requirements. In this case, we arbitrarily select the conservative value of 0.50 to avoid unpleasant surprises resulting from the hit ratio. We thus obtain the cost model given in Eq. 5.4.

Equation 5.4   The cost model for changed reuse of requirements for the classic waterfall development process

```
cost = .125 * (nonreuse costs to develop)
       +
       .50 * (nonreuse costs to develop)
```

```
+
integration and maintenance costs of
a nonreuse-based system
```

Finally, for systems that have so many changes to the requirements that redesign is necessary, attempting to reuse a large number of the requirements would lead to a cost as given in Eq. 5.5.

Equation 5.5   The cost model for new reuse of requirements for the classic waterfall development process

```
cost = .125 * (nonreuse costs to develop)
       +
       1.0 * (nonreuse costs to develop)
       +
       integration and maintenance costs of
       a nonreuse-based system
```

Of course, this is the same model as for new development with collection and analysis of metrics and reuse information.

5.2.3   Reuse in the design phase

Reuse at the design phase does not have the same potential for total life cycle cost savings. The potentially reusable software artifact appears at a later point in the life cycle than before, and hence there are costs both before and after the identification of the reusable artifact.

The cost of setting requirements is (presumably) known within the organization since this stage preceded the reuse of the artifact's design. Since we will reuse a design, the code and testing activities (planning, test cases, and test results) will automatically be reused, and thus the only major issue is the integration with other interoperable systems. Documentation can be inserted into larger system documentation for the most part without changes.

The cost model now becomes

```
cost = cost to set requirements for system +
       cost to reuse system +
       cost to integrate system +
       cost to maintain system
```

Of course, the additional overhead of a systematic reuse program with its need for additional analysis and data collection must be added. This overhead is still assumed to be 12.5 percent.

Thus, we have four cost models for reuse of designs, one for each of the four situations of transportable, adaptable, changed, or new designs. The four cost models are given in Eqs. 5.6 through 5.9.

Equation 5.6   The cost model for transportable reuse of designs for the classic waterfall development process

```
cost = cost to set requirements for system
       +
       .125 * (cost to design nonreuse system)
       +
       cost to integrate system
       +
       cost to maintain system
```

Equation 5.7   The cost model for adaptable reuse of designs for the classic waterfall development process

```
cost = cost to set requirements for system
       +
       .125 * (cost to design nonreuse system)
       ┆
       .25 * (cost to design nonreuse system)
       +
       cost to integrate system
       +
       cost to maintain system
```

Equation 5.8   The cost model for changed reuse of designs for the classic waterfall development process

```
cost = cost to set requirements for system
       +
       .125 * (cost to design nonreuse system)
       +
       .50 * (cost to design nonreuse system)
       +
       cost to integrate system
       +
       cost to maintain system
```

Equation 5.9   The cost model for new reuse of designs for the classic waterfall development process

```
cost = cost to set requirements for system
       +
       .125 * (cost to design nonreuse system)
       +
       1.0 * (cost to design nonreuse system)
       +
       cost to integrate system
       +
       cost to maintain system
```

As with new requirements, the cost for new designs is the cost to redesign a system from scratch.

5.2.3 Reuse in the coding phase

Reuse at this phase does not have the same potential for total life cycle cost savings as did the previous two phases. There are costs both before and after the identification of the reusable artifact.

There is an advantage to estimating costs associated with reuse at this phase, however. Source code is the most familiar software artifact and the most suited to evaluation by existing metrics, such as lines of code (in all its forms). In addition, the costs to develop requirements and designs are known at this point. Only the two phases (1) testing and integration and (2) maintenance remain to have their costs estimated.

There is almost as much opportunity for reuse of documentation here as in the previous cases. Most of the high-level information in users' guides can be reused without change. The internal documentation of the individual source code modules to be reused is not likely to be changed if it follows the detailed PDL of these modules.

The simple basic cost model now becomes

```
cost = cost to set requirements for system +
       cost to design system +
       cost to reuse system +
       cost to integrate system +
       cost to maintain system
```

Of course, the additional overhead of a systematic reuse program with its need for additional analysis and appropriate data collection must be added. However, a question about the amount of overhead to be considered naturally arises, since many metrics are applied only at source code level. We will present the cost models as we have previously, charging the costs for a complete program at all phases of the software life cycle.

The four cost models for transportable, adaptable, changed, or new reuse of source code are given in Eqs. 5.10 through 5.13.

Equation 5.10   The cost model for transportable reuse of source code for the classic waterfall development process

```
cost = cost of requirements for nonreuse system
       +
       cost to design nonreuse system
       +
       .125 * (cost to code nonreuse system)
       +
       cost to integrate system
       +
       cost to maintain system
```

Equation 5.11   The cost model for adaptable reuse of source code for the classic waterfall development process

```
cost = cost of requirements for nonreuse system
       +
       cost to design nonreuse system
       +
       .125 * (cost to code nonreuse system)
       +
       .25 * (cost to code nonreuse system)
       +
       cost to integrate system
       +
       cost to maintain system
```

Equation 5.12   The cost model for changed reuse of source code for the classic waterfall development process

```
cost = cost of requirements for nonreuse system
       +
       cost to design nonreuse system
       +
       .125 * (cost to code nonreuse system)
       +
       .50 * (cost to code nonreuse system)
       +
       cost to integrate system
       +
       cost to maintain system
```

Equation 5.13   The cost model for new reuse of source code for the classic waterfall development process

```
cost = cost of requirements for nonreuse system
       +
       cost to design nonreuse system
       +
       .125 * (cost to code nonreuse system)
       +
       1.0 * (cost to code nonreuse system)
       +
       cost to integrate system
       +
       cost to maintain system
```

As with new requirements and designs, the cost for new source code is the cost to recode a system from scratch.

5.2.4   Reuse in the testing and integration phase

Reuse in the testing and integration phase is likely to be the least efficient application of reuse since it occurs so late in the life cycle.

However, there are likely to be fewer problems with reuse at this level because of the reduced possibility for errors.

Plans are the most commonly reused artifacts in this phase. Examples of reusable plans are an integration checklist for a complex system and a compiler test plan such as the Ada Compiler Validation Suite (ACVS). Sets of test cases can also be reused easily. Note that the well-known technique of regression testing is a special case of the inclusion of a reusable set of test plans or test data.

The cost model for the effect of reuse in the testing and integration phase now becomes

```
cost = cost to set requirements for system +
       cost to design system +
       cost to code system +
       cost to test system +
       cost to reuse system +
       cost to integrate system +
       cost to maintain system
```

Of course, the additional overhead of a systematic reuse program with its need for additional analysis and data collection must be added. However, in this case, we believe most of the metrics are front loaded into the earlier phases of the life cycle.

The cost models are given in Eqs. 5.14 through 5.17. In the context of these four equations, the term *develop* means to set requirements, design the system, code the system and then test it.

Equation 5.14   The cost model for transportable reuse of test data for the classic waterfall development process

```
cost = cost of requirements for nonreuse system
       +
       cost to design nonreuse system
       +
       cost to code nonreuse system
       +
       .125 * (cost to develop nonreuse system)
       +
       cost to integrate system
       +
       cost to maintain system
```

Equation 5.15   The cost model for adaptable reuse of test data for the classic waterfall development process

```
cost = cost of requirements for nonreuse system
       +
       cost to design nonreuse system
       +
       cost to code nonreuse system
```

```
+
.125 * (cost to develop nonreuse system)
+
.25 * cost to test nonreuse system
+
cost to integrate system
+
cost to maintain system
```

Equation 5.16   The cost model for changed reuse of test data for the classic waterfall development process

```
cost = cost of requirements for nonreuse system
+
cost to design nonreuse system
+
cost to code nonreuse system
+
.125 * (cost to develop nonreuse system)
+
.5 * cost to test nonreuse system
+
cost to integrate system
+
cost to maintain system
```

Equation 5.17   The cost model for new reuse of test data for the classic waterfall development process

```
cost = cost of requirements for nonreuse system
+
cost to design nonreuse system
+
cost to code nonreuse system
+
.125 * (cost to develop nonreuse system)
+
1.0 * cost to test nonreuse system
+
cost to integrate system
+
cost to maintain system
```

5.2.5   Reuse in the maintenance phase

We will not present any models of maintenance costs. However, we do believe that these costs will be lower for reused systems. Of course, the additional overhead of a systematic reuse program with its need for additional analysis and data collection must be added to any fair measurement of maintenance phase costs in order to verify this opinion.

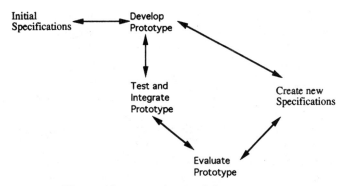

Figure 5.2   The rapid prototyping model

5.3   A Cost Model for Reuse Using the Rapid Prototyping Model

The rapid prototyping model of software development is appealing because it allows the potential user to interact with the system before it is complete. This should result in software systems that are easier to use.

Perhaps more importantly, this method allows changes to be made based on the user's actual requirements rather than his or her perceived needs. Hopefully, this is done at lower cost than if there were no user interaction before the finished product was delivered.

Any prototyping model for software development is highly dynamic and will pose several problems for the measurement of savings due to software reuse. The problem here is that it is difficult to certify the quality of larger software components. (The certification of small software components, such as library modules, is not likely to be very difficult, especially in the case of modern components such as object-oriented components.)

Figure 5.2 illustrates the rapid prototyping model.

The apparently endless cycle of development terminates when the evaluation step indicates that no further changes in the latest prototype are needed to meet the requirements.

The rapid change of requirements, design, and source code in incremental models of software development require different cost models to predict the effect of software reuse on total costs.

Testing and integration costs can be most severe in this environment. Here the use of standards is absolutely essential, especially for interfaces.

An important issue in reuse with rapid prototyping is the "stability" of the underlying components. Stability refers to the relative changes in the component. This can be determined from the reliability of the component as well as from other fault information. Note than an unstable component would not have been certified and thus should not have been placed into a reuse library.

To simplify our cost models for software development using the rapid prototyping model, we will assume that the components have been certified for correctness.

Since the rapid prototyping software development model has fewer distinct phases than the classic waterfall life cycle model, fewer cost models will be needed. However, additional problems arise when estimating costs using the rapid prototyping software development method.

We can illustrate these problems by considering the role of the initial requirements at the start of the prototyping cycle. There is clearly a difference between the initial step of getting system requirements and determining requirements after one or more prototypes have been produced.

If there is a systematic program of software reuse in place in the organization a reused set of initial requirements should automatically lead to a reused system, assuming that the pattern of new requirements prepared after each prototype is developed is the same as expected from the previously created system. However, there may be significant deviations from the previous system's development path because of the different requirements set after each evaluation of a prototype. Remember the adage "users never know what they want until they see it." And keep in mind Murphy's Law, "If something can go wrong it will."

The most optimistic cost model for the rapid prototyping method at the time that the initial requirements are set is given in Eq. 5.18.

Equation 5.18   The optimistic cost model for transportable reuse of source code using the rapid prototyping method

```
cost = cost of requirements for nonreuse system
       +
       .125 * (cost to evaluate nonreuse system)
       +
       cost to maintain system
```

The pessimistic cost model for the rapid prototyping method at the time the initial requirements are set is given in Eq. 5.19. It assumes that there will be a great divergence between the development path of the previous system and the new system because of major changes in requirements when prototypes are evaluated. Note that the development costs for the new system should be based on costs of software development using the rapid prototyping model, not the waterfall life cycle model.

Equation 5.19   The pessimistic cost model for transportable reuse of source code using the rapid prototyping method

```
cost = cost of requirements for nonreuse system
       +
       .125 * (cost to evaluate nonreuse system)
       +
       1.0 * (cost to develop nonreuse system)
       +
       cost to maintain system
```

Fortunately for us, the pessimistic model is not very realistic. It assumes that there is no relation between the future development path of the system and the initial requirements. This is not very likely.

A more realistic assumption is that the requirements will change only slightly from the requirements of the system to be reused. In a systematic reuse environment, the effect of relative changes to requirements will be evaluated in future efforts.

We note that the effect of requirements changes can be estimated at each evaluation of a prototype. At each evaluation, we can determine the relationship of the new requirements to the old ones. Specifically, we can use the terminology given earlier in this chapter and ask if the requirements are transportable, adaptable, changed, or new.

The cost estimates for the rapid prototyping model are therefore best expressed as a sum of the costs at each different cycle depicted in the rapid prototyping model graph in Fig. 5.2. We call this model an *incremental model* for obvious reasons.

We present the model in Eq. 5.20. In this equation, the quantity called *reuse factor* represents the four quantities used for requirements reuse in Sec. 5.2: transportable, adaptable, changed, and new code. These values are 0.0, 0.25, 0.50, and 1.0, respectively.

Equation 5.20   The incremental cost model for transportable reuse of source code using the rapid prototyping method

```
cost = cost of requirements for nonreuse system
       +
       sum (for all prototypes) of
       {
       .125 * (cost to evaluate nonreuse system)
       +
       reuse factor * (cost to develop prototype)
       +
       integration costs (nonreuse-based system)
       }
```

+

```
cost to maintain system
```

Note the continued appearance of the overhead of reuse and other metrics data collection. We view this as essential for the success of any reuse program, systematic or otherwise, in the rapid prototyping software development environment.

5.4   A Cost Model for Reuse for a System Developed Using the Spiral Model

The spiral model of software development has many of the features of the rapid prototyping model. Boehm described the spiral model in an important 1988 paper [BOEH88]. As in the rapid prototyping model, creation of software is an iterative process, with considerable user interaction.

Boehm's primary goal was to develop a model that included the formality of the classical waterfall model but that was flexible enough to allow development in the most common development environments. In these environments, the requirements are difficult to set before design is underway, and the user has a chance to react to an initial interpretation of his or her real and perceived software needs.

The spiral model of the software development process allows precise milestones to be set during an iterative software development process. The model is illustrated in Fig. 5.3.

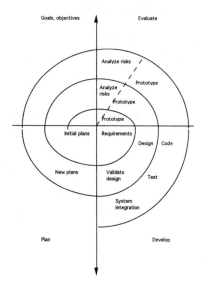

Figure 5.3 The spiral model of software development

Because the spiral model is iterative it has little in common with the waterfall model, especially at the early stages of the process. Clearly reuse-based cost estimation models based on the waterfall approach cannot be applied directly to software developed using this process.

The most important difference between the spiral and rapid prototyping development models is that the initial software in the spiral model is not considered to be a prototype that will probably be discarded. Instead, the initial prototype is considered to be the basis for future development. Note that there is an initial life cycle plan in the spiral model; such a plan is not usually present in a rapid prototyping environment.

Since there are many similar activities for these two development models the cost models will have many similar features. The important differences between these two software development models are risk analysis for each prototype and the heavy emphasis placed on acceptance testing in the spiral model.

The risk analysis required for each prototype must take into account the expected reliability of the prototype's reusable components in order to determine the system's acceptability, even before extensive testing. This effectively mandates the existence of an evaluation process that includes reliability and other metrics data. In short, the risk analysis presumes that there is some sort of certification process already in place for the reusable components.

There are many activities entailed in the spiral model:

- Requirements plan
- Life cycle plan
- Initial requirements analysis
- Initial prototype
- Initial operational concept
- Prototypes (many)
- Software requirements
- Requirements validation
- Development plan
- Risk analysis
- Software product design
- Design validation and verification
- Integration and test
- Operational prototype

- Detailed design
- Code
- Testing and integration

Each of these activities presents an opportunity for reuse, and therefore a cost model can be given for the reuse of any one of these activities. Since the individual steps and the order in which they are applied varies so much from organization to organization, we will not give detailed cost models for a reuse-based spiral development process. Instead, we will present a set of guidelines for applications of the cost models described in my discussion of the rapid prototyping process. These models will apply at different times in the spiral process. Of course, the amount of the artifact being reused will influence the cost estimation you use.

For example, suppose that we use a completely reusable (transportable, or verbatim reuse) subsystem as part of the original prototype. This system's known requirements and performance (assuming it has been certified) affect the rest of the spiral process. The risk analysis step for each prototype can essentially ignore this subsystem, thereby saving money and resources at the prototype development and risk analysis steps of each iteration.

In the case of lower levels of reuse of the subsystem, such as adaptable, changed, or new reuse, the cost savings will certainly be less. The primary effects will clearly be on the coding required for the prototype development. The risk analysis activity also offers an opportunity for reuse and the associated cost savings, particularly if the analysis is linked to some of the test plans and test cases used at later steps in the spiral process.

In the absence of more accurate information, the reuse factors of 0.0, 0.25, 0.50, and 1.0 should be used for transportable, adaptable, changed, and new code, respectively. As we have seen many times before, the greatest cost savings in a reuse-based program will be obtained when there is the greatest life cycle leverage.

Finally, after a detailed design has been developed for the system the remaining portions of the process are the same as those of the waterfall model, and appropriate cost models can be used.

5.5 A Cost Model for Reuse for a System Using Only COTS

At first glance there appears to be very little cost in a system that uses only COTS products. It would seem that the only important costs are those to purchase the individual software. Reuse would seem to be easy and maintenance a nonissue. For several reasons, however, this is not the case.

There is generally a substantial integration cost. Consider the cost of a UNIX-based system of COTS products, in which each COTS application reads its input from the standard input file stdin and writes its output to the standard output file stdout. Assume also that each COTS application acts as a filter on some data, as in the hypothetical UNIX shell command

```
cat data > COTS_app1 | COTS_app2 | COTS_app3>
```

(The UNIX cat command sends the data, which is assumed to be in a file named data, to its output, which is stdout.)

The input to the COTS application COTS_app1 is read from the output of the file stdout. In turn, the COTS application COTS_app1 writes its output to the input of the COTS application COTS_app2, and so on.

In this situation, there is little or no integration problem because the different components have restricted interfaces, and each of these interfaces is standard within the UNIX environment. However, most COTS applications do not fit this situation, even in the UNIX world. Many applications are transaction-oriented rather than following the stream-oriented model described above.

Applications often access the operating system's services by using system calls, for example. As such, essential system resources, such as the maximum number of open files or runnable processes at any one time, may be exceeded.

The situation is much worse in a modern, distributed environment, such as one based on the client-server paradigm. There may be some problem with the number of remote procedures that can be operating at any one time because of a limit on the number of available socket descriptors. There may be other problems due to concurrency and associated synchronization problems. Thus, any systems integrator must know the level of resources required for the application.

Another point must be made before we discuss a cost model for systems built out of COTS products. Everyone with experience in the computer industry is aware of the high failure rate for many companies, even some that were household names with a large share of the market for a particular application. Thus, even an investment in COTS application does not guarantee that it will be easy to maintain the system over time.

Many purchasers of COTS systems will therefore only buy systems for which source code is available. This ensures that maintenance will still be possible if the COTS vendor leaves the business or stops supporting the product. However, this strategy greatly increases the initial costs of purchasing the COTS application.

The inputs to a cost model based on the use of COTS software would include the quality assessment of the COTS software, the requirements, and some metrics, including assessments of integration costs and maintenance costs. The maintenance costs would include the availability of source code for the COTS product. Ideally, the cost model for COTS software would be used in conjunction with a model for the rest (non-COTS-based) of the system to be created.

Equation 5.21 shows a cost model for COTS-based systems.

Equation 5.21   A cost model for COTS-based systems

```
cost = cost of requirements for nonreuse system
       +
       sum (for all COTS products) of
       {
       .125 * (cost to evaluate COTS system)
       +
       cost to obtain COTS system
       +
       cost to obtain source code (if available)
       +
       integration costs
       +
       cost of annual maintenance for COTS
       }
       +
       cost to maintain system
```

There are three implicit assumptions in Eq. 5.21. We have used the same maintenance cost that would occur for a non-COTS system of the same size. As we pointed out earlier, there are several possibilities for software maintenance, depending upon whether we wish to purchase source code and do our own maintenance or allow the maintenance cost to be amortized across the COTS vendor's installed base.

The first implicit assumption in Eq. 5.21 is that the maintenance costs would have been the same for both COTS source code and software developed in house. This might not be true in the initial portion of the maintenance of the software because the preponderance of maintenance costs is associated with program understanding.

In many organizations some of the development team is assigned to maintenance for a short time after the system is delivered. These software engineers have an easier time understanding the source code because they are already familiar with at least some portion of the software. Thus, these people would have an easier time fixing software faults than people unfamiliar with the software. This potential disadvantage of COTS maintenance will be eliminated over time as more of the original development team moves away from maintenance of a non-COTS product.

Perhaps the last term in Eq. 5.21 should be broken down further as

```
cost to maintain non-COTS system
    =
1.1 * (cost to maintain non-COTS system)
+
cost to maintain system in subsequent years
```

Here the factor of 1.1 represents a projected higher maintenance cost for the COTS-based system in the first year. We chose a factor of 1.1 because 10 percent seems likely as the added cost of maintenance due to other maintenance efforts on the COTS system elsewhere.

The second implicit assumption in Eq. 5.21 is that we no longer need a reuse library because we will be purchasing larger systems and subsystems than those likely to be in a reuse library. Using only COTS should lead to the integration of a small number of systems and subsystems. In this environment, domain analysis is probably less important than detailed analysis of the available COTS products.

The final implicit assumption in Eq. 5.21 is that there is a choice in the maintenance process; that is, we can either do the maintenance ourselves or let the COTS vendor do it. In the event that the vendor decides to stop supporting the product the most likely scenario is that we would have to perform the maintenance ourselves. Of course, the situation is much worse if the vendor goes out of business.

The cost models for hybrid systems that consist of both COTS and software developed in house (including reusable components) will be straightforward combinations of the models for pure COTS and conventional systems, weighted by the appropriate percentages.

In a recent paper [ELLI95], Ellis of Lockheed Martin Federal Systems commented that the standard use of measurements such as lines of code is completely inappropriate for COTS-based software development. (Others have also noted this.) Ellis recommends the use of the Albrecht function point metrics [ALBR79] to determine the amount of effort needed for the filters or glueware necessary to bridge nonstandard interfaces between COTS products.

Ellis also presents some guidelines for estimating integration costs based on assessments of items such as the maturity of the COTS product and the stability of the COTS vendor. The cost estimation process for COTS products uses a weighted numerical scale. The basic assumption is that a useful scale can be determined for COTS products on each of several dimensions that reflect different attributes of the COTS product. The interface and functionality as measured by the function point metric are just two of the factors considered (probably the most important ones). The values of these attributes are then multiplied by various weights, and the sum reflects a description of the software used to estimate costs. The selection for COTS products is done by a simple linear ordering of the values of those products evaluated; those products with higher values are considered better candidates for insertion into a system.

Any cost model that uses a weighted linear scale must be validated against actual data. At the time this section was written, Ellis had validated his model against six different COTS-based development projects at Lockheed Martin Federal Systems, and there was a continuing effort to validate the weights in his model on additional projects. Unfortunately, for proprietary reasons the scale and weighting factors cannot be presented here.

Kontio at the University of Maryland, College Park, has a different view of measurement of COTS-based software [KONT95]. This work avoids the use of a single linear scale for cost modeling. It is based on a general comparison technique called the Analytic Hierarchy Process (AHP) that was originally presented by Saaty [SAAT80]. Saaty designed this technique to assess preferences among sets of potential choices. Kontio was one of the first to use the AHP technique to provide assessments of the applicability of COTS products.

The basic idea of Saaty's AHP technique is to develop a hierarchy of desirable features of objects in a universe of potential choices. The hierarchy is chosen to reflect the importance of certain attributes determined by the creator of the hierarchy. Within the same level of this hierarchy, different objects from the selection universe are compared in pairs according to preferences. The reason for the preference at each level is left up to the evaluator.

Some of the comparisons in the AHP technique might take the following form:

Which of the COTS products has a better interface to SQL?

Which has a smaller interface to the operating system, as measured by the number of operating system calls?

Which has a better user interface?

Some of the questions asked in the AHP approach have readily quantifiable answers; others do not.

Note that no absolute linear scale is possible in most instances of the AHP method. The final outcome of Kontio's application of the AHP process is a COTS product that is "more suitable" than others on a variety of measurements.

We note that the COTS-based cost estimation models presented in this section are consistent with both the Ellis and Kontio measurement approaches.

5.6   Other Reuse-Based Cost Estimation Models

In this section we will describe a more detailed cost model than those presented previously. In particular, we will assume that the cost estimating procedure is sufficiently refined so as to be able to provide a more precise description of the costs of certain activities.

We will base the discussion in this section primarily on the paper by Bollinger and Pfleeger [BOLL90]. Some related work can be found in the papers by Bollinger [BOLL95] and Lim [LIM94].

Bollinger and Pfleeger represent the first approximation of the costs of a systematic program of software reuse in terms of the potential benefit, which is given as

Equation 5.22   The Bollinger-Pfleeger basic model for the benefits of software reuse

```
benefit = sum (for all products) of
          {
          development - adaptation
          }
          +
          reuse investment
```

Here the term *investment* refers to the total cost of resources applied specifically to making the product or set of products that are considered to be reusable.

Bollinger and Pfleeger then extend the basic model of Eq. 5.21 to several situations. They use the term *inclusion effect* instead of my term *life cycle leverage* to describe the increase in cost savings that result when reuse of a software component occurs at an early phase of an organization's software development life cycle, thereby reducing the need for later life cycle steps. You should note that the inclusion effect is indicated in Eqs. 5.1 through 5.5 for the waterfall model of the software life cycle. There are similar inclusion effects related to the cost models for the rapid prototyping and spiral models of software development that were presented in Secs. 5.3 and 5.4, respectively. The COTS-based models in Sec. 5.5 are the most extreme case of the inclusion effect in software reuse.

Bollinger and Pfleeger note a management problem that was addressed earlier in this chapter: how to distribute the costs of a systematic reuse program across a set of projects that may access the same set of reusable software artifacts. When we discussed this point, we left the responsibility for proper accounting of all reuse-based activities in the hands of the project manager, who then was asked to educate his or her division managers. Bollinger and Pfleeger present a more concrete suggestion.

They introduce the concept of a "cost sharing domain" to address this issue. They suggest an analogy to a bank creating new assets within a cost sharing domain. In this concept, an investment in a systematic reuse plan is made using funds that are independent of individual projects. This is clearly most appropriate for reuse in the same application domain (vertical reuse).

Clearly the development of a "bank" of expenses for pooled resources of potentially reusable components is as much a managerial issue as a technical one. We will not discuss the issue any further but will refer the reader to Bollinger and Pfleeger's paper.

Frakes and Fox have methods of cost estimation across an entire life cycle [FRAK95A] that are similar in function to the methods described in this chapter. Finally, the reader should consult a recent paper by Lim [LIM94] and a subsequent book [LIM95] in which he describes some cost modeling problems in large organizations.

5.7   Estimation of Other Resources in Reuse-Based Environments

In this section we will describe some of the other organizational resources that are impacted by a reuse-based environment. The primary effects are the time needed to bring a system to market and the amount of computer facilities and personnel needed. Quantitative models will not be presented because of the large variation in different organizations. Instead, we will be content with qualitative models, which is satisfactory because the data is so incomplete.

We first consider the savings in time. There are two essential factors here:

- The time overhead of a reuse program
- The time saved by reusing a software artifact

In most organizations, the time penalty appears to be the sum of two factors: a general overhead of measurement and analysis and a specific time to examine a reuse library. We can approximate the general time overhead factor using the same factor we employed for the cost overhead of reuse, namely 12.5 percent.

The specific time required to examine a reuse library depends on the number of software artifacts in the reuse library and the amount of time needed for domain analysis. This time should be added to the expected time for the project.

The time saved by reusing a software artifact depends upon the life cycle phase in which the artifact is reused and the amount of the artifact that is reused. Reuse of a high-quality artifact such as in the requirements phase has the greatest potential for cost savings. For smaller degrees of reuse we suggest time savings at the low end of the range.

Thus, reuse of 75 to 99 percent of the requirements would involve a 75 percent saving of the rest of the time needed for the project, and reuse of 50 to 75 percent of the requirements would involve a 50 percent saving of the rest of the time needed. The same pattern holds for reuse at other life cycle phases.

The extra computer resources will fall into two categories:

- Additional disk space for reuse libraries
- Additional execution time for general purpose instead of custom software

The first is directly predictable. It is the size of the reuse library. The execution overhead is only relevant in systems with hard real-time deadlines.

The personnel costs associated with reuse are hard to generalize. We will be content with the observation that the following tasks are required:

- Reuse process expert
- Domain analyst
- Reuse library manager
- COTS technology assessor
- System integrator

It is likely that reuse-based software development environments will emphasize COTS and system integration much more in the future than they do now. It is clear that organizations with systematic software reuse plans will need fewer lower-level programmers than before.

5.8   The Economic Reuse Quantity

The title of this section is based on an analogy with inventory management systems. We will argue that there is an optimum component size for reusable components based on the costs of entering components in a reuse library, maintaining the library, and accessing the library.

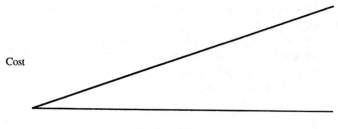

Cost

Number of Components

Figure 5.4 The relationship between maintenance costs and the number of components

The idea is that the same amount of reusable information can be packaged many different ways. Hopefully, the ideas in this section will provide some guidance in efficient packaging.

Figure 5.4 shows the relationship between the cost of maintaining a number of components in a reuse library and the number of components. Note that for the same fixed amount of information, the library maintenance cost can be made smaller by having fewer components.

However, the cost of receiving the many small components into the library will increase as will the cost of processing many small components. The amount of information, number of components, and average amount of information per component are related by the equation

```
total amount = (average information per component)
               *
               (number of components)
```

Therefore, the receiving cost looks something like what is shown in Fig. 5.5, where we have indicated the relationship between the ordering cost and the size of an order.

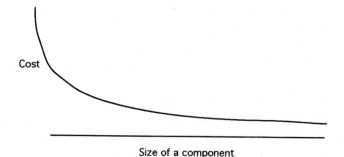

Cost

Size of a component

Figure 5.5 The relationship between the cost of receiving components and the size of a component.

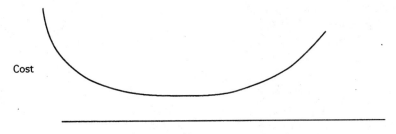

Figure 5.6 The relationship between the total cost of receiving and maintaining a reuse library and the size of a component

The sum of the two costs represents the total cost of maintaining an appropriate reuse library. This cost is shown in Fig. 5.6.

It is clear from the figure that there is an optimal component size that minimizes the cost. We now compute this component size.

Let A be the cost of placing a component into the reuse library, B the cost of maintaining a single item in the reuse library for the given time period, and T the total amount of information provided in the reusable artifact. The cost of each of these three quantities can be estimated within certain limits of precision by techniques given in this and previous chapters.

For example, T, which is the total amount of information in a reusable software artifact, can be measured by the number of function points or the number of individual requirements listed in a requirements document; the number of lines of code or Halstead metrics for a source code module; the number of lines, words, or paragraphs for documentation; or some other appropriate measurement of the size of an artifact.

The constant A represents the cost of placing a component into the reuse library. This cost involves performing the domain analysis of the software artifact, checking for legal ownership of the component, obtaining proper permissions for use of the component, checking that all available items associated with the component are present (such as checking for the source code associated with a set of reusable requirements), and formally placing the component into the reuse library.

The constant B represents the cost of maintenance of the component within the library. This may be estimated as a percentage of the total maintenance costs for the entire reuse library.

In our model, it is important to treat certification costs consistently. If the reuse library is operated under the "certify-on-demand" approach, or if library components can be recertified after placement in the reuse library, then the costs of continuing certification should also be prorated and considered as part of the value of B. If all certification is done before the component is placed into the library, then this should be reflected in the value of A.

If we use the symbol Q to represent the number of components, then my previous discussion indicates that the total cost, C, is given by the formula

$$C = A * T/Q + B * Q$$

The derivative of C with respect to Q is

$$-A * T/(Q^2) + B$$

and therefore the minimum value of Q occurs when

$$Q = sqrt(A * T/B).$$

It is clear from Fig. 5.6 that this value represents a minimum cost rather than a maximum.

Now that we have obtained a theoretical estimate of the optimal size of a reuse library component, it remains to determine the practical implications. Three quantities are needed to compute the optimal size of a reusable component: A, T, and B. There are obviously some accounting issues involved in determining the values of these quantities. However, the presence of the square root operation in the equation means that a relative error of 20 percent in any of the values of A, B, or T yields only about an 11 percent error in the computed value of Q. Thus, the economic reuse quantity is still a meaningful number in many applications.

Summary

Most software cost models do not include information on software reuse. This is true for the classical waterfall, rapid prototyping, and spiral models of software development.

As with many things in the field of software engineering, the actual cost savings of reuse are sometimes illusory. There are several reasons for this discrepancy, depending on the life cycle model used, namely:

- Development history
- Initial costs for a systematic software reuse program
- Reuse library costs
- Percentage and level of reuse in the system being reused

There are four levels of reuse.

1. The software artifact is used as is. This is called *transportable*.

2. The software artifact has minor changes totaling less than 25 percent. This is called *adaptable* or having *few changes*.

3. The software artifact has more than 25 percent, but fewer than 50 percent, changes. This is called *substantial changes*.

4. The software is *new*.

Each of these factors influences the cost savings of a systematic reuse program. The cost savings are always highest if the reusable software artifact is incorporated into the system in the early parts of the system's software life cycle.

Each of the three general software development models (classic waterfall, rapid prototyping, and spiral) has its own cost estimation models. There are different cost estimation models depending on the place in the life cycle in which the reusable artifact is used and the relative amount of reuse in the artifact. Each of the models includes an estimate of the costs of a systematic reuse program, including the collection and analysis of some software metrics.

An important factor in cost models is the use of COTS software. It is possible to design some systems using only COTS.

Other resources are affected by a systematic reuse program. The time for product development is affected by a general overhead and a time savings that is a function of the life cycle phase in which the software artifact is reused as well as the amount of the artifact reused.

Each potentially reusable component has a size that is optimal for minimizing software costs. A module that is too large is likely to have limited applicability and thus little potential for reuse. On the other hand, a module that is too small may not be worth the trouble of searching for it in a reuse library. The optimal size for a reusable source code component is called the *economic reuse quantity*.

Further Reading

Perhaps the most widely read book on software cost modeling is Boehm's classic *Software Engineering Economics* [BOEH81]. This book predates the current systematic reuse efforts. It also predates the current emphasis on rapid prototyping and Boehm's own spiral model of software development [BOEH88]. This is must reading for anyone interested in software cost and resource estimation.

A recent book by Gaffney and Cruickshank [GAFF91] emphasizes the modeling work done by the Software Productivity Consortium in the economics of software reuse. This book has many complex linear models of the savings possible with systematic programs of software reuse. A spreadsheet version of their models is available from the ASSET library.

The papers by Barnes and Bollinger [BARN91], Bollinger and Pfleeger [BOLL90], Frakes and Fox [FRAK95A], Pfleeger [PFLE96], and Lim [LIM94] also should be consulted for more information on reuse-based cost modeling. Lim's book [LIM95] describes some of the issues in reuse-based cost modeling at Hewlett-Packard.

There is little generally available literature on the subject of cost modeling of COTS-based systems in a reuse environment. The paper by Ellis [ELLI95] and a related paper by Waund [WAUN95] both provide good advice for COTS-based systems. These two papers are based on their authors' work at Lockheed Martin Federal Systems. Other work on COTS-based modeling can be found in Kontio [KONT95].

Exercises

1. (*This exercise is intended for experienced software professionals only.*) Determine how reuse is used in software cost estimation in your organization. What are the overhead factors?

2. (*This exercise is intended for both students and experienced software professionals.*) Examine some software you wrote recently. Based on an estimate of 4 to 10 documented, tested lines of code per hour, estimate how long the project might have taken. After you have done this, reexamine the code for possible software reuse. Based on these savings in code, indicate the cost savings you would expect. Use an estimate of $50 per hour, which is a typical industry average for salary-plus-benefits for all types of software employees (including some support staff). What cost model did you use?

3. Consider the following statement: "The more you spend on an original component, the more you save when you reuse it." Discuss this statement's validity. In your discussion be sure to consider the effect of the component's size and volatility and the likelihood that the component will be reused.

6

Reengineering

Many different definitions of reengineering are common in the technical literature. All seem to have one thing in common: improving the design of existing systems. Sometimes the process is described by an adjective that indicates the particular application domain, as in "business process reengineering." We will focus here on software reengineering, which we will define broadly as improving the design of existing software systems.

There is often some confusion between the terms *software reengineering* and *reverse software reengineering*. The two terms are related but do not describe the same engineering process.

The software reengineering process includes the following activities:

- Extracting knowledge from an existing system
- Recovering the program design, even if documents have been lost (or were never made). This is necessary to maintain the code.

The reverse engineering process includes the same steps as reengineering and at least one additional one:

- Producing an "equivalent" product by working backward from the external behavior to determine how to code a new system that is identical in function to the old one.

One difficulty arises if the new system is developed by a group that does not have legal rights to use the original code. In this situation, the intention is to develop an equivalent product either to compete commercially with an existing one or to avoid the cost of completely new development of an equivalent system whose functionality is considered important. We will not discuss reverse engineering in this book.

Note that reengineering is related to potential software reuse. A program that performed its duties acceptably and presented no maintenance problems is more likely to be reengineered if all or part of it is likely to be reused in other systems. Thus, the amount of potential reuse influences the decision to reengineer.

On the other hand, a program that is poorly documented, with an overly complex structure, or is written in an obsolete language is a poor candidate for reuse. Thus, the quality of the software engineering of the system and the decision to reengineer will both influence the amount of potential reuse.

There are some major pressures currently driving the software reengineering process. The desire to reduce maintenance costs has focused attention on a few languages and standards. Software systems that only work on obsolete hardware must be reengineered before they can be used. The same situation holds for software systems that have large interfaces with obsolete applications or operating systems.

Technology advances have caused other pressures. Many older software systems were written in languages that are not popular today, and thus there is pressure to rewrite systems in either Ada or C++. The object orientation and other software engineering features of these two programming languages can create some major difficulties when translating from systems written in programming languages without these features.

This chapter will emphasize some of the issues in software reengineering. We will briefly discuss the general process of program translation in Sec. 6.1.

Section 6.2 will include a description of a reengineering scheme that is based on semantic reasoning and a sequence of program transformations. The intermediate program translations are analyzed and compared to the original in order to measure program understanding.

The remainder of the chapter (Secs. 6.3 to 6.10) will discuss an example of the process of reengineering a program written in a procedural programming language (C) to an object-oriented programming language (C++).

6.1   Program Translation

The easiest way to reengineer a program written in an older programming language is to translate it into a modern one. This activity is critical for many legacy systems, especially if the original source language is not currently supported widely in the software industry. We use the term *legacy system* to mean a system that was developed before the current software development methodology of the organization. Frequently, legacy systems have little available documentation and are hard to understand. Hence, any change, especially to a new methodology such as object orientation, involves a great deal of effort just to understand the existing system.

Since programming languages have precise syntax, the translation process would appear to be easy. Formal descriptions of the syntax of the source and target languages are readily available for most languages. A parser could be built using these descriptions together with a parser generator tool such as the UNIX `lex` and `yacc` or the similar Ada language tool `Alex` and `Ayace`. Software reengineering based on the use of such translators is called *automatic program translation.*

Unfortunately, syntax analysis of programs does not appear to lead to programs that are easy to understand or modify. Some reasons for this are fairly obvious. A program written in FORTRAN IV (before the use of structured loops) does not map well to languages that don't use GOTOs very often.

In addition, older programming languages frequently do not support modern software constructs. Therefore, determining relevant objects is very difficult if programs in FORTRAN, Pascal, COBOL, or even the original version of Ada (Ada83) are to be translated automatically into object-oriented languages and have object-oriented features. The term *AdaTRAN* is frequently used to describe the results of line-by-line syntactic translations of FORTRAN to Ada.

Clearly, some type of semantic analysis is needed. The semantic analysis often produces products that are not quite identical to the original source code. For example, several languages deliberately leave undefined the order of evaluation of operands in expressions. If the target language specifies the order of evaluation of operands as being, say, left to right, then the two programs cannot be completely identical, and at least this portion of the translation process cannot be reversed.

More serious difficulties occur if the source language has features that are not available in the target language. Typical situations where this can occur are pointers, recursion, and structured data types (especially variant records).

Most tools for automatic program translation attempt at least some form of semantic analysis. The tools developed by Scandura Systems have better performance than those publicly available in the Public Ada Library (see App. 2) for automatic translation from FORTRAN to Ada, or from C to Ada. These tools generally create new programs in the target languages that are syntactically equivalent to the source programs.

However, none of these tools have sufficient semantic information to fully automate the process of program translation. The resulting translated systems are often poorly structured themselves, requiring additional analysis, which is usually done manually. The tools generally require additional analysis to restructure the resulting code in the target language. We discuss some typical other reasoning in the remaining sections of this chapter.

Automatic program translators have improved considerably in the past few years. It is likely these improvements will continue.

6.2   An Example of Semantic Reasoning in Reengineering

In a paper presented at the 1992 IEEE Conference on Software Maintenance, Pleszkoch, Linger, and Hevner examined the results of a formal transformation scheme [PLES92]. The purpose of their work was to demonstrate the feasibility of transforming the relatively unstructured versions of the code into a more structured model. Their primary concern was reducing the number of untraversable paths from the code fragments.

It is well known that a major portion of the time spent in software maintenance activities is devoted to program understanding. Thus, any simple method that restructures programs and improves program understanding is likely to be beneficial to the maintenance process. Certainly, removing untraversable paths from a program should improve program maintenance.

Pleszkoch and colleagues considered four versions of a small program fragment called "Structured Long," "GOTOs," "Unstructured Short," and "Structured Short." The formal method used a special representation for providing the transformations from the original version ("Structured Long"). The new representation of the program is based on a set of regular expressions. Relevant symbols in the grammar of the regular expression include the statements in which functions are performed, decision statements, and the testing and setting of control flow variables. Each of the labels in the programs of Examples 6.1 through 6.4 is used as part of the alphabet of the regular expressions.

The transformation process had the following steps, each of which resulted in a new program fragment equivalent to the old in functionality:

1. Develop a formal set of regular expressions to indicate the structure of the program.

2. Create a new program based on the regular expressions created in step 1.

3. Examine the regular expression describing the program for potential untraversable paths and remove unnecessary control variables.

4. Remove all untraversable program paths and unnecessary control variables.

5. Examine the new program with the goal of determining a simpler regular expression describing the program.

6. Convert the regular expression in step 5 to a program. The program at this stage will generally be unstructured.

7. Change the (probably) unstructured program of step 6 to a structured one.

For more information about the transformation process, consult Pleszkoch, Linger, and Hevner [PLES92].
The program specifications are as follows:

```
For each i in 1..N, search A(i,1), A(i,2), A(i,3),
..., for the first nonzero entry. Place the position
of the first nonzero entry in W(i), and the type (+1
for positive, -1 for negative) in T(i). Assume that
there will always be a nonzero entry.
```

The four program fragments are given in Examples 6.1 through 6.4. The changes in the control structure of these program fragments are illustrated by the changes in the program graphs, which are given in Figs. 6.1 through 6.4, respectively.

Example 6.1 "Structured Long" version of the code

```
i := 1;                                         -- f1
done := false;
new := true;
while not done loop
        if new then
                if (i <= N) then                -- p1
                        j := 1;                 -- f2
                        new := false;
                        rest := false;
                else
                        done := true;
                end if;
        else
                if rest then
                        j := j + 1;             -- f3
                        rest := false;
                else
                        W(i) := j;              -- f4
                        if A(i,j) > 0 then      -- p2
                                T(i) := 1;      -- f5
                                new := true;
                        else
                                if (A(i.j) < 0 then   -- p3
                                        T(i) := -1;   -- f6
                                        new := true;
                                else
                                        rest := true;
```

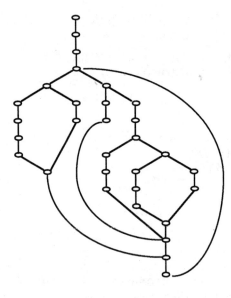

Figure 6.1 The program graph of the code in Example 6.1

```
                    end if;
              end if;
        end if;
        if new then
                i := i + 1;                    -- f7
        end if;
      end if;
  end loop;
```

The program structure of the code in Example 6.1 is relatively complex, as Fig. 6.1 shows.

Note that the code fragment of Example 6.1 is somewhat complex relative to its size. The McCabe cyclomatic complexity is 7 for this code. (See App. 1 for more information about the McCabe cyclomatic complexity and its relation to the number of test cases needed for branch testing.)

Example 6.2 "GOTOs" version of the code

```
<<LF1>>      i := 1;                  -- f1
             goto LP1;
<<LF2>>      j := 1;                  -- f2
             goto LF4;
<<LF3>>      j := j + 1;              -- f3
             goto LF4;
<<LF4>>      W(i) := j;               -- f4
             goto LP2;
<<LF5>>      T(i) := 1;               -- f5
             goto LP1;
<<LF6>>      T(i) := -1;              -- f6
```

```
                goto LP1;
<<LP1>>         i := i + 1;
                if (i <= N) then              -- p1
                    goto LF2;
                else
                    goto EXIT;
                end if;
<<LP2>>         if (A(i,j) > 0) then          -- p2
                    goto LF5;
                else
                    goto LP3;
                end if;
<<LP3>>         if (A(i,j) < 0) then          -- p3
                    goto LF6;
                else
                    goto LF3;
                end if;
<<EXIT>>
```

The graph shown in Fig. 6.2 appears more complex than the program actually is. Note that the graph is not planar, and therefore there are many arcs that appear to intersect.

The code fragment in Example 6.2 is unappealing because of the large number of GOTO statements. The McCabe cyclomatic complexity for this code fragment is relatively large. Note also that the code has a single entry point and a single exit.

Example 6.3   "Unstructured Short" version of the code

```
i := 1;                                -- f1
while ( (i <= N) loop                  -- p1
```

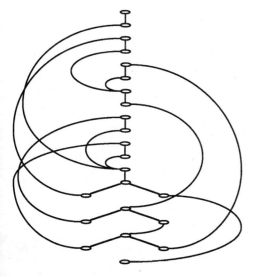

Figure 6.2 The program graph of the code in Example 6.2

```
j := 1;                                      -- f2
loop
      W(i) := j;                             -- f4
      if A(i,j) > 0 then                     -- p1
            T(i) := 1;                       -- f5
            exit;
      else
            if A(i,j) < 0 then               -- p3
                  T(i) := -1;                -- f6
                  exit;
            else
                  j := j + 1;                -- f3
            end if;
      end if;
   end loop;
   i := i + 1;                               -- f7
end loop;
```

The McCabe cyclomatic complexity for the fragment of Example 6.3 is only 4, which is relatively low. (The McCabe cyclomatic complexity metric is increased by 2 for each potential exit point in the program.) However, the code has two possible exit points, which is considered poor software engineering practice. Joining the two exit points to a single exit would increase the McCabe cyclomatic complexity to 5, which is still low. (We do not do this here in order that we may be consistent with the original program translation techniques.)

Example 6.4 "Structured Short" version of the code

```
i := 1;                                      -- f1
while (i <= N) loop                          -- p1
      j := 1;                                -- f2
      flag := true;
      while (flag) loop
            W(i) := j;                       -- f4
            if A(i,j) > 0 then               -- p2
                  T(i) := 1;                 -- f5
                  flag := false;
```

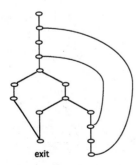

exit

Figure 6.3 The program graph of the code in Example 6.3

```
        else
                if A(i,j) < 0 then           -- p3
                        T(i) := -1;          -- f6
                        flag := false;
                else
                        j := j + 1;          -- f3
                end if;
        end if;
    end loop;
    i := i + 1;                              -- f7
end loop;
```

The code fragment in Example 6.4 has a McCabe cyclomatic complexity of 5, which is an improvement over some of the other versions.
The code also has the advantage of having only a single point of en-
trance and a single point of exit.

It is clear that this program restructuring method has potential
benefits for improving program understanding.

6.3 Transitioning to an Object-Oriented System

In this section we describe a common problem: reengineering an existing, procedurally developed legacy system to an object-oriented system. Our approach is to use the rapid prototyping software development model. In this method, the system is designed to meet a
minimal set of requirements. The system is then either changed or
discarded and built anew as new specifications or requirements are
changed or added. Support for rapid prototyping is considered to be
one of the major advantages of C++ as a programming language.

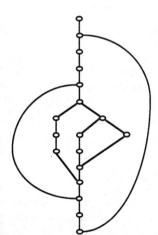

Figure 6.4 The program graph
of the code in Example 6.4

Prototyping is especially important when updating legacy systems. The documentation may be missing or not consistent with the code, which is likely to have had many changes made to it during its lifetime. The fact that the original computer hardware and most of the software that the system had to be interoperable with are very much out of date is much more important.

In the rest of this chapter we will describe a software system that was already built in the C programming language. The software provides a simulation of a file system, which is a major component of an operating system. We will also consider the actual disk movement as well as the writing of data to and from computer memory.

The remainder of this chapter is organized as follows. In the next section (Sec. 6.4), we will describe procedurally based specifications for a simulation of a file system. In Sec. 6.5, we will describe the high-level design of the procedurally based simulation, using a well-documented main program and set of procedures. Input and output in the original C program have been changed to use the C++ I/O operators $<<$ and $>>$ to operate on iostreams.

The details of the procedurally based implementations of disk operations, memory-disk transfers, and I/O are discussed in Sec. 6.6. This section can be omitted by readers more interested in the steps used in a reengineering process than in the details of source code.

In Sec. 6.7, we will describe additional features of the procedurally based design that allow a more complex structure of the simulated disk, using a hierarchical organization for the simulated file system. This section can be omitted by a reader uninterested in source code.

In Sec. 6.8, we study the process of transforming the procedurally based simulation into one that is object oriented in nature. Here we describe changing procedurally based requirements into object-oriented requirements.

In Sec. 6.9, we will present some of the code for an object-oriented program to perform the file system simulation. As with Sec. 6.6, this section can be omitted by readers more interested in the steps used in a reengineering process than in the details of source code.

Finally, in Sec. 6.10 we compare the two sets of requirements and designs. We also discuss general issues that are likely to arise when transforming procedurally described systems into object-oriented ones.

6.4   Specifications for a File System Simulation

The initial requirements are that the system will be able to move blocks of data from memory to the disk and from the disk to memory. We will concentrate on the actions that our program will perform and on how we will communicate our wishes to various portions of the program.

The most important thing needed at this point is a discussion of a user interface. The program is to be totally interactive and should prompt the user to enter data in a predetermined form. There is an initial message explaining the system and then the user is prompted for input from a small set of options. A high-quality user interface should also provide checking of the input for errors and provide a method for the user to correct any input errors. Since we are designing a simple system, let us assume that the user is perfect and never makes errors. Thus, no error checking of input is needed.

The input commands will allow data to be entered into memory directly. Data can be entered into memory directly, sent from memory to disk, or sent from disk to memory in units called *blocks*. Our system will be able to move data in blocks accessed in memory by identifying a starting memory location of a block and to access blocks of data on the disk by the track and sector numbers identifying them.

A limited set of the specifications of the system is thus:

Functional requirements

Provide opening message to user.

Move data into memory directly, from memory to disk, or from disk to memory in fixed-sized units called blocks. Any movement of data to or from the disk must access the block using the `track` and `sector` numbers that uniquely identify the block. A block in memory is specified by identifying the starting position.

Obtain input commands interactively. The input is read in one line at a time. If the first input character is `'i'`, then the next input line is a variable of type `int`, which is the type that we are using for data. The function `put_in_memory()` is then called with the parameter data that was read in. After the function `put_in_memory()` is called, then control returns to the main program.

If the input is `'d'`, then the next three input lines will contain variables of type `int`. These three lines represent the values of the memory location `mem_loc` and the disk location specified by `track` and `sector`, respectively. The function `mem_to_disk()` is then called with the parameters `mem_loc`, `track`, and `sector` read in. After the function `mem_to_disk()` is called, then control returns to the main program.

If the input is `'m'`, then the next three input lines will contain variables of type `int`. These three lines represent the values of the memory location `mem_loc` and the disk location specified by `track` and `sector`, respectively. The function `disk_to_mem()` is then called with the parameters `mem_loc`, `track`, and `sector` read in.

After the function `disk_to_mem()` is called, then control returns to the main program.

Input is read in without error checking.

Some of the functions we will need are

```
void print_disk();
void print_mem();
void mem_to_disk(int mem_loc, int track, int sector);
void disk_to_mem(int mem_loc, int track, sector);
```

The functions `print_disk()` and `print_mem()` are used to display the contents of the simulated memory and disk on the screen. The functions `mem_to_disk()` and `disk_to_mem()` are actually used to move blocks of data from memory to disk or from disk to memory. The three parameters `mem_loc`, `track`, and `sector` are each of type `int` and indicate the starting locations of the blocks of data in memory or on the simulated disk.

The user will have to be able to tell the software if data are to be moved from memory to disk or from disk to memory. In our system, data need to be placed in memory before they can be sent to the disk. Thus, we need some additional functions:

```
opening_message()
get_data()
put_in_memory()
```

To make life as simple as possible, we will require that the input commands are entered one per line, with `'i'` for input into memory, `'d'` for writing to disk from memory, and `'m'` for writing from disk to memory. A command of `'d'` or `'m'` means that three additional parameters are needed to specify the memory location `mem_loc` and the two parameters `track` and `sector` are needed to specify a disk location. The command `'i'` means that data are to be sent to memory from the keyboard and this is to be followed by the data. We will assume that the data are of type `int` and that only one such data item will follow the command `'i'`.

Functions:

```
void opening_message(void)
```

Presents an opening message explaining the system and its purpose to a user. `opening_message()` has no parameters and returns no value.

```
void get_data(void)
```

This function has no parameters. It reads its input one line at a time. It has no parameters and returns no value.

If the input is `'i'`, then the next input line contains a variable of type `int`, which is the type of data we are using for the disk. The function `put_in_memory()` is then called with the parameter data that are read in. After the function `put_in_memory()` is called, control returns to the main program.

If the input is `'d'`, then the next three input lines will contain variables of type `int`. These three lines represent the values of the memory location called `mem_loc` that is used to mark the start of a block of memory as well as the `track` and `sector` that are used to mark the start of a disk block. The function `mem_to_disk()` is then called with the parameters `mem_loc`, `track`, and `sector` that were read in. After the function `mem_to_disk()` is called, control returns to the main program.

If the input is `'m'`, then the next three input lines will contain variables of type `int`. These three lines represent the values of the memory location called `mem_loc` that is used to mark the start of a block of memory as well as the `track` and `sector` that are used to mark the start of a disk block. The function `disk_to_mem()` is then called with the parameters `mem_loc`, `track`, and `sector` that were read in. After the function `disk_to_mem()` is called, control returns to the main program.

If the input is `'p'`, the contents of the simulated memory will be printed.

If the input is `'P'`, the contents of the simulated disk will be printed.

If the input is either `'q'` or `'Q'`, the program will terminate.

```
void put_in_memory(int data)
```

Parameter is of the type of data that we will enter into memory. It returns no value.

```
void disk_to_mem(int mem_loc, int track, int sector)
```

Parameters are of type `int`. It returns no value.

```
void mem_to_disk(int mem_loc, int track, int sector)
```

Parameters are of type `int`. It returns no value.

```
void print_disk(void)
```

Prints the contents of the array simulating the disk. It returns no value.

```
void print_mem(void)
```

Prints the contents of the array simulating memory. It returns no value.

We will write the design in two parts. The top-down design will indicate the major modules of the system and their relationship. The data-flow design will show some of the flow of data through the system, using text to simulate the boxes and lines that would be part of a graphical model, keeping the representation as part of the source file for the system.

We will use a top-down approach to our design by choosing appropriate functions and by "stubbing in" their definitions. *Stubbing in* means that even if we do not know precisely how the function will perform its actions, we include a description of the function in the design. Stubbing in requires that all parameters to a function be described in the function header. It is good practice to include documentation of the name, type, and purpose of each parameter used inside a function.

6.5 Procedurally Based System Design

We now show the high-level procedural design of the system. It has three parts: documentation of the top-down design of the system, documentation of the flow of data through the system, and a stubbed-in set of functions.

To facilitate the discussion of the transition to an object-oriented system later in this chapter, we will illustrate the code using the C++ I/O features with `cout` and `cin` instead of the C language functions `printf()` and `scanf()` that were originally used in the C code. We have also used a C++ comment style instead of the comment style typically used in the C language. We note that both these steps can be easily automated. See the exercises at the end of this chapter for more information.

In a realistic programming environment, these two steps might be useful if the existing C source code will be reused to a large extent in the development of the object-oriented system in C++. On the other hand, the effort needed to carry out these two steps might be wasted if most of the code has to be rewritten to emphasize an object-oriented approach. Clearly, the amount of potential reuse is the deciding factor.

Example 6.5   Initial System (with modifications)

```
//
// DESIGN OF DISK/MEMORY MANAGEMENT SYSTEM PROTOTYPE
// DESIGN TEAM: A. B. See
//             C. D. Eff
//             G. H. Eye
// DESIGN LEADER:
//             A. B. See
//
// DESIGN DATE: February 30, 1995
//
// HOST COMPUTER: Sun SPARC 2
//
// OPERATING SYSTEM: SunOS 4.1.3 (Solaris 1.1)
//
// COMPILER: UNIX C++ Compiler v 3.0
//
//
// FUNCTION BLOCK DESIGN:
//
//    |-----------|
//    |   main()  |
//    |-----------|
//         |
//         |
//         |
//    |--------------------|
//    |   opening_message()|
//    |--------------------|
//         |
//         |
//         |
//    |--------------|
//    |   get_data() |
//    |--------------|
//         |
//         |
//         |
// -----------  |-------------------------------------------
// |         |        |           |           |
// |         |        |           |           |
// ----------      | -------------  | -------------
// put_in_memory()  | disk_to_mem()  | print_mem()
// ----------       | -----------    | -----------
//
//         |              |
//         |              |
//      ------------    -----------
//      mem_to_disk()   print_disk()
//      ------------    -----------
//
//
```

```
//
//                    DATA FLOW DESIGN


// input choice:
// --- 'i', data --> put_in_memory()

// --- 'd', mem_loc, track, sector --> mem_to_disk()

// --- 'm', mem_loc, track, sector --> disk_to_mem()

// --- 'p' --> print_mem()

// --- 'P' --> print_disk()

//



//
//
//              MAIN

//
//
// List of functions in program.

void opening_message(void ) ;
void get_data(void ) ;
void put_in_memory(int data) ;
void mem_to_disk(int mem_loc, int track, int sector) ;
void disk_to_mem(int mem_loc, int track, int sector) ;
void print_mem(void ) ;
void print_disk(void ) ;
#include <iostream.h>
main(void)
{
  char ch;

  opening_message();
  get_data();
}


//
// FUNCTION opening_message()
// This function prints an opening message.
// CALLED BY: main()
// FUNCTIONS CALLED: none
// PARAMETERS : none
// VALUE RETURNED: none
//

void opening_message(void )
{
  cout <<"Welcome to the FILE SIMULATION SYSTEM \n\n";
```

```
    cout << "The purpose of the system is to demonstrate";
    cout << "some of the\n";
    cout << "features of a file system.\n\n";
    cout << "This first phase will show some of the";
    cout << "commands\n";
    cout << "to move data to and from simulated memory";
    cout << "and disk.\n\n\n";
}


//
// FUNCTION get_data()
//

// This function gets input data for the system. It will
// accept data of the form 'i', 'd', 'm', 'p', 'P', 'q', or
// 'Q'.

// If the input is 'i', then the next parameter will be of
// type int and will be used to fill up a memory block by
// calling the function put_data().

// If the input is 'd', then the next three variables will
// be passed to the function mem_to_disk() as the parameters
// mem_loc, track, and sector.

// If the input is 'm', then the next three variables will
// be passed to the function disk_to_mem() as the parameters
// mem_loc, track, and sector.

// If the input is 'p', then the function print_mem() will
// be called without any parameters.

// If the input is 'P', then the function print_disk() will
// be called without any parameters.

// If the input is 'q' or 'Q', then the function will
// terminate and return control to the main program.

// If the input is not either 'q' or 'Q', then the function
// get_data() will continue execution, calling the
// appropriate functions.

// The function will repeat the evaluation of input until a
// 'q' or 'Q' is entered, at which point the function
// returns control to the main program.

//
//
// CALLED BY: main()
//
// FUNCTIONS CALLED:
//          put_in_memory()
//          mem_to_disk()
//          disk_to_mem()
```

```
//          print_mem()
//          print_disk()
//
// PARAMETERS : none
//
// VALUE RETURNED: none
//
//


void get_data(void )
{
  char ch;           // for input command
  int data, mem_loc, track, sector;

  // loop runs forever until a quit command is given
  for( ; ; )
    {
    cout << "\n\n";
    cout << "Select an option:\n";
    cout << "\n";
    cout << "i.........insert directly into memory .\n";
    cout << "d.........move data from memory to disk\n";
    cout << "m.........move data from disk to mem\n";
    cout << "p.........print memory\n";
    cout << "P.........print disk\n";
    cout << "q.........quit\n";
    cout << "\n\n";
    cin >> ch ;
      switch (ch)
      {
      case 'i'://  place data directly into memory block
         cin >> data;
        put_in_memory(data);
        break;
      case 'd': // need three parameters
        cin >> mem_loc;
        cin >> track;
        cin >> sector;
        mem_to_disk(mem_loc, track, sector);
        break;
      case 'm': // need three parameters
        cin >> mem_loc;
        cin >> track;
        cin >> sector;
        disk_to_mem(mem_loc, track, sector);
        break;
      case 'p':
        print_mem();
        break;
      case 'P':
        print_disk();
        break;
      case 'q':               // exit get_data()
```

```
      case 'Q':
        return;
      }                    // end switch
    }                      // end for
  }                        // end get_data


/////////////////////////////////////////////////////////////
// FUNCTION put_in_memory()
/////////////////////////////////////////////////////////////

// This function places data into memory initially.
// It has a parameter that represents the data that are to be
// placed into each of the memory locations forming the
// first available block.
// CALLED BY: get_data()
//
// FUNCTIONS CALLED:none
//
// PARAMETERS: data (type int)
//
// VALUE RETURNED: none
//
/////////////////////////////////////////////////////////////

void put_in_memory(int data)
{
  cout << "In put_in_memory - parameter is";
  cout << data << "\n";
}



/////////////////////////////////////////////////////////////
// FUNCTION mem_to_disk()
/////////////////////////////////////////////////////////////
// This function controls the movement of blocks of data
// from the simulated memory to the simulated disk. It has
// three parameters: mem_loc, track, and sector.
//
// CALLED BY: get_data()
//
// FUNCTIONS CALLED: none
//
// PARAMETERS : mem_loc, track, sector
//
// VALUE RETURNED: none
//
/////////////////////////////////////////////////////////////
void mem_to_disk(int mem_loc, int track, int sector)
// int mem_loc is the starting point of memory block
{
  cout << "In mem_to_disk - parameters are";
  cout << mem_loc << track << sector << "\n";
}
```

```
/////////////////////////////////////////////////////////
// FUNCTION disk_to_mem()
/////////////////////////////////////////////////////////
//
// This function controls the movement of blocks of data
// from the simulated disk to the simulated memory. It has
// three parameters: mem_loc, track, and sector.
//
// CALLED BY: get_data()
//
// FUNCTIONS CALLED: none/
//
// PARAMETERS : mem_loc, track, sector
//
// VALUE RETURNED: none
/
/////////////////////////////////////////////////////////

void disk_to_mem(int mem_loc, int track, int sector)
// int mem_loc is starting point of memory block.
{
  cout << "In disk_to_mem -");
  cout << "parameters are %d %d %d \n";
  cout << mem_loc, track, sector);
}


/////////////////////////////////////////////////////////
// FUNCTION print_mem()
/////////////////////////////////////////////////////////
// This function prints the contents of simulated memory.
// CALLED BY: get_data()
// FUNCTIONS CALLED: none
// PARAMETERS : none
// VALUE RETURNED: none
/////////////////////////////////////////////////////////
void print_mem(void )
{
  cout << "In print_mem\n";
}


/////////////////////////////////////////////////////////
// FUNCTION print_disk()
/////////////////////////////////////////////////////////
// This function prints the contents of the simulated disk.

// CALLED BY: main()

// FUNCTIONS CALLED: none

// PARAMETERS : none

// VALUE RETURNED: none
```

```
//////////////////////////////////////////////////////
void print_disk(void )
{
  cout << "In print_disk\n";
}


//////////////////////////////////////////////////////
// END OF PROGRAM
//////////////////////////////////////////////////////
```

It is important to note the use of some simple design principles in this first prototype. We have chosen to write a modular design, with each of the functions needed stubbed in.

Note that the design is in the form of a documented program. This is because we want to avoid duplication of effort. It will be easier to test our program by testing the component functions individually and then placing them into the final program.

6.6   Implementation Details for a Procedurally Based Disk Simulation (Optional)

We can start to flesh out the bodies of the two functions mem_to_disk() and disk_to_mem() that were stubbed in earlier. We interpret memory as a two-dimensional array of data elements whose type is the same as we considered earlier, that is, the data are of type int. The contents of memory locations are addressed by simply giving their location. Since we will be moving blocks of data from memory to disk and from disk to memory, we also want to think of memory as being composed of blocks that can be accessed by knowing the starting location of a block and the number of elements in the block. Hence, we will also want to be able to view memory as a two-dimensional array of blocks of data.

The disk is a more complex system since a disk is inherently a two-dimensional object. We access elements on the disk by determining the disk block in which they occur. A disk block has its position determined by two parameters—the track and sector of the block. Think of a disk as being a set of concentric rings. Each ring is assumed to have the same capacity for storing data even though the rings of smaller diameter have the data packed more densely. By analogy to a phonograph record, these concentric rings are called tracks. There is another division of the disk into sectors. Each of the tracks is considered to be divided into the same number of sectors.

In actual disks, there is a read/write head that moves relative to the disk. The head can move along a particular track through various sectors or can move to different tracks while remaining along the same sector. For our purposes, it doesn't matter if the read/write head is fixed and the disk spins or if the disk is fixed and the head moves. A fixed-head system allows the disk to move along a sector, and the head can move in and out, reading data as necessary. A fixed-disk system has the head move along tracks or read different sectors by moving along rays emanating from the center of the disk. In most large computers, there are many read/write heads and many "platters" making up a disk system; for the sake of simplicity we consider only one platter and one read/write head.

The natural way of simulating the disk is by a two-dimensional array of data elements. On most computer disks, movement of the read/write head in and out while staying in the same sector is slower than changing sectors while staying in the same track. Therefore we will access a block of data by reference to the pair (track, sector) instead of the pair (sector, track). An element of the disk is then found by knowing the track and sector numbers that tell which block the element is in and the offset of the element from the start of the block.

As with memory, there is another way of treating the disk. We can consider a disk to be a three-dimensional array of data, with the data indexed by three numbers: the track, sector, and offset from the start of the disk block.

We will fix the following constants shown in Example 6.6 for use in our setting of the system requirements.

Example 6.6   Constants for the file system simulation.

```
constant int BLOCKSIZE = 10 ;
constant int NUM_TRACKS = 50 ;
constant int NUM_SECTORS = 4 ;
constant int NUM_MEM_BLOCKS = 10 ;
constant int MEMSIZE = 100; //NUM_MEM_BLOCKS*BLOCKSIZE
```

There are additional specifications.

Data movement

Movement from memory to disk and from disk to memory is determined by specifying the track index and sector index on the disk and the memory block index in memory for each block. The track index is in the range 0..NUM_TRACKS - 1. The sector index is in the range 0..NUM_SECTORS - 1. The memory block index is in the range 0..NUM_MEM_BLOCKS - 1.

Note that there is a lot of leeway in the specifications given so far for this project. All the lower-level decisions such as how the disk and

memory are to be organized, how to error check, or how to implement
the parsing of input are left to be determined during the design of the
system. The design involves decisions about the following functions:

```
disk_to_mem(int mem_loc,int track, int sector)
```

Parameters are of type int. The first parameter represents a memory
location in the range 0..NUM_MEM_BLOCKS - 1. The second parameter represents a track number in the range 0..NUM_TRACKS - 1,
and the third parameter represents a sector number in the range
0..NUM_SECTORS - 1. This function will move a block of data that is
specified by a track and a sector number to a memory location
specified by the parameter mem_loc.

```
mem_to_disk(int mem_loc, int track, int sector)
```

Parameters are of type int. The first parameter represents a memory
location in the range 0..MEMSIZE - 1. The second parameter represents a track number in the range 0..NUM_TRACKS - 1, and the
third parameter represents a sector number in the range 0..NUM_
SECTORS - 1. This function will move a block of data that is specified
by a memory location to a disk block that is specified by a track
number and a sector number.

```
void print_disk(void)
```

Prints the contents of the array simulating the disk. Details are
given later.

```
void print_mem(void)
```

Prints the contents of the array simulating memory. Details are
given later.

We have several choices here depending on the organization of the
disk and memory. One solution is to have one-dimensional arrays for
both the simulated memory and the simulated disk. The corresponding declarations are

```
MEMSIZE = NUM_MEM_BLOCKS * BLOCKSIZE;
DISK_SIZE = NUM_TRACKS * NUM_SECTORS * BLOCKSIZE ;
int data
int track , sector;    // track and sector parameters
int mem[MEMSIZE];      // a one-dimensional array
int disk[DISK_SIZE];
int mem_loc;
```

If we use this organization, we will have to impose the disk and memory structures upon the program commands as they execute. This organization does not support the availability of high-level structures in the C language.

If we wish to preserve the block structure, one alternative is to design the disk as a two-dimensional array and to require that the memory organization should be in the form of a one-dimensional array.

```
int data
int track , sector;   // track and sector parameters
int mem[MEMSIZE];     // a one-dimensional array
int disk[NUM_TRACKS][NUM_SECTORS];
int mem_loc;
```

This causes one problem—we don't have any way of indicating the contents of a block. For now, we can't use this organization.

If we use a three-dimensional array for the disk, we will be able to access every disk element directly. Clearly, we should use a similar arrangement for the organization of memory, so we could have memory declared as a two-dimensional array. In this organization, the structure of a block of data is relatively unimportant, since it has been incorporated into the disk itself. This is the organization we will use for this project.

```
int data
int track, sector; // track and sector parameters
int mem[NUM_MEM_BLOCKS][BLOCKSIZE];
int disk[NUM_TRACKS][NUM_SECTORS][BLOCKSIZE]
int mem_loc;
```

What are the ramifications for the rest of the design? If we consider the disk as a three-dimensional array, then we can use the first two parameters to act as identifiers of blocks and the third dimension as a counter for indexing the elements in the block. The simulated memory can be handled in a similar manner using the first parameter to identify the block and the second one to act as an index of the block elements. Because of the modular way the program has been written, no changes need to be made to the main program or to the functions get_data() or opening_message().

The functions print_mem() and print_disk() are the easiest to implement, so we consider them first. They require no parameters, and the disk and memory organizations make them easy to design. In fact, the coding of these two functions is so simple that we can do it right now.

The original functions were stubbed in and looked like this:

```
print_mem(void)
{
  cout << "In print_mem\n";
}
print_disk(void)
{
  cout << "In print_disk\n";
}
```

The output statements can be removed, and the simple loops to allow us to print the contents can be inserted easily.

```
void print_mem(void)
{
  int i, j;
  for(i = 0; i < NUM_MEM_BLOCKS; i++)
    {
    for (j = 0; j < BLOCKSIZE; j++)
      cout << mem[i][j];
    cout << "\n";
    }
}

void print_disk(void)
{
int i, j, k;
for(i = 0; i < NUM_TRACKS; i++)
  {
  for (j = 0; j < NUM_SECTORS; j++)
    {
    for (k = 0; k < BLOCKSIZE; k++)
      cout << mem[i][j][k];
    cout << "\n";
    }
  cout << "\n";
  }
}
```

This coding is somewhat minimal in that there is no appropriate heading for the output. This might be marginally acceptable for a system in which the output is written to a file, but it is not at all appropriate for an interactive system. The formatting of output should be done at a later stage since it is not yet critical to the design. We will not consider it here.

It is now time to look more closely at the structure of memory and the disk. We have a situation something like that shown in Fig. 6.5, assuming a value of 10 for BLOCKSIZE and a value for NUM_MEM_BLOCKS of at least 9.

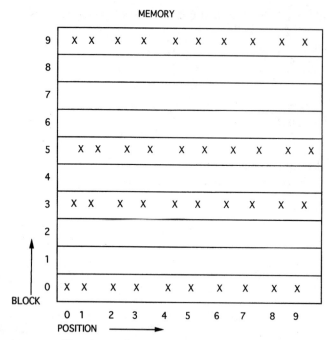

Figure 6.5 Structure of memory

An element in memory is then found by directly specifying the block_number and the offset from the start of the block. For example, if the value of BLOCKSIZE is 10 and the value of NUM_MEM_BLOCKS is 10, then the last element in memory can be found by specifying a value of 9 for the block_number and a value of 9 for the offset. The next to last element has a block_number of 9 but an offset of 8, and so on.

We can relate the value of the variable mem_loc we have used previously to the values of the block_number and offset by the formulas

```
mem_loc = block_number * BLOCKSIZE ;
block_number = mem_loc / BLOCKSIZE;
offset = mem_loc % BLOCKSIZE;
```

Note that the values of MEMSIZE or NUM_MEM_BLOCKS do not figure into these formulas. Note also that the location of a particular memory element is found by adding the offset of the element from the starting position in the block to the value of mem_loc.

What about the three remaining functions, put_in_memory(), mem_to_disk(), and disk_to_mem()? In each case, we need to make a decision about where the block of data should be placed. There are several ways of doing this.

Consider the problem of placing a block of data into memory. We need to be able to find an available place for the insertion of a new block. There are two situations we need to consider: one or more blocks available or nothing available.

If one or more memory blocks are available, then we have a situation something like that shown in Fig. 6.5. In Fig. 6.5, an uppercase X indicates that the memory location is already in use while a blank space means that the space is available for insertion of data. Recall that we are assuming that data are transferred in blocks and not as individual memory locations.

Our system will use the "first fit" method of inserting blocks into memory. In the first-fit method, we start at the beginning of memory and ask for the first available block that is large enough for the data to be inserted.

The result of using this method on the insertion of the

$$Y\,Y\,Y\,Y\,Y\,Y\,Y\,Y\,Y$$

into the memory configuration displayed in Fig. 6.5 is shown in Fig. 6.6.

We still have to consider the disk. We will use the same method of first-fit to find available blocks but with a slight difference. We will choose to fill up the disk by filling up all blocks on the first track, then all blocks on the second track, and so on. On each track we will fill up the sectors in increasing numerical order. This is the first-fit method applied to both the tracks and sectors, in order.

This takes care of the situation in which there is room in memory for the storage of the desired data. If there is no room, we have three choices. (1) We can terminate the program with an appropriate error action. (2) We can continue the program execution by swapping the block of data from memory to the disk and thus free up the memory block. The third option is unacceptable: (3) we continue execution of the program in an error state. Options 1 and 2 are used in many computer systems. We will arbitrarily choose the second option if memory is full; that is, we write a memory block of data onto the disk.

A similar problem occurs when the disk is full. In this case, we have no place to put extra data, so we select the first strategy of terminating execution of our program with an appropriate error action.

Everything looks fine from the point of view of how blocks of data can be accessed on the simulated disk or simulated memory. However, there are some things we have overlooked. For example, we need to have some mechanism for determining if a block of space in memory

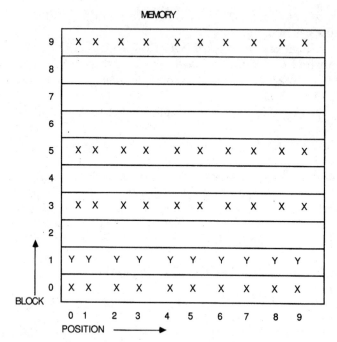

Figure 6.6 Result of insertion using the first-fit method

or on the disk is available. We have to store such information some-where and access it somehow. Finally, we have to know the state of the simulated disk and memory initially; that is, we have to initialize the system.

Real operating systems store information about what space is avail-able in memory in what is historically called a free list or free vector. We will use an array to store the information for memory; this array will contain as many entries as there are blocks in memory, NUM_MEM_BLOCKS. Recall that the dimension of the simulated memory is MEM-SIZE, which is the product of NUM_MEM_BLOCKS and MEMSIZE. Simi-larly, the availability of blocks on the disk is kept in a two-dimensional array. Thus, we need two new data declarations,

```
int free_mem_list[NUM_MEM_BLOCKS];
int free_disk_list[NUM_TRACKS][NUM_SECTORS];
```

to keep a record of the available blocks. If a block is available, we should have a 0 in the corresponding "list"; if the block is in use, we should have something else, such as a 1, in the appropriate place.

We now know enough to do the design. We will follow the general principle of using a function to encapsulate an action that is repeated.

The two functions `put_in_memory()` and `disk_to_mem()` require us to find an available memory block. Therefore, we will define a new function, `find_mem_block()`. This function uses the first-fit algorithm for obtaining a free block. We have to check the array called `free_mem_list`. The algorithm seems simple:

```
mem_block_number = 0
do
    {
    test free_mem_list[mem_block_number]
    mem_block_number ++
    }
while free_mem_list[mem_block_number] != 0
```

This works perfectly if there is a free block. If none is available, we would continue searching until we exceeded the amount of memory allotted to our running program. The correct algorithm also tests for failure:

```
mem_block_number = 0
do
    {
    test free_mem_list[mem_block_number]
    mem_block_number ++
    }
while (free_mem_list[mem_block_number] != 0) &&
                (mem_block_number < NUM_MEM_BLOCKS);

if (mem_block_number == NUM_MEM_BLOCKS)
    printf("Error - no available memory blocks\n");
```

We will need to perform a similar search for free blocks on the disk. For the disk, the algorithm is

```
track_number = 0;
sector_number = 0;
do
    // search each track, one sector at a time
    do
        {
        // search a complete track
        test free_disk_list[track_number][sector_number];
                sector_number] ++;
        }
    while ( free_disk_list[track_number][sector_number] != 0 )
                && (sector_number < NUM_SECTORS);

    track_number ++;
    sector_number = 0;
while (free_disk_list[track_number][sector_number] != 0 ) &&
                (track_number < NUM_TRACKS) ;
```

```
if (track_number == NUM_TRACKS)
    cerr << "Error - no available disk blocks\n";
```

It is time to take stock of our progress. We have designed a fairly elaborate system for moving data blocks to and from memory. Let us suppose that we have actually coded the program to carry out the algorithms and data structures in the design. It is important to note that we really cannot do exhaustive testing of any major software project because of the complexity of the system. For example, there are NUM_MEM_BLOCKS possible memory blocks. The number of possible combinations of memory block availability includes

one case of no blocks available

NUM_MEM_BLOCKS cases of exactly one block available

NUM_MEM_BLOCKS * (NUM_MEM_BLOCKS - 1) / 2 cases of exactly two blocks

and so on for a total of two raised to the power of NUM_MEM_BLOCKS possible groupings of memory alone. The number of possible disk block combinations is exponential in the number NUM_TRACKS + NUM_SECTORS, and the total number of combinations to be tested is astronomical. It is quite common to have systems so complex that complete testing would take centuries.

As we mentioned earlier in this chapter, the original source code for the system has been changed to C++ from C code by replacing the calls to the functions printf(), scanf(), and getchar() by the C++ I/O operators << and >>, using the standard iostreams cout and cin. For simplicity, the file-based I/O using pure C language constructions has been left unchanged.

6.7   Source Code for Procedural System

The code presented in this section is based on a procedural design of the system and will be given in Examples 6.8 through 6.13. The overall organizational structure of the code is indicated by the Makefile presented in Example 6.7. The source code performs the appropriate disk operations such as moving blocks of data between simulated memory, the simulated disk, and a user. This is the lowest level of the file system simulation.

Robin Morris of AT&T provided some help in the original C language implementation of this program using the design given in the previous sections of this chapter.

Example 6.7 `Makefile` **for a procedurally oriented file system simulation**

```
## makefile for disk simulation program
## the executable file is named disk_mem

disk_mem: memory.o move_dat.o print.o disk.o main.o
        cc -o disk_mem memory.o move_data.o print.o disk.o\
        main.o

memory.o: memory.c header.h
        cc -O -c memory.c
move_dat.o: move_dat.c header.h
        cc -O -c move_dat.c
print.o: print.c header.h
        cc -O -c print.c
disk.o: disk.c header.h
        cc -O -c disk.c
main.o: main.c header.h
        cc -O -c main.c
```

In Example 6.8, we present the header file common to all source code files for this system.

Example 6.8   Header file `header.h` **for a procedurally oriented file system simulation**

```
/**********************************************************/
/** HEADER FILE header.h **/
/**********************************************************/

#define NUM_MEM_BLOCKS 10
#define NUM_TRACKS 50
#define NUM_SECTORS 10
#define Blocksize 10
#define MEMSIZE 100

int data;
int track,sector;
int mem[10][10];
int disk[50][10][10];
int mem_loc,location;
int free_mem_list[10];
int free_disk_list[50][10];

struct disk_info
{
   int track_no;
   int sector_no;
};

struct FIFO
{
   int block;
   struct FIFO *next;
}*mem_que;
```

```
/* Function prototypes */
void initialization(void);
void opening_message(void);
void get_data(void);
void print_disk(void);
void print_mem(void);
put_in_mem(int data);
disk_to_mem(int track,int sector);
mem_to_disk(int mem_loc);
```

Example 6.9   File main.c for a procedurally oriented file system simulation

```
/*************************************************************/
/****                      MAIN                        ****/
/*************************************************************/

#include "header.h"
#include <iostream.h>

main()
{
  initialization();
  opening_message();
  get_data();
}


/*************************************************************/
/****        FUNCTION initialization()        *******/
/****                                         *******/
/**** CALLED BY: main()                       *******/
/****                                         *******/
/**** FUNCTIONS CALLED: none                  *******/
/****                                         *******/
/**** PARAMETERS: none                        *******/
/****                                         *******/
/**** VALUE RETURNED: none                    *******/
/*************************************************************/

void initialization(void)
{
  int i,j,k;

  for (i = 0; i < NUM_MEM_BLOCKS; i++)
    {
    free_mem_list[i] = 0;
    for (j = 0; j < Blocksize; j++)
      mem[i][j] = -99;
    }

    for (i = 0; i < NUM_TRACKS; i++)
      for (j = 0; j < NUM_SECTORS; j++)
        {
        free_disk_list[i][j];
```

```
        for (k = 0; k < Blocksize; k++)
        disk[i][j][k] = -99;
        }
   mem_que = (struct FIFO *)NULL;
}


/****************************************************************/
/****              FUNCTION opening_message()       *******/
/****                                               *******/
/**** This function prints an opening message.      *******/
/****                                               *******/
/**** CALLED BY: main()                             *******/
/****                                               *******/
/**** FUNCTIONS CALLED: none                        *******/
/****                                               *******/
/**** PARAMETERS: none                              *******/
/****                                               *******/
/**** VALUE RETURNED: none                          *******/
/****************************************************************/

void opening_message(void)
{
   cout << "Welcome to the FILE SIMULATION SYSTEM.\n"
     << "The purpose of the system is to demonstrate some"
     << "of the.\n"
     << "features of a file system.\n\n"
     << "This first phase will show some of the commands"
     << " necessary\n"
     << "to move data to and from simulated memory and"
     << "disk.\n\n\n";
}


/****************************************************************/
/****                                               *******/
/****              FUNCTION get_data()              *******/
/****                                               *******/
/**** CALLED BY: get_data()                         *******/
/****                                               *******/
/**** FUNCTIONS CALLED: many                        *******/
/****                                               *******/
/**** PARAMETERS: none                              *******/
/****                                               *******/
/**** VALUE RETURNED: none                          *******/
/****************************************************************/

void get_data(void)
{
   int ch;
   int data,mem_loc,track,sector;

   for(;;)
     {
```

```
cout << "\n\nSelect an option:\n";
cout << "i......insert data into memory directly.\n";
cout << "d......move data from memory to disk\n";
cout << "m......move block from disk to memory\n";
cout << "p......print memory\n";
cout << "P......print disk\n";
cout << "q......quit\n";
cout << "\n\nEnter Option >> ";
cin >> ch;
cout << "\n\n");
switch(ch)
  {
  case 'i':
    cout << "Enter data:\n";
    cin >> data;
    if (put_in_memory(data) != -1)
      break;
    else
      return;
  case 'd':
    cout << "Enter mem_loc, track, sector:\n";
    cin >> mem_loc >> track >> sector;
    mem_to_disk(mem_loc,track,sector);
    break;
  case 'm':
    cout << "Enter mem_loc, track, sector:\n";
    cin >> mem_loc >> track >> sector;
    disk_to_mem(mem_loc,track,sector);
    break;
  case 'p':
    print_mem();
    break;
  case 'P':
    print_disk();
    break;
  case 'q':
  case 'Q':
    return;
  default:
    cout << "Invalid Selection, Try Again\n";
    break;
  } /* end switch */
} /* end big for loop */
}
```

Example 6.10   File `memory.c` for a procedurally oriented file system simulation

```
#include "header.h"
#include <iostream.h>

/*************************************************************/
/**** FILE memory.c                                      ***/
/*************************************************************/
```

```
int find_mem_block()
{
  int mem_block_number = 0;

  do
    {
    if (free_mem_list[mem_block_number] != 0)
      mem_block_number++;

  while ((free_mem_list[mem_block_number] != 0) &&
          (mem_block_number < NUM_MEM_BLOCKS));

  if (mem_block_number == NUM_MEM_BLOCKS)
    {
    printf("Error - no available memory blocks\n");
    return(-1);
    }
  else
    return(mem_block_number);
}


int free_memory(void)
{
  struct disk_info disk_block;
  int block_num,i;
  disk_block = find_disk_block();
  if (disk_block.track_no == -1)
    {
    cout << "Memory and Disk full \n";
    return(-1);
    }

  block_num = mem_que->block;
  mem_que = mem_que->next;
  for (i = 0; i < Blocksize; i++)
    disk[disk_block.track_no][disk_block.sector_no][i] =
                 mem[block_num][i];
  free_disk_list[disk_block.track_no][disk_block.sector_no]
             = 1;
  for (i = 0; i < Blocksize; i++)
    mem[block_num][i] = 0;
  free_mem_list[block_num] = 0;
}

update_mem_info(int location)
{
  struct FIFO *current,*new_node;

  free_mem_list[location] = 1;

     /* Adds location which is the block just filled
     to the mem_que so that we can keep up with which
     location was filled in first (order). */
```

```
new_node = (struct FIFO *) malloc (sizeof(struct FIFO));
new_node->block = location;
new_node->next = (struct FIFO *)NULL;
current = mem_que;
if (current == (struct FIFO *)NULL)
  mem_que = new_node;
else
  {
  while (current->next != (struct FIFO*)NULL)
  current = current->next;
  current->next = new_node;
  }
}
```

Example 6.11   File disk.c for a procedurally oriented file system simulation

```
/**************************************************************/
/***** FILE: disk.c                                    ****/
/**************************************************************/

#include "header.h"
#include <stdio.h>

struct disk_info find_disk_block()
{
  int track_num = 3;
  int sector_num = 0;
  struct disk_info block;

  do
    {
    do
      {
      if (free_disk_list[track_num][sector_num] != 0)
        sector_num++;
      }
    while ((free_disk_list[track_num][sector_num] != 0) &&
             (sector_num < NUM_SECTORS));

    if (free_disk_list[track_num][sector_num] != 0)
      {
      track_num++;
      sector_num = 0;
      }
    }
  while ((free_disk_list[track_num][sector_num] != 0) &&
           (track_num < NUM_TRACKS));

  if (track_num == NUM_TRACKS)
    {
    cout << "Error-no available disk blocks \n";
    block.track_no = -1;
    block.sector_no = -1;
    }
```

```
  else
    {
    block.track_no = track_num;
    block.sector_no = sector_num;
    }
  return(block);
}
```

Example 6.12   File move_dat.c for a procedurally oriented file system simulation

```
#include "header.h"

/***************************************************************/
/***    FILE: put_dat.c                                 ****/
/***************************************************************/

int put_in_memory(int data)
{
  int loc_found = -1;
  int i;

  if ((loc_found = find_mem_block()) == -1)
    {
    if (free_memory() == -1)
      return(-1);
    else
      loc_found = find_mem_block();
    }
  for (i = 0;i < Blocksize;i++)
    mem[loc_found][i] = data;
  update_mem_info(loc_found);
  cout << "Information stored in memory\n";
}

mem_to_disk(int mem_loc, int track, int sector)
{
  int block_num,i;
  int chances = 0;

  do
    {
    if (free_disk_list[track][sector] != 0)
      {
      cout << "Information is already stored at track"
        << track
        << " and sector" << sector << endl;
      cout << "Enter new track and sector numbers:\n";
      cin >> track >> sector;
      chances++;
      }
    }
  while ((free_disk_list[track][sector] != 0) &&
          (chances < 2));
```

```
if (chances != 2)
  {
  block_num = mem_loc/Blocksize;
  for (i = 0; i < Blocksize; i++)
    disk[track][sector][i] = mem[block_num][i];
  free_disk_list[track][sector] = 1;
  free_mem_list[block_num] = 0;
  for (i = 0; i < Blocksize; i++)
    mem[block_num][i] = 0;
  }
}


disk_to_mem(int mem_loc, int track)
int sector;
{
  int block_num,offset,i;
  int chances = 0;

  do
    {
    block_num = mem_loc/Blocksize;
    offset = mem_loc%Blocksize;
    if (free_mem_list[block_num] != 0)
      {
      cout << "The mem_loc specified is not available\n";
      cout << "Enter mem_loc:\n";
      cin >> mem_loc;
      chances++;
      }
    }
    while ((free_mem_list[block_num] != 0) &&
                (chances < 2));

  if (chances != 2)
    {
    for (i = 0; i < Blocksize; i++)
      mem[block_num][i] = disk[track][sector][i];
    update_mem_info(block_num);
    }
}
```

Example 6.13   File print.c for a procedurally oriented file system simulation

```
/*************************************************************/
/***        FUNCTION print_mem()                  *******/
/**** This function prints an opening message.    *******/
/****                                             *******/
/**** PARAMETERS: none                            *******/
/****                                             *******/
/**** VALUE RETURNED: none                        *******/
/*************************************************************/

#include "header.h"
```

```
void print_mem(void)
{
  int i,j;

  cout << "          LAYOUT OF MEMORY  \n\n\n";
  for (i = 0;i < NUM_MEM_BLOCKS;i++)
    {
    cout << "Block = " << i ;
    for (j = 0;j < Blocksize; j++)
      if (mem[i][j] != -99)
        cout << mem[i][j]);
    cout << "\n";
    }
  cout << "\n\n\n";
}


/*****************************************************************/
/****             FUNCTION print_disk()            *******/
/****                                              *******/
/**** PARAMETERS: none                             *******/
/****                                              *******/
/**** VALUE RETURNED: none                         *******/
/*****************************************************************/

void print_disk(void)
{
  int i,j,k;

  cout << "  LAYOUT OF DISK \n\n\n";
  for (i = 0; i < NUM_TRACKS; i++)
    for (j = 0; j < NUM_SECTORS; j++)
      {
      if (free_disk_list[i][j] != 0)
        {
        cout << "Track " << i << "Sector " << j ;
        for (k = 0; k < Blocksize; k++)
          {
          if (disk[i][j][k] != -99)
            cout << disk[i][j][k];
          }
      cout << endl;
        }
      }
  cout << "\n*** All Tracks and Sectors not Printed are"
       << "Empty ***\n\n";
}
```

6.8 Reengineering a Procedurally Based System into an Object-Oriented One

The subject of this section is one of the most difficult problems in the field of object-oriented software. While there have been many articles written on the subject, there is little consensus on appropriate methodologies for performing this transformation generally. It is not completely clear that any of the existing methodologies are general or if they succeeded in particular situations because of the nature of the application domain of the software.

The fundamental issue is whether we should develop an entirely new set of requirements for our system, obtaining the design from the new requirements, or use the existing, procedurally oriented ones to develop a new design. In each case, we would use the new design as the basis for the remainder of activities during the software's life cycle.

In our example, the object-oriented requirements naturally suggest some objects. These objects will lead to a potential organization for the objects that represent the data used in the program. The organization is usually a hierarchy because of the inheritance structure of many objects.

However, we have to be careful to distinguish the object hierarchy of the data from the hierarchy of the program. Even with an object-oriented approach, the program must begin its execution somewhere and must maintain a flow of control. The control flow of the program is what is commonly referred to as the *program hierarchy*.

We will transform the procedural requirements of the simulation system to object-oriented requirements by using the following guidelines. They are based on the domain analysis techniques described in Chap. 2:

1. List all major actions performed by the system in complete sentences.

2. Group the nouns in the sentences by placing them into one of three categories: medium, object, or system.

3. Determine all parallel relationships between the actions of the sentences and the three classes of nouns determined in the previous step.

4. Use these relationships as the initial set of candidates for objects. (This will be similar, but not identical, to the set of objects determined in step 1.)

These guidelines should be taken as a starting point, with more specific steps generally being necessary.

The relevant terms found are as follows:

action	medium	object	system
print	memory	memory	memory
print	disk	disk	disk
put	disk	block	disk
insert	disk	block	disk
insert	memory	block	memory
delete	disk	block	disk
write	memory	block	memory
delete	memory	block	memory
write	disk	block	disk

The two subsystems of our memory-disk simulation are the disk and memory subsystems. There are two "mediums" in our system: the "disk" and "memory." The rest of the terminology is straightforward.

An examination of this data suggests that there are only a few actions applied to objects: printing, reading, and writing. Deleting appears to be a misnomer—we are only overwriting the information in a memory block. Note also that we can combine printing of the disk and memory into repeated printing of the individual blocks that make up these simulated "media." Reading and writing can take several forms, often including some sort of initialization.

6.9 An Object-Oriented Disk Simulation Program (Optional)

The class organization causes several changes to the existing, procedurally developed solution. These changes affect the number and type of operations given as member functions, the placement of functions into files, and documentation. Of course, the code itself will change considerably. Nonetheless, its roots in the procedural system remain clear.

The program will have three important types of objects: block, disk, and memory. These objects will be organized so that the classes `Disk` and `Memory` can inherit from the base class `Block`.

The organization of the object-oriented design is different from that of the procedural one. The use of an object of type `Block` as the primary object allows the routines `mem_to_disk()` and `disk_to_mem()` to be simplified considerably. Other routines can be replaced by simple function calls.

For example, the header file can be eliminated, since there is no need for prototypes for member functions, and the `Block` class contains the common structure. All functions in the file `move_dat.c` can be placed into other files as member functions or developed as simple compositions of functions relating the disk to memory.

In this section we will present some C++ code that describes the procedurally based simulation of the file system. The code will perform the appropriate disk operations such as moving blocks of data between simulated memory, the simulated disk, and a user. The documentation has been changed to reflect the information hiding and abstraction available in object-oriented programming.

Our new system will have three files, which are shown in Examples 6.14, 6.15, and 6.16. The algorithms for disk and memory operations are the same as in the procedural version of the system.

Most of the code is straightforward. However, you should note the use of conditional compilation using the #ifndef; ... #endif construction in Example 6.15 to make sure that a header file is included only once. You should also note the use of the include file iomanip.h in order to format the output using C++ I/O.

Example 6.14   File Block.cpp for object-oriented file system simulation

```
//
// FILE block.cpp
//


#include <iostream.h>
#include <iomanip.h>

//
// Description of base class Block.
//
class Block
{
private:
#define BLOCKSIZE 10
  int contents[BLOCKSIZE];
public:
  Block();
  void init();
  void clear();
  void put(int info); // Put info into each entry.
  int get(); // Returns info in block.
  void print();
};


Block:: Block()
{
  init();
}

void Block:: init()
{
```

```
   int i;
   for (i = 0; i < BLOCKSIZE; i++)
     contents[i] = -1;
}


void Block:: clear()
{
   int i;
   for(i = 0; i < BLOCKSIZE; i++)
     contents[i] = 0;
}


int Block:: get()
{
   return (contents[0]);
}


void Block:: put(int info)
{
   int i;
   for (i = 0; i < BLOCKSIZE; i++)
     contents[i] = info;
}


void Block :: print()
{
   int i;
   for (i = 0; i < BLOCKSIZE; i++)
     cout << setw(4) << contents[i];
   cout << endl;
}
```

Example 6.15   File disk_mem.cpp for object-oriented file system simulation

```
#ifndef block_cpp
#include "block.cpp"
#endif
#include <iostream.h>
//
// Description of the class Disk.
//

class Disk: public Block
{
private:
   #define NUM_TRACKS 50
   #define NUM_SECTORS 10
   Block contents[NUM_TRACKS][NUM_SECTORS];
   int free_disk_list[NUM_TRACKS][NUM_SECTORS];

public:
   int track,sector;
```

```
   Disk();
   void init();
   struct disk_info find_disk_block();
   Block get(int trck, int sec);
   void put(int trk, int sec, Block b);
   void clear(int trk, int sec);
   void print();
};


struct disk_info
{
   int track_no;
   int sector_no;
};

Disk :: Disk()
{
   init();
}


void Disk:: init()
{
   int i, j;

   for (i = 0; i < NUM_TRACKS; i++)
      for (j = 0; j < NUM_SECTORS; j++)
         {
         free_disk_list[i][j];
         contents[i][j].init();
         }
}


struct disk_info Disk :: find_disk_block()
{
   int track_num = 3; // Reserve first 2 tracks.
   int sector_num = 0;
struct disk_info d_info;

do
   {
   do
      {
      if (free_disk_list[track_num][sector_num] != 0)
             sector_num++;
      }
   while ((free_disk_list[track_num][sector_num] != 0) &&
          (sector_num < NUM_SECTORS));

   if (free_disk_list[track_num][sector_num] != 0)
      {
      track_num++;
      sector_num = 0;
      }
   }
```

```
while ((free_disk_list[track_num][sector_num] != 0) &&
        (track_num < NUM_TRACKS));

if (track_num == NUM_TRACKS)
  {
  cout << "Error-no available disk blocks \n";
  d_info.track_no = -1;
  d_info.sector_no = -1;
  }
  else
    {
    d_info.track_no = track;
    d_info.sector_no = sector;
    }
  return(d_info);
}


////////////////////////////////////////////////
Block Disk :: get(int trck, int sec)
{
  Block temp;
  int i, j;
  temp.put(contents[trck][sec].get() );
  return temp;
}


////////////////////////////////////////////////
void Disk :: put(int trk, int sec, Block b)
{
  contents[trk][sec].put( b.get());
}

void Disk::print(void)
{
  int i,j,k;
  cout << " LAYOUT OF DISK \n\n\n";
  for (i = 0; i < NUM_TRACKS; i++)
    for (j = 0; j < NUM_SECTORS; j++)
      {
      if (free_disk_list[i][j] != 0)
      {
      cout << "Track " << i << "Sector " << j ;
      contents[i][j].print();
      cout << endl;
      }
      }
  cout << "\n*** All Tracks and Sectors not Printed are"
       << "Empty ***\n\n";
}


//
// Description of the class memory.
//
```

```
class Memory: public Block
{
public:
  #define NUM_MEM_BLOCKS 10
  Block memory[NUM_MEM_BLOCKS];
  struct FIFO
    {
    int block;
    struct FIFO *next;
    } *mem_que;
public:
  // Constructor
  Memory();
  void init();
  int free_mem_list[NUM_MEM_BLOCKS];
  int find_mem_block(); // Returns a block number.
  void free_memory();

  // Functions to update memory.
  void update_mem_info(int location);
  void put(int loc, Block b);
  Block get (int loc);
  int mem_loc;
  void print();
};


/////////////////////////////////////////////
Memory :: Memory()
{
  init();
}


/////////////////////////////////////////////
void Memory :: init()
{
  int i,j,k;

  for (i = 0; i < NUM_MEM_BLOCKS; i++)
    {
    free_mem_list[i] = 0;
    memory[i].init(); // Uses Block :: init()
    }
  mem_que = (struct FIFO *)NULL;
}


/////////////////////////////////////////////
void Memory ::put(int loc, Block b)
{
  memory[loc].put( b.get() );
  }
```

```
////////////////////////////////////////////////
Block Memory ::get (int loc)
{
  Block temp;
  temp.put(memory[loc].get() );
  return temp;
}


////////////////////////////////////////////////
int Memory :: find_mem_block()
{
  int mem_block_number = 0;

  do
    {
    if (free_mem_list[mem_block_number] != 0)
      mem_block_number++;
    }
  while ((free_mem_list[mem_block_number] != 0) &&
          (mem_block_number < NUM_MEM_BLOCKS));

  if (mem_block_number == NUM_MEM_BLOCKS)
    {
    cout << "Error - no available memory blocks\n";
    return(-1);
    }
  else
    return(mem_block_number);
}


////////////////////////////////////////////////
void Memory :: free_memory(void)
{
  struct disk_info disk_block;
  int block_num, i;
  Block b;

  block_num = mem_que->block;
  mem_que = mem_que->next;
  memory[block_num].init();
  free_mem_list[block_num] = 0;
}


////////////////////////////////////////////////
void Memory :: update_mem_info(int location)
{
  struct FIFO *current;
  free_mem_list[location] = 1;
```

```
        /* Adds location which is the block just filled
        to the mem_que so that we can keep up with which
        location was filled in first (order). */

    struct FIFO * new_node = new (struct FIFO) ;
    new_node->block = location;
    new_node->next = (struct FIFO *)NULL;
    current = mem_que;
    if (current == (struct FIFO *)NULL)
      mem_que = new_node;
    else
      {
      while (current->next != (struct FIFO*)NULL)
        current = current->next;
      current->next = new_node;
      }
}


///////////////////////////////////////////////////
void Memory:: print(void)
{
  int i,j;

  cout << " LAYOUT OF MEMORY \n\n\n";
  for (i = 0;i < NUM_MEM_BLOCKS;i++)
    {
    cout << "Block = " << i ;
    if ( memory[i].get() >= 0 )
      memory[i].print();
    cout << "\n";
    }
    cout << "\n\n\n";
}
```

Example 6.16   File main.cpp for object-oriented file system simulation

```
//
// File main.cpp
//

#include "disk_mem.cpp"
#include <iostream.h>

// Global variables.
Disk disk;
Memory memory;
Block temp; // For temporary storage.

// Function prototypes.
void opening_message(void);
void get_data(void)
```

```
main()
{
  opening_message();
  memory.init();
  disk.init();
  get_data();
}


//////////////////////////////////////////////////////////
// FUNCTION opening_message()
//

void opening_message(void)
{
  cout << "Welcome to the FILE SIMULATION SYSTEM.\n"
    << "The purpose of the system is to demonstrate some"
    << "of the.\n"
    << "features of a file system.\n\n"
    << "This first phase will show some of the commands"
    << " necessary\n"
    << "to move data to and from simulated memory and"
    << "disk.\n\n\n";
}

//
// FUNCTION get_data()
//

void get_data(void)
{
  char ch;
  int data, mem_loc, trk, sect;

  for(;;)
    {
    cout << "\n\nSelect an option:\n";
    cout << "i......insert data into memory directly.\n";
    cout << "d......move data from memory to disk\n";
    cout << "m......move block from disk to memory\n";
    cout << "p......print memory\n";
    cout << "P......print disk\n";
    cout << "q......quit\n";
    cout << "\n\nEnter Option >> " ;
    cin >> ch;
    cout << "\n\n";
    switch(ch)
      {

      case 'i':
        cout << "Enter data:\n";
        cin >> data;
        temp.put(data);
```

```
          memory.put(memory.find_mem_block(), temp);
          break;

     case 'd':
          cout << "Enter mem_loc, track, sector:\n";
          cin >> mem_loc >> trk >> sect;
          temp = memory.get(mem_loc);
          disk.put(trk, sect, temp);
          break;

     case 'm':
          cout << "Enter mem_loc, track, sector:\n";
          cin >> mem_loc >> trk >> sect;
          temp = disk.get(trk, sect);
          memory.put(mem_loc, temp);
          break;

     case 'p':
          memory.print();
          break;

     case 'P':
          disk.print();
          break;

     case 'q':
     case 'Q':
          return;

     default:
          cout << "Invalid Selection, Try Again\n";
          break;
     } /* end switch */
   } /* end big for loop */
 }
```

6.10 Comparison of Object-Oriented and Procedural Solutions

Let's examine the two proposed organizations for the system. The C language, procedurally designed organization presented in this chapter uses arrays and structures to represent data. It is very easy to manipulate lower-level details that should be hidden from a programmer. For example, it is easy to write I/O functions that directly act upon the individual members of a disk block, defeating the block orientation of the procedural system.

The C code consists of approximately 317 lines of code. (We have used the measure NCNB, or noncommented, nonblank lines of code.) Any measurement of lines of code should be taken as a reasonable approximation and not as an absolute number.

On the other hand, the object-oriented C++ program provides a higher level of abstraction and information hiding. Access to private data is only allowed by using member functions.

The C++ code consists of approximately 301 NCNB lines of code. These are broken into many small member functions, including several functions that were not present in the original, procedurally developed system coded in C.

At first glance, the systems would appear to have the same level of complexity since the number of NCNB lines of code is essentially the same for each system development. However, the C++ system is less complex because its functions are simpler.

The C++ code combines some of the member functions to eliminate several of the more complex routines in the C source code. The C source code consists of 12 functions, with an average size of 317/12 or 26.25 NCNB lines of code per function. On the other hand, the C++ code consists of 25 functions, of which 23 are member functions that can be reused easily. This is an average of approximately 12 NCNB lines of code per function.

Clearly, the C++ implementation of this system is easier to understand than the C implementation.

Summary

Software reengineering is the process of transforming an existing software system into a form perceived to be more useful than the existing one. Reengineering can involve automatic program translation or transformations with more semantic analysis.

We described a program restructuring experiment in order to present examples of alternative views of a small system. We illustrated the reengineering process illustrated by developing two designs for a simulation of the operation of a simple disk-memory system. The first design was a procedurally oriented one, which we took to be the description of an existing system. We reengineered the procedurally oriented design by the simple method of examining the operations of the existing system and changing them into object-oriented actions.

Further Reading

The best place to find information on the software reengineering process is the tutorial by Arnold [ARNO92], *Software Reengineering.* Information on particular automatic program projects can be found in Arnold's technical documentation. The paper by Pleszkoch, Linger, and Hevner describes an interesting view of program translation

[PLES92] from the perspective of program understanding and code improvement. Pfleeger's book [PFLE96] *Software Engineering* discusses the distinction between software reuse and software reengineering in more detail.

Much of the conference literature on software reengineering is presented in general forums. Nearly every conference on software engineering with Ada, object-oriented techniques, software testing, or maintenance includes at least one paper or tutorial on reengineering. Such sources present excellent opportunities to obtain state-of-the-art and state-of-the-practice information.

A general approach to software reengineering is the recent *Software Reengineering Assessment Handbook* [SRAH96], which is available from the Internet at http://www.stsc.hill.af.mil.

Exercises

1. List the characteristics that distinguish candidates for software reuse from candidates for software reengineering. Consider a legacy system available to you from the perspective of convincing your management that the system should be reengineered. What information would you expect to present? Why?

2. Choose any computer language you are familiar with that has undergone important changes during its lifetime. List all potential problems in translating code from the older version to the newer one. Some language families you might consider are FORTRAN (FORTRAN IV, FORTRAN 77, FORTRAN 90), C (Kernighan & Ritchie C and ANSI C), and Ada (Ada83 and Ada95).

3. Choose any procedural language and any object-oriented language. Describe the potential difficulties in reengineering code from the procedural language to the object-oriented one. Were all the difficulties encountered in the example presented in this chapter?

4. Implement the free list for access to memory blocks in the disk simulation project as a bit vector. A bit vector is a memory unit used to simulate the contents of a Boolean array. The bits are either 0 or 1, and this means that the memory location corresponding to the position of the bit is either empty or full.

The function that manages the free list should use each bit to represent a specific memory block. We can determine the first bit that has a value of 0, using a function to select the bit by shifting the input until the bitwise exclusive OR of the number and the octal number 0000 has the value xxx1, where we don't care about the first three octal digits. The exclusive OR operator will return a value of the form xxx1 if the rightmost bit is a 0, which is the situation that we want.

The header for the new function find_free_block() should be of the form

```
find_free_block(list_vector)
double list_vector;
```

```
{
// The body of find_free_block goes here.
}
```

with the free list passed as a parameter named `list_vector`.
Are there any differences implementing this in the procedural versus in the object-oriented system?

5. Change the system to have two possible environments—a user-friendly one, in which the user is prompted for input with an opportunity user to correct incorrect or missing data, and an environment in which a user has no interaction because all the commands come from a file. This second situation is commonly called a *batch system*. Specifically, the software should be able to take either of two execution paths. If the system receives the command for interactive input and response, then the software should respond as before. However, if the command is for the software to act as a batch system, then all the user interface commands and prompts should be removed from the software.

The information concerning whether the system is to be interactive or batch should be obtained as early as possible in the execution of the program. The command line

```
program1
```

means the program is interactive; the command line

```
program1 input
```

means the program is batch and reads commands from a file named `input`; and the command line

```
program1 input output
```

means the output should be written to a file named `output`. This means that our program should be able to handle the case of one, two, or three command-line arguments. If the number of arguments is one, then the program is meant to be interactive. If there is more than one argument, then the program is a batch program, and the second command-line argument is the name of the input file. If a third command-line argument is given, it represents the name of the file to which output is to be written. If there are any additional command-line arguments, they should be ignored.

Are there any differences implementing this in the procedural versus in the object-oriented system?

6. Assume that the additional features of the procedurally oriented system include simulation of higher levels of the file system: that is, grouping disk blocks into files and lacing the files into directory structures.

   a. Determine the fundamental data objects in this system. Are the fundamental objects the disk, the memory, disk or memory blocks, single data elements for either disk or memory, or something else? As part of your analysis, include the possibility of reusing libraries of transformations on these data objects and the possibility of having new classes of objects inherit properties from existing classes of objects.

b. Determine the allowable operations on each of the classes you determined in the first part of this problem.

7. Write a translation tool to take as input one or more files containing C language source code that constitute a program and produce as output an equivalent C++ program with the following changes:

a. All comments are to be written in C++ form using the `//` delimiter instead of `/*` and `*/`.

b. All input and output to the standard streams `stdin`, `stdout`, and `stderr` are to be done using the C++ I/O streams `cin`, `cout`, and `cerr`.

c. All formatted output using `scanf()` is to be done using an equivalent statement utilizing manipulators available in the file `iomanip.h`.

d. File I/O is also to be changed using the facilities available in the files `iostream.h`, `fstream.h`, and related files.

e. Any other constants such as `EOF` in the file `stdio.h` should be available to the new C++ program.

f. No other changes should be made to the C source code files used as input.

g. The resulting C++ program will have exactly the same output as the original C program when given the same input.

7

Case Studies

In this chapter we describe some software reuse activities in government and industry. The examples chosen will help illustrate the range of situations in which reuse is an important part of the software engineering process.

Several case studies will be presented. The NASA system, which involves the unique (in the literature) case of efficient incorporation of software reuse into a rapidly evolving software environment, will be described in fairly complete detail, primarily because I have had considerable experience with this reuse effort.

The other case studies, of reuse experiences and programs at AT&T, Battelle Laboratory, and Hewlett-Packard are presented more concisely as they are based on secondary sources such as informal discussions, reports, and other publications.

The AT&T case study describes reuse in the context of a companywide effort supported at the highest levels.

The Battelle Pacific Northwest Laboratory case describes reuse in the context of a high degree of domain expertise combined with a desire to reuse higher level components than just source code modules. The software environment has a large proportion of numerical FORTRAN code, and this influences the reuse program there.

The Hewlett-Packard (HP) case study describes reuse in the context of a companywide policy of software metrics. The widespread, corporate-level support for software reuse is reflected by the eight papers from that organization presented at the 1992 Workshop on Software Reuse and HP's continued high levels of participation.

To give a more balanced view of software reuse, we will present a negative experience with software reuse. To preserve the participants' anonymity, the material described here is a hybrid of several actual organizational experiences. My intention is to represent everything that can go wrong in software reuse.

In each case, only a high-level view will be presented in order to preserve confidentiality. The intention is to provide an overview of some interesting practices in software reuse, not duplicate the level of detail available in internal technical reports. In particular, we do not intend to violate any organizational confidentiality requirements or divulge any trade secrets.

7.1   Some Reuse Activities at NASA

In this section, we describe a project supported by NASA at the Goddard Space Flight Center (GSFC) in Greenbelt, Maryland. The work has continued for many years and is currently directed by NASA's Judith Bruner, Ronald Mahmot, Henry Murray, and Jack Koslosky. Several other people, primarily Barbara Schwarz and Donald Slater, were also heavily involved. The primary nongovernmental contractors were Computer Sciences Corporation (CSC) and Integral Systems, Inc. (ISI).

The purpose of the project was to analyze an existing system, with the primary emphasis on cost estimation and metrics, especially in the areas of reliability analysis and certification of reusable software components.

Since a large contract with a nongovernment contractor for software development was already in place when this research project began, no coding was necessary for the TPOCC (Transportable Payload Operations Control Center) system as part of the research project.

The topic of this research project was the status and cost-effectiveness of software reuse programs, specifically in the mission control software for which the Control Center Systems Branch at GSFC (Code 511) was responsible. The major effort in software reuse in this organization is the TPOCC project.

7.1.1   Introduction

The Control Center Systems Branch at NASA's GSFC in Greenbelt, Maryland, is responsible for the ground systems that control the initial interface between a spacecraft and ground-based computer control centers. The control system software consists of large amounts of code to perform the following operations (among others):

- Determine the current position of the spacecraft.
- Control the operation of the spacecraft.
- Receive and relay telemetry information from the spacecraft.
- Detect significant events in spacecraft operation.
- Display the status of the system.

The system that implements these operations can be organized into several subsystems.

These operations are often centered around a control room. A control room contains many display facilities and recording devices, with computer control performed by one or more human operators. The operators have periods of intensive work when a spacecraft is close to some position, such as a receiving antenna, or its orbit is close to the target, if we are providing a satellite-based view of the Earth's vegetation. At other times the activity is less intense and consists primarily of monitoring systems to detect anomalous situations early.

The typical operation of a control room and its related software must meet the needs of the human operators, who are generally very experienced in the area of control room operation. It must also meet the special needs of the spacecraft, including monitoring all channels used for communication, interfacing between data channels on the spacecraft to other data capture systems, and providing interfaces to standard systems.

Space system software is extremely complex because it has severe requirements for fault-tolerance, must interface with many other systems, and has some real-time requirements as well. An additional complexity is that the software must begin development far in advance of the projected launch of a spacecraft, and therefore the level of technology of both hardware and support software (operating system, compilers, tools, commercial software, etc.) is not easy to determine during the beginning of development.

The technology of control rooms has evolved considerably. For example, prior to the mid 1980s, control center operation was mainframe-based, and nearly all displays consisted of columns of alphanumeric data that were written to character-based terminals. Each launch of a spacecraft required the development of new control room software beca use the missions did not appear to have much in common. Much of the software was coded in dialects of FORTRAN that were highly related to specific hardware architectures.

An operator could view many different "pages" of displays by hitting a switch on the display control panel, which would make visible a page that was previously hidden. An operator's work area in a control room would have several large, rack-mounted monitors for displaying multiple pages.

Graphics terminals were available but were very expensive and were generally reserved for displays of the position of the spacecraft, its antennas, and the Earth. From a human factors perspective, there was an urgent need to move to a more visual environment for the operators.

There was also great confusion in the area of graphics standards, with the SIGGRAPH CORE system competing with GKS, PHIGS, and other standards. Workstations with 1 to 4 MIPS performance were becoming available at this time.

Reuse has been a concern for many years. However, the changing demands of spacecraft, the fluidity of graphics standards, the need for isolation from networks such as the Internet for security purposes, the long lead time for projects, and the need for severe restrictions on weight of onboard computers all have made the development of a reuse program more difficult.

There is a positive side, however. The fundamental business of this portion of NASA has been clearly defined for many years, and there is a high level of expertise in the Control Center Systems Branch. Thus, the initial step in any program of software reuse—domain analysis— is facilitated by a core of domain experts. Further, the domain experts were already motivated by financial pressures and their desire to produce software efficiently.

Thus, in 1985 a talented group consisting of NASA employees and contractor personnel from CSC and ISI met with the intention of determining a reusable core of spacecraft control software.

TPOCC consists of a core of software that is common to multiple missions. Thus, the general description of control center software is that it contains a generic core (TPOCC) and mission-specific software. This situation is depicted in Fig. 7.1.

After several discussions with GSFC and contractor personnel, it was determined that the initial focus of the research would be on quality and process issues.

The quality issues discussed included analysis of the TPOCC generic software and some other mission-related control center software.

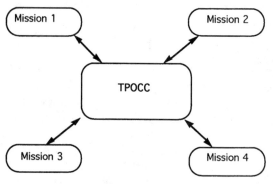

Figure 7.1 Typical structure of control room software.

We also analyzed general software available in the public domain for the purposes of comparing some of the metrics values.

In the next few subsections we will provide a preliminary assessment of the quality of the software used in the TPOCC system from the perspective of software reuse and potential cost savings associated with reuse. Some conclusions and general recommendations about reuse practices will be included in this discussion.

7.1.2 Methodology used for the collection of metrics data

All source code data analyzed for this project were available on HP workstations either at GSFC or at CSC's Laurel, Maryland, facility.

The data obtained from analysis of the source code were written to a collection of data files that was transferred to a Macintosh Quadra for analysis using the Excel spreadsheet.

Several automated tools were used for data collection during this research project. The tools used consisted of simple UNIX shell scripts using standard utilities, lexical and semantic analysis tools based on the syntax of the C language dialect used in the source code analyzed by the tool, and a commercial product available from SET Laboratories.

Each of these tools produced an analysis of source code and computed certain metrics, describing the source code at a single point in time. Another metric that measures the changes in source code over several different releases was also used. This metric provided an assessment of the volatility and stability of source code over a period of several different releases. Stability of code is one of the attributes expected of a reusable software component.

The UNIX shell scripts are all based on the use of the UNIX find command to recursively search directories in order to identify subdirectories and source code files. These commands were discussed in Chap. 2.

Several line-counting utilities written by Tim McDermott of CSC were used to provide more detailed information than is available in the UNIX wc utility. His utilities provide an analysis of a file and produce the following output:

- SLOC (source lines of code)
- DSI (delivered source instructions)
- ESI (executable source instructions)
- CLOC (commented lines of code)
- Number of files per directory
- Number of functions

The definitions of the counting standards in McDermott's tool are slightly different from those of certain code-counting tools previously used, and therefore the results will be somewhat different from those of previous counting tools. However, the results are highly correlated, and it seemed reasonable to use these since the tool was readily available to the research project. The definitions used in McDermott's tool can be inferred from the lexical conventions used in his utilities.

His tool also computed several of the Halstead complexity metrics. The Halstead complexity metrics describe the number of operators and operands in a program, ignoring program structure, control flow, or internal interfaces.

The BVA metric was used to provide an assessment of the degree of coupling between program modules. The use of this metric was discussed in Chap. 4. See App. 1 for a detailed discussion of how the BVA metric is computed.

Because of its definition, the BVA metric is expected to have high correlation with the effort needed for testing. It describes the degree to which data are passed between modules. As such, a low value for this metric for a program module suggests relatively easier integration with other systems than does a program module with a higher value for the BVA metric. It should be noted that the BVA metric values reported in this book were computed by a prototype tool that deliberately undercounts the contribution made by complex data structures to the number of test cases necessary for complete white-box testing.

The final metric applied to the available source code is the SPA system from SET Laboratories. This metric computes the standard lines of code metrics (SLOC, DSI, ESI, NCNB LOC, etc.), although the counting method is slightly different from the one described earlier. The percentage of comments (a measure of the quality and quantity of documentation) and the number of GOTO statements (a measure of coding practice) are also computed by this tool.

The SPA tool also computes the McCabe cyclomatic complexity and the extended cyclomatic complexity. (The cyclomatic complexity metric is a measurement of the control flow of the program. It is discussed in App. 1.)

The volatility of the source code was also estimated using the UNIX prs utility discussed in Chap. 4. No anomalies were found.

7.1.3 Results

The metrics were applied to several different systems for which source code was available, including several systems in the public domain, such as the GNU gcc compiler and some Motif code. The public

Figure 7.2 Growth of TPOCC DSI in releases 1.0 through 11.0.

domain code was used as a baseline for comparing the average values of the BVA and other metrics.

The TPOCC system has grown considerably during its history. The increase in DSI is shown in Fig. 7.2.

Each release that has a substantial increase in the DSI corresponds to a major release that includes a considerable amount of new functionality due to a more complex mission using TPOCC. It is clear from Fig. 7.2 that new functionality was added in versions 4.0, 9.0, and 11.0 of TPOCC. It is natural to expect that the TPOCC system would increase in size because of these demands.

Several other metrics (ESI, number of functions, number of files, and number of directories) show growth patterns similar to the growth in the DSI over different releases. The pattern is similar for all measures that are similar to the lines of code metric. The pattern has also been observed in several of the Halstead counting metrics, which will not be presented in this book for reasons of space.

The control flow complexity was computed by the SPA tool, and the results are given in Figs. 7.3 through 7.5.

The results of both types of cyclomatic complexity measurements are similar (correlation is .991) and are within acceptable standards.

Figure 7.5 shows the SPA tool's estimate of nesting level. This metric reports the level of nested if statements. Clearly, a low value for the nesting level metric suggests a simple control flow. The results here are consistent with the results observed for the cyclomatic complexity measurements (correlation is .919) and again are acceptable.

The results illustrated in Figs. 7.3, 7.4, and 7.5 suggest that the effort made by the contract monitors to require extensive tests of all branches of program's control flow are very successful and are resulting in a product with excellent control flow design.

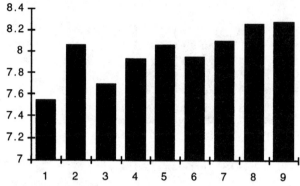

Figure 7.3 Changes in the cyclomatic complexity for TPOCC releases 1.0 through 9.0.

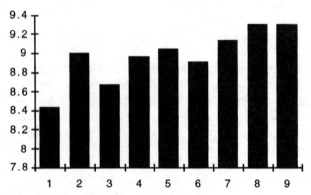

Figure 7.4 Changes in the extended cyclomatic complexity for TPOCC releases 1.0 through 9.0.

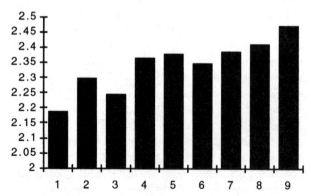

Figure 7.5 Changes to the values of the nesting level for TPOCC versions 1.0 through 9.0.

Another strong indication of a good coding practice is high-quality documentation. Experience has shown that poorly documented systems are difficult to maintain. The SPA tool reports the percentage of comments per line of code. In spite of the continuing time pressures to meet launch deadlines and be interoperable with other systems, the percentage of lines of comment embedded in TPOCC source code has increased from approximately 30 percent in release 1.0 to over 64 percent in release 9.0. Thus, the level of internal documentation of TPOCC has become quite high. The readability of the TPOCC internal documentation has not been measured, but it would appear to be high, based on the relatively complete guidelines given in the Software Systems Development Methodology (SSDM) document of CSC.

Several other measurements could be applied to the documentation, both internal and external to the code. Such measures include several different types of measurement of readability levels. They are unlikely to be worth the effort to collect the data.

It should be noted that a very clever, low-tech approach has been taken with respect to documentation. There are "generic" portions of the external documentation that are to be "cut and pasted" as appropriate, thereby saving enormous amounts of paper.

The increasing amount of internal documentation is shown in Fig. 7.6.

There is one metric whose growth during different releases of TPOCC causes concern—the BVA metric. This metric provides one measure of the interconnectivity of program modules. The value of this metric is an assessment of the number of test cases needed for complete black-box testing of a module based solely on the module's specifications. As such,

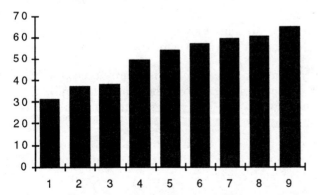

Figure 7.6 Changes to the percentages of comments for TPOCC versions 1.0 through 9.0.

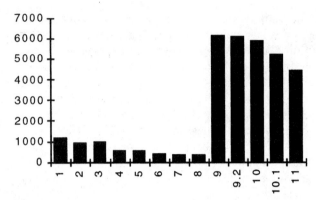

Figure 7.7 Changes to the average BVA value of TPOCC releases 1.0 through 11.0.

a low value for the average value of the BVA per file suggests a modular system, whereas a higher value suggests a more complex interface, which is to be avoided in reusable software.

There have been several unusual changes in the value of this metric in the last few TPOCC releases. They are illustrated in Fig. 7.7.

The average BVA changed from 355 in TPOCC release 8.0 to 6159 in TPOCC release 9.0. It is clear that the TPOCC system became more complex in this release, in addition to becoming larger. On the positive side, the average BVA value has decreased from its high of 6159 in release 9.0 to the current value of 4432 in release 11.0.

These numbers should be compared to the values of 2632, 3488, 3428, 3946 for the ISTP, POLAR, SOHO, and TRMM systems, respectively, which are similar software systems, and the 3299 value for the source code of the Motif system.

It is impossible to draw absolute conclusions from the values obtained from these values of the BVA metric for the following reasons:

- The tool used to compute the BVA metric is a prototype that computed the results for each file, rather than evaluating individual functions, so that files with high BVA values could be flagged as requiring additional attention.

- The tool arbitrarily assigned the value 10 to the testing complexity of each C `struct` rather than determining the number of test cases based on the details of the `struct`.

- The tool was not calibrated. Thus, the fact that the average BVA value of 6159 for TPOCC release 9.0 was 1.87 times larger than the average BVA value of 3299 for the Motif code being evaluated does not necessarily mean that the TPOCC release is 1.87 times more likely to have errors.

The results are very suggestive. An unusual change in the values of any metric for any system suggests a need for a careful look. A problem indicated by a metric that is related to the number of test cases is likely to be more serious than one with a less well-defined property.

The problem may be more serious in view of the efficient way in which TPOCC and related systems are released. One of the changes in the software practices associated with the reusable TPOCC core is that testing occurs during shorter intervals. The current testing practice is to have a careful testing effort on individual source code files. This effort is based on the decision paths in the source code and extensive design and code reviews. Unit testing is eliminated and is replaced by extensive testing of the entire system. (The term *unit testing* refers to testing portions of code larger than single files or functions but smaller than an entire system.) After a system is completed, it is made available for extensive system testing, but such testing cannot hope to cover all possible test cases involving the interface between highly coupled source code modules.

At the very least, modules with high BVA values should be subjected to a higher level of testing than ordinary modules since they have more opportunities for errors. The determination of the threshold value at which additional testing is necessary has not yet been determined, but values far from the norm are easy to spot. This point is addressed in Sec. 7.1.4 where we offer recommendations.

The standard UNIX utility `lint` was run on different releases of TPOCC. This utility is designed to produce more information about potential inconsistencies in the code than is produced by the standard C compiler. The purpose of this activity was to test for coding standards as part of the certification process. Typical output from `lint` includes information about mismatches on the number and type of arguments to functions, the return values of functions, possible unreachable code, unused variables, and variables that may be used before they are assigned values.

Because of the internal limitations of `lint`, it was not run on the entire set of source code in a release of TPOCC. Instead, it was run on a directory-by-directory basis. Thus, inconsistencies between use of a function in a different directory and the one in which it was defined will not be detected by this approach.

The problems tested for in this process include inconsistent number and type of arguments to functions and inconsistencies in the return types of functions. The following is a brief summary of the results obtained:

```
            Release
LINT DATA       10.0     10.1     11.0
inconsistent    147      142      161
variable        193      226      228
number          123      121      136
```

It should be noted that the inconsistencies detected by lint would not have occurred if the system were compiled with a strict ANSI C standard compiler or even if the flag -Aa were used on the HP. The compilation process would not succeed if inconsistencies in the number and type of function arguments or function return types were present in the source code. This is probably the best way to handle this situation since it produces a higher-quality product with minimal effort.

The final certification step was examining the atomicity of functions used to access shared resources such as shared memory. The basic idea is that the use of a shared resource by a UNIX process should not be preempted by another process unless the shared resource is in a safe state and no data can be lost by a switch of processes.

The problem detected in the code was that there are several functions in it that serve as interfaces to certain UNIX system calls for shared memory (and perhaps other nonshareable resources). If there is a "context switch" (change of process) by the scheduling algorithm, then the status of the shared resource has changed, and the function that serves as an interface to the shared resource is also supposed to change to reflect the new state of the resource.

The problem can arise only if the action of the UNIX system call has completed, but the function acting as an interface has not returned. This will occur very infrequently and probably cannot be detected by testing. It is likely to corrupt a small portion of the shared resource (such as a small portion of a block of shared memory). Because of the nature of the control system software, the error state is likely to continue only until the next rescheduling of the interrupted process, when the synchronization is complete. (The error state would continue for longer intervals if the problem occurred while running a real-time scheduler.)

This potential error has been observed in the TPOCC code in the interface to some of the shared memory system calls.

It should be noted that these logical errors are very hard to detect and are not well understood in the UNIX literature. As far as we are aware, only two UNIX-oriented books, Stevens [STEV92] and Leach [LEAC94A], address this issue properly. The proper treatment of atomicity of system calls *is* discussed correctly in most operating systems books.

7.1.4   Recommendations

I made several simple recommendations for improving the quality of the software product. These recommendations were influenced by the success of the TPOCC system as a generic core. They are also influenced by the need to minimize any additional costs that may be incurred by following these recommendations.

My recommendations have been preceded by many discussions with contractor and GSFC personnel, observations of software practice as indicated at meetings, careful reading of standards and practices documents, and the measurements summarized in this chapter. The recommendations are as follows:

1. Use an ANSI C compiler.

Rationale: One of the major successes of TPOCC is its adherence to the philosophy of open systems and industry standards. The use of UNIX, TCP/IP, Motif, X Windows, and Oracle has greatly aided in productivity. ANSI C is the standard because it supports function prototypes and extended type checking at compilation time. No books on the pre-ANSI version of C have been published since 1992, and this is now the dominant version of the C language.

2. Use the ANSI C compiler provided by the workstation vendor or a compiler with equivalent linkage to the installed version of UNIX.

Rationale: The HP C compiler allows easy access to UNIX system calls under HP-UX, with a smoother interface than several other compilers available for the HP series of workstations. UNIX is a moving target, especially given the movement toward POSIX and the need to continue support for older systems developed prior to these standards. This approach can help to improve portability problems.

3. Use `lint` on all source code files and directories and on such subsystems as is feasible.

Rationale: The TPOCC development process attains some of its efficiency by "eliminating unnecessary reviews." There is no formal procedure between the extensive module test and the system test. Therefore, any inconsistencies between function definitions and function calls should be resolved before system test so that testing can proceed on the basis of correct operation.

4. Use a measurement of module coupling to select modules likely to cause interconnection problems or to be inadequately tested.

Rationale: The BVA metric predicts the number of test cases necessary for complete white-box testing if modules are tested for those inputs for which logical errors are most likely to occur. A BVA value for a file or subsystem much larger than the average suggests a need for further checking in much the same way as the McCabe cyclomatic complexity is used to suggest modules with complex control flow. Other coupling measures may also be used to indicate the degree of modularity.

5. Code that uses UNIX system calls to control shareable resources should be atomic and should avoid extra statements between the return from the system call and the return from the function.

Rationale: Such code can lead to errors that occur very infrequently but are extremely hard to detect by any testing method.

6. Each source code module that is intended for reuse should be subjected to several metrics including lines of code (or DSI), McCabe cyclomatic complexity, and some form of coupling metric (possibly the BVA metric). High values of these metrics are a warning that the module is unusually complex and is a candidate for redesign.

Rationale: The values of these metrics can be useful in detecting source code modules that are very complex and are likely to require high levels of effort in testing and/or integration or else are the cause of undetected software errors. The Halstead metrics and other metrics appear to have high correlation with DSI and are unlikely to contribute any information that justifies the effort required for data collection.

Recommendations 1, 3, 4, 5, and 6 can be summarized in recommendation 7.

7. Each module placed in the reuse library should be certified by a formal certification procedure.

Rationale: Certification of source code modules will guarantee that the module is of high quality and is not likely to cause many problems when integrated into systems other than the one for which it was originally intended. The certification will indicate a relatively small interface and a high degree of functionality.

7.2   Some Reuse Activities at AT&T

Experience at AT&T with a process approach to software development has demonstrated that substantial improvements in interval, costs, and product performance can be achieved. By applying a new process for introducing a new product, AT&T's Operations Systems business unit focused the entire organization's effort on developing software more quickly and improving software quality. This is commonly known as "reengineering the corporation."

The leaders of the different AT&T business units attempted to define and improve their software development process in order to achieve the following goals:

- Reduce product development costs
- Increase product quality
- Decrease produce time to market

(This is often stated as "cheaper, better, faster.")

The mechanisms created for organizations emphasize the process and its components. These mechanisms also allow a software development organization to choose the most appropriate practices, technology, and platforms to support its processes and efficiently measure the results of using these choices. As a result, the average interval from identification of a customer's need to the delivery of an Operations Systems product has been cut in half in less than two years [GELM92].

AT&T product development units are under constant market pressure, and they can only excel by satisfying customer needs while simultaneously reducing intervals, improving product quality, and gaining standards certification.

Project teams have achieved these goals by identifying and implementing process improvements throughout the product life cycle. Also, it is well known that "a key way to improve processes is with sound process engineering disciplines."

One attempt to improve process capability at AT&T was a project called MOSAIC. The MOSAIC project attempted to create a process asset library that could capture and integrate knowledge about practices, platforms, and technology into an overall software process. This library consists of a generic life cycle process model and also contains information about task descriptions, tools, and methods. (Note that this MOSAIC project is not related to the Internet browsing tool of the same name available from the National Center for Supercomputing Applications [NCSA].)

Over the past several years, AT&T's Software Technology Center has collected information on process architecture and engineering from both internal and external sources.

From within AT&T, the MOSAIC Process Asset Library draws knowledge from:

- Best current practices
- Best area practices
- Quality gate criteria from various organizations
- New product introduction guidelines

- Research advances and tools
- Jump-start services aimed at helping to integrate new technologies into a project's processes quickly

This project makes heavy use of what is essentially a certification process for potentially reusable software components and practices. For example, the MOSAIC Process Asset Library draws knowledge from external benchmarking standards as seen as best-in-class processes. Among these standards and practices are

- International standards such as ISO9000
- The Software Engineering Institute's Capability Maturity Model (CMM)
- The NASA/Goddard Software Engineering Laboratory "Process Capability Model" and "Experience Factory"
- Other software quality and productivity activities

Mosaic is aimed at deploying current best-in-class processes in all AT&T business units. The MOSAIC process engineering team can accelerate this aim by helping project teams more quickly define processes, improve them, establish a local process engineering function, and take advantage of reusable assets such as those in the Mosaic Process Asset Library.

Project teams have been getting a head start with the help of MOSAIC project engineers. MOSAIC engineers work with both management and technical staff to help "fine-tune" and socialize the plan, finding ways to bypass roadblocks and thus reach consensus and commitment. They also help to establish and track process metrics. To help the project develop project-specific plans, the process engineers have at their disposal the wide range of materials available in the MOSAIC Process Asset Library.

Parallel to the efforts of the MOSAIC library, AT&T is also working on a project called "Silver Bullet" whose goal is to achieve radical improvements in product development intervals. The project is aimed at providing a next-generation environment for the development of Operations Systems products. Based in North Carolina, Project Silver Bullet is an organization specifically designed to execute highly advanced processes.

In an article titled, "Architectures for Large-Scale Reuse," Beck discusses AT&T's basic approach to software reuse and the process changes associated with it [BECK92]. Platforms, modular reuse goals, frameworks, reusable assets and components, and libraries are all considered approaches to handling reuse.

Again, object-oriented technology, a valuable asset to AT&T's product development cycle, has resulted in significant reuse of code, design, and analysis; reduced development cycles; and simplified system integration. AT&T believes that software reuse will be promoted by the object-oriented paradigm in two ways: through the use of code directly or through specializing.

Supporting this viewpoint is the experience of AT&T's call attempt data collection system (CADCS). The CADCS project consists of about 350,000 lines of code and reported the following: "Software and methodology reuse has resulted in a quality product delivered in a short time frame."

For the CADCS system, the modification request (MR) density, that is, the number of MRs per thousand lines of source code, was calculated to be less than 0.1 percent. This rate is much lower than that projected from experiential data for such systems. While the entire reduction cannot be attributed to object-oriented technology, it seems to have played an important role.

A later system, which will not be identified, used the CADCS software as a basis for development. The new system's development team estimated that had the new system been developed from the ground up and not based on CADCS, it would have grown approximately 180 to 220 percent more in budget and approximately 150 to 200 percent more in development time.

The general consensus was that planned reuse resulted not only in savings in development errors but also in integration and testing efficiencies, leading to an overall cycle reduction. Object-oriented technology eased the modification and reuse of existing CADCS code for the new system, allowing AT&T to leverage the technology investment in CADCS.

An important group in the AT&T reuse effort is the advanced software products group, or ADSOFT, whose work also provides a platform for improving software fault tolerance. A recent book by Krishnamurthy describes the importance of advanced UNIX-based tools for reuse [KRIS95]. The selection of Krishnamurthy's book in 1995 as a dual main selection by a major computer book club provides further evidence of the importance of reuse (and the growth of UNIX software tools) to the software engineering community. It also illustrates the importance of small, well-defined interfaces between systems that are intended to be interoperable with other software.

The UNIX environment encourages the use of standard file descriptors for input and output of processes (separately running programs). A *file descriptor* is a small integer that indicates the "file" that is used for either input or output. (The term *file* in this context can mean a permanently stored file on a disk or a temporary convention to represent terminal I/O.) Many of the interfaces between multiple UNIX processes are obtained by simply connecting the output file descriptor of one process to the input file descriptor of the other.

Many other reuse efforts at AT&T are centered around the BaseWorX Application Platform. BaseWorX is so general that it should be considered as a software tool. We will discuss it in Chap. 8 when we discuss tools that support software reuse.

7.3   Some Reuse Activities at Battelle Laboratory

In this section we will briefly discuss some reuse experiences at Battelle's Pacific Northwest Laboratory. The concerns of several managers at Battelle are the same as those at many other organizations working with software reuse:

- legacy designs versus new ones
- reuse library accessibility
- identification of reusable components
- educational issues
- complexity of interaction with global data structures
- portability issues
- lack of managerial support

These concerns are familiar to us by now. However, there have been some encouraging signs. A group of software managers at Battelle have begun a characterization of the architecture of software systems that have a potential for reuse of higher-level artifacts than just source code modules. This has been done from the ground up by means of informal seminars and brown-bag lunches.

These managers see several features common to the Battelle systems as having high reuse potential:

- Client-server architecture, generally with a UNIX-based server and a PC-based client
- The systems' integrated capabilities, using a GIS (geographic information system) and a relational database. These are frequently COTS products
- The systems' extensive use of commercial tools, such as those for geographic display analysis, database management, reporting, modeling, and system administration

- The use of rapid prototyping, using such GUI tools as Microsoft Visual BASIC

The Battelle Computer Science Department's systems engineering process (SEP) guide is being modified to incorporate reuse activities into the life cycle. Formal reuse programs are being used in certain environments, even without the commonly used terminology.

The statement of an anonymous project manager that we gave in Chap. 1 is especially relevant here: "People think that source code modules can be thrown into libraries and reused whenever they need them, but this is not the case." For example, the Tank Waste Information Network System (TWINS) has an architecture such as the ideal one described earlier. This system is being designed to encourage reuse and portability to other applications. The Federal Emergency Management Information System (FEMIS) was built using several portions of the TWINS system at higher levels than simple source code modules. This is a high level or reuse.

Unfortunately, because of the relative newness of these systematic reuse activities, there is little hard data on the cost savings due to reuse. However, there is reasonable satisfaction with those software systems that have been built recently.

We note that the numerical computations, which are so important at government laboratories, are still coded primarily in FORTRAN. The heavy reuse of numerical libraries and algorithms provides an excellent experience base for expanding software reuse practices to the distributed systems of the future.

The current economic pressures on government laboratories mandate that cost saving efforts continue, and hence the reuse program is likely to become more widespread in these organizations.

7.4 Some Reuse Activities at Hewlett-Packard

Hewlett-Packard recognized the importance of software metrics relatively early. After several pilot projects that demonstrated the positive effect of metrics information on the software development process, it began a companywide program of collecting and using software metrics. Details of the implementation of that program are given in *Software Metrics* by Grady and Caswell [GRAD87].

It is not surprising that software reuse is being treated in the same systematic way at HP. Its approach is one of determining measurable goals in different business units.

A good example of HP's approach is the paper by Collins for the Fifth Workshop on Software Reuse in 1992 [COLL92]. In that paper, Collins described the difficulties in fitting a single, "one size fits all" reuse methodology into existing software development environments. She described the approach as using project teams as a "living laboratory," with heavy emphasis on lessons learned and the scientific analysis of results.

Note that improvements in both software product and process are much easier to measure in an environment that emphasizes the collection, analysis, and use of metrics as a companywide policy.

Collins identified five activities as essential:

- Development of a set of objectives for a systematic software reuse program
- Development of a plan to carry out these objectives
- Domain analysis
- Development requirements using reusability
- Certification

These activities are discussed in more detail in a paper by Collins and Zimmer [COLL95]. Their method for reuse metrics adoption that reflects the identification method is a refinement of Basili and Rombach's GQM (Goals, Questions, Metrics) paradigm [BASI88]. Basili and Rombach's goal statement activity is extended to include explicit alignment of reuse goals with business goals. The questions and metrics identification are guided by the desire to manage the risk of the reuse adoption as well as by organizational limits.

The HP Software Initiative's Evolutionary Reuse Metrics Adoption (ERMA) method is based on GQM identification and implementation and the management of metrics.

The ERMA method keeps the GQM process highly focused on delivering metrics that provide the information needed to manage progress toward critical goals. The innovations of ERMA are as follows:

- Explicitly state the goals as well-formed, strategic objectives.
- Identify which objectives require metrics support so that progress toward that objective can be managed. Justify the critical metrics for each goal selected.
- Identify one or two key assessment questions for each objective. (The assessment questions must align with the well-formed objective, and the answer to the question must enable the organization to assess progress toward the objective.)
- Identify criteria for which metrics will be used (e.g., the organization's readiness, ease of data collection).

- Identify one or two metrics for the question(s) deemed to be most critical for managing reuse adoption.

Other aspects of HP's program involve goal clarification; a domain analysis workshop; and interviews with users, producers, and marketers.

For one group at HP, the Software Initiative developed an evolutionary GQM approach based on the same principles as a pruned search algorithm. A "cost" was established for pursuing a particular goal, question, or metric, and an attempt was made to get the most return from implementing a particular metric.

The ERMA team established criteria for pursuing one goal, question, or metric over another. These criteria (in order of priority) stipulated that they would pursue a path if

1. The organization has a strong need to manage progress toward the associated goal.

2. The information needed to manage progress is not currently available.

3. Having answers to the associated assessment question would significantly improve the organization's ability to manage progress toward the goal.

4. The cost-benefit of implementing the metric is acceptable to the organization.

The reuse effort was a tactic for achieving several important business goals. Of these, the group identified three critical ones, toward which progress could be made with a substantial contribution from metrics. Asking only one or two key questions about each goal led the group to a small set of metrics that were feasible and would provide the data needed for analysis. Future phases of evolutionary metrics adoption will employ the same method to implement and utilize additional metrics.

Of course, the development of a measurable set of goals and objectives is consistent with the GQM metaphor of Basili and Rombach [BASI88]. It is clearly well suited to an organization with a company-wide metrics policy.

However, even in a company that encourages and uses feedback from the measurement of both process and product, there is resistance to some aspects of a systematic software reuse program. In a 1995 article, Collins and Zimmer noted that

> We found strong cultural resistance to implementing a classification scheme, even when there were 200–300 work products in use. In HP, the typical number of reusable components in a library is 10–20. [COLL95]

This view is consistent with our observations about the TPOCC project at NASA's Goddard Space Flight Center. There is more acceptance of the activities at the back end of the reuse process, when a product exists, than in front-end activities, where there is a perceived danger of having too much analysis and modeling and not enough product.

Other reuse issues are raised in the conference papers of Beach [BEAC92], Collins [COLL93], Griss [GRIS92], Johnson, Ornburn, and Rugaber [JOHN92B], Lea and de Champeaux [LEA92], Malan [MALA93], Navarro [NAVA92], Rix [RIX92], and Wentzel [WENT92]. All these papers are available in electronic form on the Internet and will not be summarized here.

Some conclusions can be drawn from the reuse activities at HP. Different technical groups are encouraged to experiment with this technology and attempt to fit it into their software development procedures. Reuse is incorporated whenever it makes sense to do so.

HP has developed what is called a "corporate engineering reuse program." Some of the elements of this reuse program are discussed in Griss [GRIS92]. An important aspect of this program is the development of a software reuse handbook. This is consistent with the experiences described in the other case studies in which training in reuse concepts and the "culture of reuse" is considered essential.

The companywide goals are specified in some detail in the handbooks but leave some flexibility for local variations depending upon the needs of the group's customers. There is no attempt to force everyone to follow the same rigid life cycle model or the same procedures in developing a reuse program.

In addition, there is a considerable amount of experimentation with different models of computing. There are experiments on higher-level systems for user interaction. The intention is to increase life cycle leverage and to remove some of the restrictions on user interfaces that are imposed with current GUI tools, which restrict users to menu-based systems.

We have seen the importance of having reuse influence requirements in the NASA case study presented in this chapter and in the discussion of cost models for reuse using COTS products in Chap. 5.

It is interesting to note that several of the research teams for pilot projects in reuse are interdisciplinary. This is due in part to the feeling that many of the problems associated with reuse are cultural and not especially technical. (This feeling is held by many in the software industry, not just at HP.)

Experiments are also underway on using spreadsheets to extend the applicability of these ubiquitous tools. This also increases cost savings through life cycle leverage.

7.5   A Hypothetical Failed Software Reuse Program

In this section, we describe a scenario in which software reuse is not effective but in fact increases costs and reduces quality. It is included here as an example of what *not* to do when implementing a software reuse program.

Company XYZ is a large company with a decentralized software development operation. Each distinct location of the company represents a different division, and each division manager is evaluated yearly on the success of his or her division rather than on the division's contribution to the company's good. Each division has different standards for software quality, documentation, and coding style. This "every tub on its bottom" approach makes it difficult to have companywide quality improvement programs.

The A and B divisions are asked to work together on a larger project because each has some expertise in the area. Each division has begun to emphasize software reuse, although they have poor quality measurement techniques. There is no formal domain analysis process in place.

The only quality measurement data available were the number of faults per thousand lines of code (KLOC). Division A reported this data per system, while division B reported the data as the number of faults per line of code in a source code file.

There was no reuse library available, and so all potentially reusable software artifacts were identified by a group of software engineers and managers during a monthlong meeting. To avoid turf battles, the meeting was held in a neutral site, a large hotel. Both divisions shared the cost of this meeting equally.

The first problem that occurred was missed opportunities. Over 35 percent of the requirements of division A's contribution can be met by high-quality subsystems developed by division B. Because of differences in requirements formats, however, none of this potential reuse of high-level artifacts occurs.

On the positive side, 25 percent of the source code in the joint project was obtained from reusable components built by division B. This reduced coding costs by only 15 percent because of the lack of training among division A's personnel.

Division B personnel obtained 10 percent of their contribution to the system by means of potentially reusable source code from division A. This reduced coding costs slightly. However, the lower quality of division A's software meant an increase in testing time. No funds were available for a companywide quality standard. The lack of standardization of interfaces meant that integration times increased considerably.

Because few of the artifacts were properly stored to enable easy access to test plans, test data, and documentation, the project came in late, with most of the documentation inconsistent with the delivered project. Of course, the maintenance costs for the delivered system were much larger than normal. The overall project was 30 percent over cost and 20 percent behind schedule.

At a postmortem, each divisional representative blamed the other division for producing poor-quality software that held their division back. However, there were no hard data to support any of the accusations made.

The only thing that central management knew for sure was that the project had been delivered late and was way over budget. It decided that the problem was the original management decision to have software reuse be a major factor in software development and thus canceling all other efforts in the company. The company's market share declined in several key areas, the value of its stock decreased by 60 percent, and it was taken over two years later, with many layoffs.

Note that the overhead of a systematic, measurement-based software reuse program would have been far cheaper than the ad hoc reuse program described in this hypothetical example.

Summary

We have presented case studies in software reuse from several different organizations. The experiences include longstanding efforts; systematic, companywide programs; and relatively new ones.

The NASA Goddard Space Flight Center case study illustrates what can be achieved even in a rapidly changing environment. The central core of the system has remained a viable part of spacecraft control systems, even with changes in the requirements for interoperable systems.

The AT&T case study illustrates what can be achieved by a companywide effort supported at the highest levels. The standardization of the UNIX I/O interface by means of file descriptors made interoperability of many tools relatively easy, thus encouraging reuse.

The Battelle Pacific Northwest Laboratory case study illustrates the effect of a high degree of domain expertise together with a desire to reuse components of a higher level than just source code modules.

The Hewlett-Packard case study illustrates what can be achieved by a companywide effort based upon the consistent collection and analysis of software metrics. Some at HP supported pilot projects that attempted to incorporate systematic reuse practices into existing software policies for different organizations. A software reuse handbook was developed as part of the corporate effort. HP made no attempt to enforce a single software development methodology to be used by all business units.

All the reuse experiences presented in this chapter were positive ones.

Further Reading

Spacecraft control systems have been studied elsewhere from a reuse perspective. The articles by Gomaa [GOMA92] and Bailn [BAIL92] are especially useful for providing a different, front-end, model-based view of the reuse process. These authors' models were not used as part of the TPOCC effort, but they do illustrate the technology efforts of some related organizations.

The best place to get more information about the success of these organizations is from technical papers, which are listed in the references section of this book, or in popular technical publications. You should compare their experiences with those in your own organization. If your organization has had an interesting experience with reuse, please send the author a report via email at rjl@scs.howard.edu, or via surface mail at

AfterMath Attn: reuse

10 E. Lee St., Suite 2101

Baltimore, MD 21202

Exercises

1. List the common elements of existing or proposed reuse programs in the successful case studies presented in this chapter. Which of these elements are missing from the hypothetical example of a failed reuse program?

2. Suppose you are an upper-level software manager. Based on the successful case studies described in this chapter, indicate some metrics that you would collect and analyze to evaluate the success of your organization's reuse plan.

8

Tools for
Software Reuse

In this chapter we describe some sample tools that can be used to support software reuse. The tools discussed here will suggest the level of support for a wide range of approaches to systematic reuse. No attempt has been made to cover the full range of available tools.

The first tool discussed, InQuisiX, is well suited to organizing and cataloging assets in a reuse library. It is also helpful in performing domain analysis. The latest version, InQuisiX Pro, is probably the commercial tool most commonly used to support software reuse. It has evolved to provide support for collaborative software development environments.

The next tool, a research prototype developed by Johnson, Ornburn, and Rugaber is a simple, text-based tool for analyzing existing source code. It can be used for reuse, maintenance, or reengineering of source code. The tool has the advantage of being essentially free (in that the underlying UNIX utilities are free). It is discussed in Sec. 8.2.

In Sec. 8.3, we will discuss the AT&T BaseWorX tool for building object-oriented management applications. The relevant features of this tool are its support for reuse by object-oriented software engineering techniques and its explicit use of standards.

In Sec. 8.4, we will discuss a knowledge-based system for support of software reuse activities. The system is being developed by Digitalk and KnowledgeWare and will be used for mainframe-based transaction processing. This tool has the advantage of not requiring that the reusable software components be written in the same language.

In Sec. 8.5, we briefly discuss some issues surrounding the use of groupware systems or the Internet as aids in a systematic software reuse process.

Even though most CASE tools include a central repository for system information, we have not discussed any general-purpose CASE tools in this chapter. Instead, we have focused our discussion on tools with a heavy reuse emphasis. We note in passing that most CASE tools do not yet incorporate easy access to reuse libraries other than those provided directly by the user, the compiler vendor, or by the vendor of the CASE tool itself.

8.1   The InQuisiX System of Reuse Tools

The InQuisiX system provides a GUI interface to a sophisticated application system for creating, searching, and managing a reuse library. The system has a highly adaptable classification and search engine that, when integrated with an existing software development environment, provides an advanced software reuse library system.

An InQuisiX reuse library system, with its set of cooperating tools, supports a software development process centered around reusing software assets rather than one based on development from scratch. InQuisiX provides high-performance classification, cataloging, searching, browsing, retrieval, and synthesis capabilities that support increased automation of the reuse process. The InQuisiX capabilities are highly flexible and support many different software development processes.

The current version of InQuisiX, InQuisiX Pro, is a suite of desktop applications for reusable software assets, including informal products such as engineering notes, markups, annotations, memos, and electronic mail. The InQuisiX Pro suite of applications runs on top of Lotus Notes, thus providing support for collaborative computing and software development.

Lotus Notes provides the common interface to a wide variety of platforms and network protocols, including all versions of Microsoft Windows, X Windows, OS/2, Mac OS, and most versions of UNIX, and a smooth interface to the World Wide Web. InQuisiX Pro includes a set of open interfaces to promote integration into the customer's software development environment.

InQuisiX Pro is based upon the view that reuse is fundamentally a collaborative activity rather than a simple producer-consumer process. The producers of reusable assets can also be the consumers. Successful software reuse occurs as a result of a long-term collaboration between developers, architects, managers, certifiers, and specifiers.

Different InQuisiX Pro applications address the capture, organization, and reuse of the full spectrum of soft assets, including formal assets such as specifications, designs, and software. In addition,

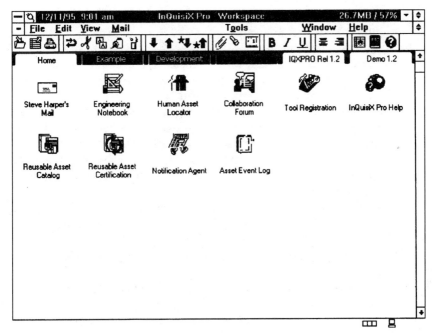

Figure 8.1 Typical InQuisiX Opening screen.

InQuisiX Pro also supports reuse of informal assets such as engineering notes or design rationale.

The opening screen of the InQuisiX Pro user interface is illustrated in Fig. 8.1. This screen clearly illustrates the interface to Lotus Notes.

The InQuisiX Pro application suite provides *notebooks* that capture and structure informal information; *forums* for collaboration and discussion of assets; and *catalogs* to describe, structure, and index soft assets. The proactive *notification agent* puts the control of notification and information flow into the hands of the recipient to help eliminate both information starvation and information overload.

An InQuisiX notebook captures and organizes informal soft assets such as ideas, engineering notes, decisions, trade studies, meeting minutes, action items, problems, unit development folders, and references. Once captured, users may view the information according to different categorizations or query to find specific information.

An InQuisiX collaboration forum provides an electronic forum for a work group to electronically discuss and exchange information on problems, issues, or topics of interest. Users post topics for discussion and respond to others. Users can interact and share information without having to meet and can do so at their own convenience. Over time, the collaboration forum becomes a valuable knowledge base that may be searched or browsed.

An InQuisiX asset catalog captures key identification, descriptive, and categorization information about soft assets of any kind. An asset catalog provides an easy way to view soft assets by different categorizations, to search for assets, to browse assets, and to check out assets for reuse. The assets may be attached directly to an asset catalog or may be referenced from the catalog but stored externally, for example, in a configuration management system. Once a user checks out an asset, the system will automatically notify him or her of new versions. A companion application automatically routes submitted assets through a certification workflow.

The various notebooks, forums, and catalogs are packaged as template applications that can be applied to a broad set of reuse problems. The user interface is illustrated in Fig. 8.2.

InQuisiX Pro provides many ways for users to organize and find information. Each application comes with a set of predefined views that organize assets in different ways (e.g., by subject, by author). The product includes a high-performance text search engine that supports comprehensive boolean, nearness, and weighted searching. Results

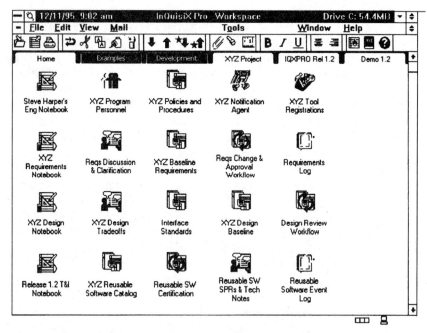

Figure 8.2 Several InQuisiX applications.

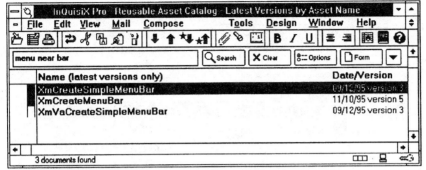

InQuisiX Pro Search Bar

Figure 8.3   An illustration of the InQuisiX search facility.

from the searches are ranked by relevance, as shown in Fig. 8.3. Users may simultaneously search multiple databases.

The ability of the search engine to return asset information in the case of inexact matches is illustrated in Fig. 8.3.

InQuisiX Pro supports the association of external files with individual documents within application databases and provides facilities to allow users to view, retrieve, check out, or otherwise manipulate these files from within InQuisiX Pro. Figure 8.4 illustrates the visibility of assets.

There are three alternative mechanisms for associating files with documents:

- Files or objects within files may be *inserted* into a document. The product supports linking and embedding objects using the native mechanisms on the various platforms:

  DDE (Dynamic Data Exchange) on Windows and OS/2

  OLE (Object Linking and Embedding) on Windows

  LEL (Link, Embed, and Launch-to-Edit) on UNIX

  Publish & Subscribe on Macintosh

- Files may be *attached* to a document. In this case, a copy of the file is ingested within the document. Once attached, a file may be *launched,* wherein its native application is launched to view or edit the file, or it may be *detached,* wherein a copy is made for the user.

- External files may be *referenced* within a special table provided in the document form. In this case, the file remains stored in its original location and no copies are made. Tools or scripts are registered with the *tool registration* facility for file operations (e.g., view, edit, mark up, execute, etc.) and for *asset checkout operations* (e.g., file

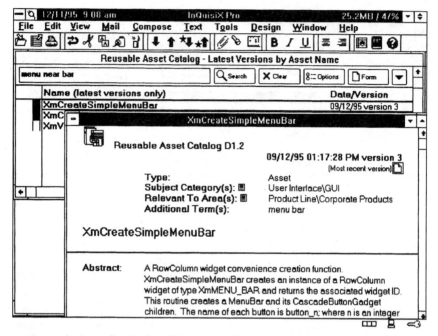

Figure 8.4 A view of an InQuisiX asset catalog entry.

copy, extract from a configuration management system, etc.). This mechanism is used for assets stored in external document management or in configuration management systems.

The InQuisiX Pro applications are proactive, notifying users about information of interest to them by means of electronic mail. The recipients can thus control the flow of information including notification of new assets in a certain interest category, notification of updates to assets, and notification of responses to important questions or issues. A notification agent maintains shared classifications against which a user may indicate interest.

The notification agent monitors the new and updated information and notifies users as new or updated information matching their interest profile is discovered. InQuisiX Pro maintains descriptive, link, and classification information about external assets while providing user access to them.

One major feature of the InQuisiX system is that a user can specify a set of keywords to be searched for using the included search routines. The user can also enter a set of synonyms for each of the keywords in order to make possible searches with incomplete or inconsistent information.

A random check of several of the UNIX commands given in Leach [LEAC94A] found that all the commands in the included example of an InQuisiX reuse catalog, which suggests that this particular reuse catalog is complete. In addition, each of the synonyms suggested by the search and analysis system were appropriate for the relevant UNIX context. It is reasonable to assume that the search process for synonyms is very good in general and that any relevant synonyms would be found by the search engine, assuming that the domain analysis was carried out properly.

This is a major step in automating the domain analysis process. As we saw in our domain analysis of the Linux operating system in Chap. 2, there are often many different synonyms for words in the reuse vocabulary. This is particularly true for the "actions" of the system under analysis, which are essential if we are to use object-oriented techniques.

Unfortunately, there is no real support for automatic analysis of source code or other software artifacts other than by the inexact selection of software assets by matching particular keywords. A sophisticated search engine is no substitute for a proper classification scheme.

In addition, there is still a large amount of data entry to be done. In UNIX environments, this can be simplified using UNIX shell scripts and redirection of input from a preexisting file instead of standard interactive input. Similar techniques can be used in MS-DOS. However, data entry is less easy using the GUIs provided with most common windowing systems.

It is likely that the InQuisiX suite of tools will be used most effectively in conjunction with a systematic reuse process that emphasizes domain analysis. Unfortunately, the lack of domain analysis support is a major drawback to the use of the InQuisiX Pro tool suite (and any other existing commercial or research tools) at the present.

8.2   A Simple Text-Based System

At the IEEE Software Maintenance Conference in Orlando, Florida, in November 1992, Johnson, Ornburn, and Rugaber described a simple system that performs automatic analysis of source code based on textual information [JOHN92A]. Their implementation of a solution to the reuse problem is considered simpler than InQuisiX because it has a limited, character-based user interface.

Their work was originally developed as an aid to software maintenance in reverse engineering. They wished to provide information to software maintainers about the content of the programs being maintained. They noted a study by Fjeldstad and Hamlen that indicated that between 47 and 62 percent of the time required for software maintenance is spent in program understanding [FJEL79].

Fjeldstad and Hamlen's system was applied to a large, real-time system written in the language PL/M. However, the ideas are applicable to the analysis of programs written in other languages. The original goal of their work was to aid in program comprehension, using simple tools. It is clear, however, that their ideas can be helpful in reuse.

Johnson, Ornburn, and Rugaber's system is based on the use of the standard UNIX utilities sed and awk. These tools are provided as part of the standard software distribution on nearly all UNIX systems. Because these two UNIX utilities are text-based, Johnson and colleagues' system will work on any character-based terminal emulator and does not require any special GUI such as X Windows or Motif. Inconsistencies in the various commercial versions of UNIX (and the relatively new Linux system) might require minor changes for the software to work on different UNIX platforms.

The sed utility is a stream-based editor, which is used in this context for transforming an input file using matching of regular expressions. This can be especially useful in treating languages that are not case sensitive. For example, a single transformation using sed can allow us to assume that the entire program is in lowercase, which can greatly simplify further analyses performed by other tools.

The transformed data are then given to a program written in the pattern matching language awk, which is then used to provide additional analyses of the software system to be analyzed.

The awk program is very simple, primarily because of the nature of the awk programming language. The awk language is a flexible language that is generally interpreted, although compiled versions of awk programs are often available.

An awk program can consist of three parts:

- Initializations taken before any tokens are read from the input.
- Actions that are taken depending on patterns matched (and logical conditions satisfied) in tokens that are read from the input. In general, each line of input is processed as a separate unit.
- Summary actions that are taken after all tokens have been read from the input.

Any of these three parts may be omitted, depending on the requirements of the situation.

Tokens are stored within awk programs as simple variables with names such as $1, $2, and the like. These internal awk variables are reset after each input line is read. The special tokens $0 and $N represent the entire line and the number of tokens on a line, respectively.

The reinitialization of the internal variables for each new line of input makes programming very easy. For example, a simple awk program to extract procedure definitions in PL/M consists of seven lines of code. Such a program is given in [JOHN92A]. This program accounted for the possibility of a procedure definition extending over several lines of program text in the input file.

It should be noted that these simple tools produce analyses based only on the syntax of the software system being analyzed. More sensitive analysis can be obtained using semantic information and parsing it through the use of semantic analysis tools such as those that can be generated by the standard UNIX utility yacc or the related UNIX utility newyacc.

These two UNIX tools for semantic analysis are used in parser generators and are the basis for many compilers. They both require a complete description of the Backus-Naur form (BNF) of the language. As Johnson, Ornburn, and Rugaber point out, this can be obtained from a language manual and entered into the proper format for these tools. More commonly, the information can be obtained from publicly available grammars that are already in the proper format for use with these tools.

The grammar rules for detecting procedure definitions in PL/M programs are as simple as adding the rule

```
proc_def :: proc_stmt block_body
[ (CALL_TREE) #1 unset_proc_name() ]
;
```

to the formal BNF description of PL/M, in addition to encoding the user-defined function unset_proc_name().

It should be noted that Johnson, Ornburn, and Rugaber used one more tool in their analysis. For consistency of analysis, they entered the results of the first two steps into a CASE tool, Software Through Pictures (STP). The purpose of this was to be able to visualize the calling tree of the original PL/M software system being analyzed.

The calling tree is an automatic product of the semantic analysis produced by any of the UNIX parser generator tools yacc, bison, or newyacc. This occurs because the parser generator must analyze its input (the PL/M program in this case) to determine if it is a valid program. Since the input is an existing system, which is known to run, the process of semantic analysis will complete successfully. A by-product of this semantic analysis is the calling tree of the input.

Thus, Johnson, Ornburn, and Rugaber were able to produce a view of the system being analyzed using standard utilities and applications software. Their approach had the additional advantage that nearly all the necessary tools and utilities were free.

We note that if the same techniques were used for C programs instead of PL/M, then the standard UNIX utility `cflow` could have been used as a basis for the call tree creation. While `cflow` does not have a standard graphical output, it does produce a view of the call tree in textual form. This may be satisfactory in many software development environments, since the software is free.

8.3 The AT&T BaseWorX Application Platform

In today's computing environments, many sophisticated management applications have many of the same features described in Chap. 7 in the discussion of the reuse program at Battelle's Pacific Northwest Laboratory.

The development of the BaseWorX application platform at AT&T was influenced by many of the goals that motivated Battelle Laboratory. Reuse strategies officially began at AT&T in 1987 through an applications platform known as RAPID/NM. Now known as BaseWorX, the applications platform is a framework that has been proven to be flexible in its applicability to software. What distinguishes BaseWorX from other development platforms is the large variety of hardware platforms on which the software operates.

The BaseWorX Applications Platform is an open, standards-based, UNIX-based software platform that enables developers to design, develop, and deploy a variety of applications quickly and cost-effectively. The platform supports both object-oriented development and procedural or functional developments.

The BaseWorX system is used to provide computer support for various management applications. As such, there is a considerable amount of overlap between the goals and environments of BaseWorX and the corresponding work at Battelle.

Their common features include the following:

- Heavily network-based systems
- A high-level system of abstraction in the system architecture, not just in the lower-level components
- Compliance with industry standards
- Cost pressures

In addition, BaseWorX has the following:

- a high-level "management information model"
- an object-oriented design that makes use of a "managed object library"

Six key objectives in the area of software reuse were incorporated into the design of the BaseWorX application development platform [BECK92]:

- The platform was conducive to prototyping and rapid development so that the developers were able to build sample prototypes for the customers to see and also to baseline the application.
- The platform was based on standard protocols like SQL and CCITT.
- Commercial components were used when applicable.
- The platform was built in the manner in which components used within the system could be selected. This objective helps customers customize their ever changing needs.
- A uniform interface and method for tracking, managing, and operating the deployed systems was built through extensive reusable operations, administration, and maintenance capabilities.
- The platform was built to operate a variety of UNIX-based systems and also complied with the relevant IEEE POSIX standards.

BaseWorX is different from many systems based on object-oriented technology because it attempts to incorporate higher levels of reuse in the managed object library. This is a higher level of reuse than the typical goal of object-oriented systems—reuse of small source code component modules.

The managed object library includes the following:

- Automatic code generation for certain tasks
- Reusable managed object classes
- Object persistence when objects are moved to and from the managed object database
- All communication between objects is completely object-oriented
- Configuration management
- Easy mapping between managed objects and user interfaces
- Flexibility across different application areas
- Strong adherence to industry standards

Many of these features have been described earlier in this book as characteristics of good reuse programs.

The core of the BaseWorX design is a management information model based on industry standards, including ISO/IEC IS standards 10040,

10164, 10165-1, and 10165-4, among others ([ISO91A], [ISO91B], [ISO91C], [ISO91D]).

The CORBA (Common Object-Oriented Request Broker Architecture) standard was also used for the objects in the libraries. The system explicitly uses the Network Management Forum's Management Information Catalog [NIST92] to avoid new code development and to foster reuse.

The BaseWorX platform is based on the concept of a software backplane that provides the OA&M communications, object support, interoperability, Multiple National Language Support (MNLS), and multiple application services for designing, developing, and running applications. The software backplane provides the main set of services needed for applications to communicate and also provides the needed management for the application by monitoring and controlling the application and the platform. The BaseWorX platform supports the development of both procedural and object-oriented applications. Surrounding this basic infrastructure, a variety of other services needed by applications are provided. Currently, these services include user interfaces, databases, and platform development tools.

The software backplane services support client-server, manager/agent (including OSI System Management), and event-driven object-oriented paradigms, thus enabling the use of the most appropriate infrastructure for applications. With these paradigms, the BaseWorX platform can be used to develop On Line.

The manager/agent model is a special type of client-server paradigm that is oriented toward OSI System Management. In this model, resources are modeled as objects. One process (the agent) provides a managed object view of managed resources to another process (the manager), which sends commands to and receives event notifications from the agent. The agent hides proprietary details of the managed objects from the management system.

The event-driven, object-oriented model views the world as a set of managed objects with specific attributes. As events occur in the application domain, object attributes change and, in turn, cause other events. Objects react to these events with predefined rules. The specific interactions of these objects make up the application. This model is very useful in many application domains and is often used for network management and OSI systems management.

Significant attributes of the BaseWorX platform include:

- Support of international standards
- Open architecture
- Support of client-server and manager/agent paradigms

- Support of multiple architecture frameworks
- Support for object-oriented platform services
- Availability on a wide variety of hardware
- Support for administration and maintenance
- Multiple national language support
- Customization capability

You should note the high level of abstraction implied by the existence of automatic code generation in this bulleted list. This is possible only if there is a high-level language that supports the range of applications.

BaseWorX uses two languages: a high-level language called GDMO (Guidelines for Definition of Managed Objects) and a more formal intermediate language called the Intermediate Object Language (IOL) that interfaces between the more abstract views and the underlying C++ and UNIX process systems. This layered architecture is consistent with the standard view of UNIX software architecture ([ANDL90], [LEAC94A]).

Higher-level objects are written in the GDMO language and then translated into the IOL. The translation is done by an MOG (managed object generator).

The IOL code can then be processed by an automatic code generator to produce C++ code with the appropriate system calls to the UNIX kernel for basic operating system services. This code generation is done by the MOSC (managed object schema compiler).

We note that other code generation tools might be used in this situation in the future, including the GEN++ analyzer generator for C++, which is a product of Bell Laboratories. The recent reorganization of AT&T together with the sale of the UNIX group UNIX Systems Laboratory to Novell makes any such change problematic, at least for the immediate future.

Both the MOG and MOSC tools are provided as part of the BaseWorX system.

Alternatively, objects written in the higher-level GDMO language can themselves interface with high-level features of a GUI builder. In particular, they can interface with the UIL (user interface language) of the Motif software system.

The expectation is that the BaseWorX system will provide the same reuse leverage that is so important in the UNIX operating system. Since UNIX views everything as either a file or a process, it is easy to develop simple applications using commonly available UNIX utilities as standard building blocks.

The same principles guide the development of BaseWorX: layered architecture, standard interfaces, and high level of abstraction in the overall system design. It remains to be seen if BaseWorX will be as much of a standard as UNIX.

We do note one BaseWorX feature that is appropriate for a global information company such as AT&T. The BaseWorX platform provides the capability to support output for all common eight-bit languages. This enables the development of applications that can support multiple languages.

8.4   A Knowledge-Based Tool for Reuse

McClure [McCL92] makes the following statement in her book *The Three R's of Software Automation:* "One of the reasons why software reusability is a technology whose time has come is that the tools needed to support it are now available." She goes on to mention that there are tools needed for building and reusing components. For building components, the tools must be able to identify components that can be widely reused, define and adapt them for reuse, classify and store the reusability components in a library, and represent them in a standard form. Likewise, for using the components, the tools should be able to find, understand, modify, combine, and incorporate the reusable components.

In addition, she states that tools will be developed to support libraries, to check standards of components before including them in a collection, to set up standard frameworks, to suggest places in a design where components could be used, and to facilitate the management of reusability-based process.

In this section we will discuss a knowledge-based tool briefly. The tool is a joint venture of Digitalk and KnowledgeWare Inc.

Digitalk developed a tool set named PARTS that makes it easier to reuse software components written in Smalltalk/V, COBOL, and C [DELR94]. (The acronym *PARTS* stands for "parts assembly and reuse tool set.")

Note that the three languages allowed by PARTS have different programming paradigms. Smalltalk is an object-oriented language that does not have the procedurally oriented facilities of C++, which was intended to work with C. COBOL is one of the oldest programming languages, with superior facilities for data file operations, especially on files containing structured data or with nonsequential access. C was originally to be a "universal assembly language," with many of the control flow methods and structured data types available in other higher-level languages ([KERN82], [KERN88], [LEAC93A]).

Since the three programming languages Smalltalk/V, COBOL, and

C are so different, any method to organize and access a reuse library will be very problematic unless it captures a high degree of abstraction together with sophisticated reasoning.

Clearly, the sort of lexically based reasoning used so elegantly in the tools of Johnson, Ornburn, and Rugaber described in Sec. 8.2 would not suffice for this new, more complex situation. Recall that Johnson, Ornburn, and Rugaber applied their analysis to programs written in PL/M. Their analysis tools would have to be modified to handle source code written in another language such as C. Either an entirely different approach to multilanguage textual analysis would have to be developed or else an intermediate language would be have to be used in order to capture the language-invariant information about reusable software components that would be obtained from each source code module, regardless of source code language.

This is the sort of problem for which a sophisticated use of artificial intelligence might be appropriate. Thus, Digitalk has joined forces on this project with KnowledgeWare Inc. The jointly developed system is called the PARTS Wrapper. As Norvin Leach (no relation to the author) has indicated, the term *Wrapper* in this context means interfaces to other languages [LEAC94A].

The combined Digitalk-KnowledgeWare system will be used for mainframe-based transaction processing. Note that the emphasis on use in software systems for mainframes is unusual in view of the rapid transition to client-server architectures. Many observers have predicted that client-server architectures are merely a temporary solution to computing problems and that the software industry trend is toward even more widely distributed application systems.

The intention is to have KnowledgeWare's Application Development Workbench (ADW) be able to process information about reusability captured automatically from Digitalk's PARTS system. The combined system will reuse existing PARTS components automatically and will create the corresponding SQL statements [MACE94].

The Wrapper will allow developers to connect PARTS applications to on-line transaction applications. This tool has been described as the first object-oriented software tool that can obtain mainframe transactions and data. It will also be capable of transforming COBOL transactions running in a CICS (Customer Information Control System) environment into reusable assets that are simply assembled graphically by linking, pointing, and clicking [DAMO93].

It would be interesting to compare this system with one based on the Draco paradigm for developing software using high-level "domain languages" that reuse abstractions. The reuse level here is source code components such as functions and data types for C or other procedural languages, file and record organizations for COBOL, and objects and associated methods for Smalltalk/V.

There is some potential for treatment of higher-level systems such as larger, procedurally built systems; higher levels of file organization; multiple files; and multifaceted objects. This step, however, must clearly wait for the lower levels of the combined Digitalk-KnowledgeWare system to become a success in the marketplace.

There is one final point worth noting about the combined Digitalk-KnowledgeWare system. It is based on standards, at least for the source code languages. There are ANSI standards for both C and COBOL. Smalltalk compiler vendors have insisted that the language not include unnecessary, procedurally oriented features. Therefore, Smalltalk, like C and COBOL, is a relatively small language and presents few semantic difficulties for a compiler vendor (at least in comparison to the complexity of Ada or PL/M).

8.5   Issues with Network-Based Tools for Software Reuse

In this section I will briefly describe some of the issues associated with the use of network-based tools for software reuse. Most of the discussion applies equally to groupware such as Lotus Notes, Ventana Systems Groupware, and the Internet itself using Java or similar languages. The Repository-Based Software Reuse project at NASA/Langley Research Flight Center is a good example of the use of network-based reuse libraries.

The key advantage of such organizations is that information can be shared easily. For example, a set of requirements for a system can be placed on line for easy access. Configuration management and access protection allow the requirements to be changed in a systematic manner if errors or omissions are found or if there are changes in technology that make some requirements obsolete.

It is much easier to analyze requirements if they are available on line. A function point analysis of a relatively large system with over a thousand distinct bulleted requirements can be obtained in a few days if the requirements are on line. It is simply necessary to download the requirements, save them in ASCII format, select the portion that represents the requirements traceability matrix, and import this into a spreadsheet. The rest of the analysis is straightforward, using standard techniques.

Note that a reuse library that is accessible from remote locations would have improved the environment described in the hypothetical case study presented in Sec. 7.5.

Summary

In this chapter we described some sample tools that can be used to support software reuse.

The InQuisiX Pro tool set is well suited to organizing and cataloging assets in a reuse library. It is implemented as a suite of tools that reside on top of the Lotus Notes system and works on most platforms that support Lotus Notes. It allows access to local repositories and to information stored on the World Wide Web. InQuisiX Pro is also helpful in performing domain analysis. It is one of the most commonly used commercial tools for software reuse.

The simple, text-based tool of Johnson, Ornburn, and Rugaber analyzes existing source code and can be used for reuse, maintenance, or reengineering of this code. The tool consists of a suite of simple programs using standard UNIX utilities such as sed, awk, and yacc.

The AT&T BaseWorX system supports reuse by object-oriented software engineering and the explicit use of standards. It is primarily intended for building object-oriented management applications. The tool works in a UNIX environment.

Many other tools are available to help with some or all aspects of a systematic process of software reuse.

Most CASE tools include a central repository for system information but do not provide easy access to reuse libraries other than those provided directly by the user, the compiler vendor, or the vendor of the CASE tool itself.

Further Reading

The best source of information for InQuisiX is the product documentation.

The paper by Johnson, Ornburn, and Rugaber was given at the IEEE software maintenance conference in Orlando, Florida. A complete reference can be found in Johnson, Ornburn, and Rugaber [JOHN92A]. Many other articles in the conference proceedings are also relevant to the topics of program understanding and restructuring.

There are several books on the UNIX utilities mentioned in this chapter. The simplest reference for awk and sed is by Dougherty [DOUG92] in the O'Reilly series on UNIX tools. The second edition of the book lex and yacc in the same series, by Levine, Mason, and Brown [LEVI92], has an excellent discussion of the technical intricacies of using yacc with other tools. The on-line documentation available on most UNIX systems is also informative, as are the standard UNIX manuals.

Information on the AT&T BaseWorX Applications Platform can be found in the relevant technical documentation and manuals. Information about the combined Digitalk-KnowledgeWare system can be obtained from either of the two vendors. Information on most of the other tools discussed in this chapter can be found in the references given in my discussion of these tools. Many of these tools are so new, however, that little other information can be found.

A recent article by Henninger [HENN95B] describes a retrieval tool named CodeFinder developed as part of a research project. The article also describes some criteria for evaluating retrieval tools.

Exercises

1. For your organization, which of the classes of tools described in this chapter is the most appropriate? Explain.

2. Locate some other tools for assisting in the software reuse process. Describe them in detail. (Get an examination copy if you can.)

3. Describe the potential use of hypertext in reuse of documentation.

References

[ADA83] American National Standards Institute, *Reference Manual for the Ada Programming Language,* ANSI-MIL-STD–1815A, 1983.

[ADA95] American National Standards Institute, *Reference Manual for the Ada Programming Language,* ISO/IEC 8652, 1995.

[ADLE95] Adler, R. M., "Emerging Standards for Component Software," *IEEE Computer,* vol. 28, no. 3, March 1995, pp. 68–77.

[AHRE95] Ahrens, J. D., and N. S. Prywes, "Transition to a Legacy- and Reuse-Based Software Life Cycle," *IEEE Computer,* vol. 28, no. 10, October 1995, pp. 27–36.

[ALBR79] Albrecht, A. J., "Measuring Application Development Productivity," *Proceedings of the IBM Applications Development Joint SHARE / GUIDE Symposium,* Monterey, California, 1979, pp. 83–92.

[ALBR83] Albrecht, A. J., and J. E. Gaffney Jr., "Source Lines of Code, and Development Effort Prediction: A Software Science Validation," *IEEE Transactions on Software Engineering,* SE-9, November 1983, pp. 639–48.

[ANDE88] Anderson, K. J., R. P. Bech, and T. E. Buonanno, "Reuse of Software Modules," *AT&T Technical Journal,* vol. 67, no. 4, July/August 1988, pp. 71–76.

[ANDL90] Andleigh, P., *UNIX System Architecture,* Prentice-Hall (Englewood Cliffs, New Jersey), 1990.

[ANSI91] American National Standards Institute "Standard Glossary of Software Engineering Terminology," ANSI/IEEE Standard 729–1991, 1991.

[ANSI92] American National Standards Institute "Recommended Practice for Software Reliability," ANSI/IEEE Standard R–012–1992, 1992.

[ANTH93] Anthes, G. H., "Software Reuse Plans Bring Paybacks," *Computerworld,* vol. 27, December 6, 1993, p. 73.

[ARNO92] Arnold, R. S., ed., *Software Reengineering,* IEEE Press (Los Alamitos, California), 1992.

[ARNO94] Arnold, T. R., and W. A. Fuson, "Testing in a Perfect World," *Communications of the ACM,* vol. 37, no. 9, September 1994, pp. 78–86.

[ATKI91] Atkinson, C., *Object-Oriented Reuse, Concurrency, and Distribution,* ACM Press (New York), 1991.

[ATT94] AT&T, *BaseWorX Applications Platform Technical Overview,* AT&T, 1994.

[BAIL92] Bailn, S., "KAPTUR, Elvis, Hendrix, and Other Acronyms: Domain Engineering at CTA," *Proceedings of the Fifth Workshop on Software Reuse,* WISR-5, 1992.

[BAKE79] Baker, A. L., and S. H. Zweben, "The Use of Software Science in Evaluating Modularity," *IEEE Transactions on Software Engineering,* SE-5, vol. 5, no. 3, 1979, pp. 110–20.

[BARB94] Barbey, S., and A. Strohmeier, "The Problematics of Testing Object-Oriented Software," *Proceedings of the Second Conference on Software Quality Management (SQM'94),* Edinburgh, Scotland, July 26–28, 1994, vol. 2, pp. 411–26.

[BARN91] Barnes, B., and T. Bollinger, "Making Reuse Cost Effective," *IEEE Software,* 1991.

[BASI88] Basili, V. R., and H. D. Rombach, "The TAME Project: Towards Improvement-Oriented Software Development," *IEEE Transactions on Software Engineering,* SE-14, vol. 14, no. 6, 1988, pp. 758–73.

[BASI90] Basili, V. R., "Viewing Maintenance as Ruse-Oriented Software Development," *IEEE Software,* vol. 7, no. 1, January 1990, pp. 19–25.

[BASI92] Basili, V. R., G. Caldiera, and G. Cantone, "A Reference Architecture for the Component Factory," *ACM Transactions on Software Engineering and Methodology,* vol. 1, no. 1, January 1992, pp. 53–80.

[BATO92] Batory, D., and S. O'Malley, "The Design and Implementation of Hierarchical Software Systems with Reusable Components," *ACM Transactions Software Engineering and Methodology,* vol. 1, no. 4, October 1992, pp. 355–98.

[BEAC92] Beach, B. W., "Declarative Programming for Component Interconnection," *Proceedings of the Fifth Workshop on Software Reuse,* WISR-5, 1992.

[BECK92] Beck, R. P., S. R. Desac, D. R. Ryan, R. W. Tower, D. Q. Vroom, and L. M. Wood, "Architectures for Large-Scale Reuse," *AT&T Technical Journal,* vol. 71, no. 6, November/December 1992, pp. 34–45.

[BEHR87] Behrens, C. A., "Measuring the Productivity of Computer Systems Development Activities with Function Points," *IEEE Transactions of Software Engineering,* SE-13, vol. 13, no. 1, 1987, pp. 311–23.

[BEIZ83] Beizer, B., *Software Testing Techniques,* Van Nostrand Reinhold (New York), 1983.

[BEIZ90] Beizer, B., *Software Testing Techniques,* 2d ed., Van Nostrand Reinhold (New York), 1990.

[BERA93] Berard, E. V., *Essays on Object-Oriented Software Engineering,* vol. 1, Prentice-Hall (Englewood Cliffs, New Jersey), 1993.

[BETH85] Bethea, R. M., B. S. Duran, and T. L. Boullon, *Statistical Methods for Engineers and Scientists,* 2d ed., Marcel Dekker (New York), 1985.

[BIEM95] Bieman, J. M., and J. X. Zhao, "Reuse through Inheritance: A Quantitative Study of C++ Software," *Proceedings of the ACM-SIGSOFT Symposium on Software Reusability,* Seattle, Washington, April 28–30, 1995.

[BIEM95] Bieman, J. M., and S. Karunanithi, "Measurement of Language-Supported Reuse in Object-Oriented and Object-Based Software," *Journal of Systems Software,* vol. 30, no. 3, September 1995, pp. 271–93.

[BIGG87] Biggerstaff, T., and C. Richter, "Reusability Framework, Assessment, and Directions," *IEEE Software,* vol. 4, no. 2, March 1987, pp. 41–49.

[BIGG89] Biggerstaff, T., and A. Perlis, eds., *Software Reusability,* vol. 1, 2, ACM Press (New York), 1989.

[BIND94] Binder, R. V., "Design for Testability in Object-Oriented Systems," *Communications of the ACM,* vol. 37, no. 9, September 1994, pp. 87–101.

[BOEH78] Boehm, B., J. R. Brown, G. J. MacLeod, and M. J. Merritt, *Characteristics of Software Quality,* Elsevier North-Holland (New York), 1978.

[BOEH81] Boehm, B., *Software Engineering Economics,* Prentice-Hall (Englewood Cliffs, New Jersey), 1981.

[BOEH88] Boehm, B., "A Spiral Model of Software Development and Enhancement," *IEEE Computer,* vol. 21, no. 2, February 1988, pp. 61–72.

[BOLL90] Bollinger, T., and S. L. Pfleeger, "Economics of Reuse: Issues and Alternatives," *Information and Software Technology,* vol. 32, no. 10, December 1990, pp. 643–52.

[BOLL95] Bollinger, T., "Quality Time Column," *IEEE Software,* vol. 12, 1995.

[BOOC83] Booch, G., *Software Engineering with Ada,* Benjamin Cummings (Menlo Park, California), 1987.

[BOOC87A] Booch, G., *Software Engineering with Ada,* 2d ed., Benjamin Cummings (Redwood City, California), 1987.

[BOOC87B] Booch, G., *Software Components with Ada: Structure, Tools, and Subsystems,* Benjamin Cummings (Menlo Park, California), 1987.

[BOOC91] Booch, G., *Software Engineering with Ada,* 3d ed., with D. Bryan and C. G. Petersen; Benjamin Cummings (Redwood City, California), 1991.

[BOOC94] Booch, G., *Object-Oriented Analysis and Design with Applications,* Benjamin Cummings (Redwood City, California), 1994.

[BOX78] Box, G. E. P., W. J. Hunter, and J. S. Hunter, *Statistics for Experimenters,* John Wiley & Sons (New York), 1978.

[BRAC95] Bracken, M. R., S. L. Hoge, C. Sary, R. Rashkin, R. D. Pendley, and R. D. Werking, "IMACCS: An Operational COTS-Based Ground System Proof-of-Concept Project," *Proceedings of the European Space Conference,* 1995, pp. 37.1–37.8.

[BROD95] Brodie, M. L., and M. Stonebreaker, *Migrating Legacy Systems: Gateways, Interfaces, and the Incremental Approach,* IEEE Press (Los Alamitos, California), 1995.

[BUCH89] Buchman, C. D., "Practical Advice for Designing Ada Systems," *Proceedings of the Seventh Annual National Conference on Ada Technology,* Atlantic City, New Jersey, March 13–16, 1989, pp. 549–56.

[BUDD94] Budd, T., *Classic Data Structures in C++,* Addison-Wesley (Reading, Massachusetts), 1994.

[BUHR90] Buhr, R., *Practical Visual Techniques in System Design with Applications in Ada,* Prentice-Hall (Englewood Cliffs, New Jersey), 1990.

[BURT87] Burton, B. A., R. W. Aragon, S. A. Bailey, K. D. Koehler, and L. A. Mayes, "The Reusable Software Library," IEEE Software, vol. 4, no. 4, July 1987, pp. 25–33.

[CALD91] Caldiera, G., and V. R. Basili, "Implementing Faceted Classification for Software Reuse," *Computer,* vol. 24, no. 2, February 1991, pp. 61–70.

[CARD86] Card, D., V. E. Church, and W. W. Agresti, "An Empirical Study of Software Design Practices," *IEEE Transactions on Software Engineering,* SE-12, vol. 12, 1986, pp. 264–271.

[CARD94] Card, D., and D. E. Comer, "Quality Time Section: Why Do So Many Reuse Projects Fail?" *IEEE Software,* vol. 11, no. 5, September 1994, pp. 114–15.

[CHIK90] Chikofsky, E., and J. Cross, "Reverse Engineering and Design Recovery: A Taxonomy," *IEEE Software,* vol. 7, no. 1, January 1990.

[COAD91] Coad, P., and E. Yourdon, *Object-Oriented Analysis,* 2d ed., Prentice-Hall (Englewood Cliffs, New Jersey), 1991.

[COLL92] Collins, P., "Considering Corporate Culture in Institutionalizing Reuse," *Proceedings of the Fifth Workshop on Software Reuse,* WISR-5, 1992.

[COLL93] Collins, P., "Toward A Reusable Domain Analysis," *Proceedings of the Sixth Workshop on Software Reuse,* WISR-6, 1993.

[COLL95] Collins, P., and B. Zimmer, "Evolutionary Metrics Adoption Method for Reuse Adoption," *Proceedings of the Seventh Workshop on Software Reuse,* WISR-7, 1995.

[CONT86] Conte, S. D., H. E. Dunsmore, and V. Y. Shen, *Software Engineering Metrics and Models,* Benjamin Cummings (Menlo Park, California), 1986.

[CORB] CORBA "Common Object-Oriented Request Broker Architecture Specification 2.0," Object Management Group, Framingham, Mass., 1995.

[CORC93] Corcoran, E., "Soft Lego," *Scientific American,* vol. 268, January 1993, p. 145.

[CSC91] Computer Sciences Corporation, "SEL Ada Reuse Study Report," CSC/TM-91-6065 (552-FDD-91-034) May 1991.

[DATE95] Date, C. J., *An Introduction to Database Systems,* 6th ed., Addison-Wesley (Reading, Massachusetts), 1995.

[DAVI95] Davis, M. J., "Adaptable, Reusable Code," *Proceedings of the Symposium on Software Reusability,* SSR'95, Seattle, Washington, April 28–30, 1995, pp. 38–46.

[DEIT94] Deitel, H. M., and P. J. Deitel, *C++ How to Program,* Prentice-Hall (Englewood Cliffs, New Jersey), 1994.

[DELR94] DelRossi, R. A., L. Schneider, and J. Spragnes, "PARTS Workbench for Win32 version 2.0," *InfoWorld,* vol. 16, February 14, 1994, p. 66.

[DEMI87] DeMillo, R. A., W. M. McCraken, R. J. Martin, and J. F. Passafiume, *Software Testing and Evaluation,* Benjamin Cummings (Menlo Park, California), 1987.

[DHAM95] Dhama, H., "Quantitative Models of Cohesion and Coupling in Software," *Journal of Systems Software,* vol. 29, 1995, pp. 65–74.

[DISA93] Defense Information Systems Agency, "Domain Analysis and Design Process," Defense Information Systems Agency Center for Information Management (CIM) Software Reuse Office, Document #1222-04-210/30.1, 1993.

[DOUG92] Dougherty, D., *sed and awk,* O'Reilly & Associates (Sebastopol, California), 1992.

[DROM95] Dromey, R. G., "A Model for Software Product Quality," *IEEE Transactions on Software Engineering,* SE-21, vol. 21, no. 2, February 1995, pp. 146–62.

[EICH96] Eichmann, D., "The RBSE Spider-Balancing Effective Search Against Web Load," *Proceedings of the First International Conference on the World Wide Web,* CERN, Geneva, Switzerland, May 25–27, 1996.

[ELLI90] Ellis, M., and B. Stroustrup, *The Annotated C++ Reference Manual,* Addison-Wesley (Reading, Massachusetts), 1990.

[ELLI95] Ellis, T., "COTS Integration in Software Solutions—a Cost Model," in *Systems Engineering in the Global Marketplace, NCOSE International Symposium,* St. Louis, Missouri, July 24–26, 1995.

[FACT88] Factor, R. M., and W. B. Smith, "A Discipline for Improving Software Productivity," *AT&T Technical Journal,* vol. 67, no. 4, July/August 1988, pp. 2–9.

[FARC94] Farchamps, D., "Organizational Factors and Reuse," *IEEE Software,* vol. 11, no. 5, September 1994, pp. 31–41.

[FENT91] Fenton, N. E., *Software Metrics: A Rigorous Approach,* Chapman & Hall (London), 1991.

[FENT96] Fenton, N. E., and S. L. Pfleeger, *Software Metrics: A Rigorous Approach,* 2d ed., International Thomson Press (London), 1996.

[FINE91] Finelli, G. B., "NASA Software Failure Characterization Experiments," in B. Littlewood and D. R. Miller, eds., *Software Reliability and Safety,* Elsevier Science Publishers (London), 1991.

[FISC87] Fischer, G., "Cognitive Views of Reuse and Redesign," *IEEE Software,* vol. 4, no. 4, July 1987, pp. 60–72.

[FJEL79] Fjeldstad, R. K., and W. T. Hamlen, "Application Program Maintenance Study: Report to Our Respondents," *Proceedings GUIDE 48,* (Philadelphia, Pennsylvania), 1979.

[FOWL95] Fowler, G. S., D. G. Korn, and K.-P. Vo, "Principles for Writing Reusable Libraries," *Proceedings of the Symposium on Software Reusability,* SSR'95, Seattle, Washington, April 28–30, 1995, pp. 150–59.

[FRAK90] Frakes, W. B., and P. B. Gandel, "Representing Reusable Software," *Information and Software Technology,* vol. 32, no. 10, December 1990, pp. 653–61.

[FRAK93A] Frakes, W. B., "A Graduate Course on Software Reuse, Domain Analysis, and Reengineering," *Proceedings of the Sixth Workshop on Software Reuse,* WISR-6, 1993.

[FRAK93B] Frakes, W. B., ed., *Advances in Software Reuse: Selected Papers from the Second International Workshop on Software Reusability,* March 24–26, 1993, Luccia, Italy.

[FRAK94A] Frakes, W. B., and S. Isoda, "Success Factors for Systematic Reuse," *IEEE Software,* vol. 11, no. 5, September 1994, pp. 14–22.

[FRAK94B] Frakes, W. B., and T. P. Pole, "An Empirical Study of Representation Methods for Reusable Software Components," *IEEE Transactions on Software Engineering,* SE-20, no. 8, August 1994, pp. 617–30.

[FRAK94C] Frakes, W. B., ed., *Advances in Software Reuse: Selected Papers from the Third International Workshop on Software Reusability,* November 1–4, 1994, Rio de Janeiro, Brazil.

[FRAK95A] Frakes, W. B., and C. J. Fox, "Modeling Reuse Across the Software Life Cycle," *Journal of Systems Software,* vol. 30, no. 3, September 1995, pp. 295–301.

[FRAK95B] Frakes, W. B., and C. J. Fox, "Sixteen Questions about Software Reuse," *Communications of the ACM,* vol. 38, no. 6, June 1995, 75–87.

[FREE83] Freeman, P., "Reusable Software Engineering: Concepts and Research Directions," *ITT Proceedings of the Workshop on Reusability in Programming,* 1983, pp. 129–37.

[FREE87] Freeman, P., "Reusable Software Engineering: Concepts and Research Directions," *Tutorial: Software Reusability,* IEEE Computer Society Press (Los Alamitos, California), 1987, pp. 10–23.

[FULL94] Fuller, T. L., *Software Reuse Analysis for the Computer Science Department of Pacific Northwest Laboratory,* Battelle Pacific Northwest Laboratory Technical Report (Richland, Washington), August 1994.

[GAFF91] Gaffney, J., and R. D. Cruickshank, *A General Economics Model for Software Reuse,* Software Productivity Consortium, 1991, Reston, Va.

[GELM92] Gelman, S. J., F. M. Lax, and J. F. Maranzano, "Competing in Large-Scale Software Development," *AT&T Technical Journal,* vol. 71, no. 6, November/ December 1992, pp. 2–11.

[GAO93] General Accounting Office, "Software Reuse—Major Issues Need to Be Resolved before Benefits Can be Achieved," *GAO Report Number GAO/IMTEC-93-16, Washington, D.C., 1993*

[GILB87] Gilb, T., *Principles of Software Engineering Management,* Addison-Wesley (Reading, Massachusetts), 1987.

[GOGU86] Goguen, J. A., "Reusing and Interconnecting Software Components," *IEEE Computer,* February 1986, pp. 16–28.

[GOLD90] Goldberg, A., and K. S. Rubin, "Taming Object-Oriented Technology," *Computer Language,* vol. 7, no. 10, October 1990, pp.34–35.

[GOMA92] Gomaa, H., "Methods and Tools for Domain-Specific Software Architectures," *Proceedings of the Fifth Workshop on Software Reuse,* WISR-5, 1992.

[GOOD93] Goodman, M. A., M. Goyal, and R. A. Massoudi, *Solaris Porting Guide,* SunSoft Press (Mountain View, California), 1993.

[GOUL95] Goulde, M., "Developing a Reuse Strategy," *Open Computing,* vol. 12, no. 8, August 1, 1995, p. 29.

[GRAD87] Grady, R. B., and D. L. Caswell, *Software Metrics: Establishing a Company-Wide Program,* Prentice-Hall (Englewood Cliffs, New Jersey), 1987.

[GRAD94] Grady, R. B., "Successfully Applying Software Metrics," *IEEE Computer,* vol. 27, no. 9, September 1994, pp. 26–28.

[GRIS92] Griss, M. L., "A Multi-Disciplinary Software Reuse Research Program," *Proceedings of the Fifth Workshop on Software Reuse,* WISR-5, 1992.

[GRIS95] Griss, M. L., and M. Wasser, "Quality Time," column, *IEEE Software,* January 1995.

[GRIS93] Griss, M. L., "Software Reuse: From Library to Factory," *IBM Systems Journal,* vol. 32, no. 4, 1993.

[GUER94] Guerrieri, E., "Case Study: Digital's Application Generator," *IEEE Software,* vol. 11, no. 5, September 1994, pp. 95–96.

[HALL92] Hall, P. A. V., *Software Reuse and Reverse Engineering in Practice,* Chapman & Hall (London), 1992.

[HALS77] Halstead, M. H., *Elements of Software Science,* Elsevier North-Holland (New York), 1977.

[HARM91] Harms, D. E., and B. W. Weide, "Copying and Swapping: Influence on the Design of Reusable Software Components," *IEEE Transactions on Software Engineering,* SE-17, vol. 17, no. 5, May 1991, pp. 424–35.

[HARR92] Harrold, M. J., J. D. McGregor, and K. J. Fitzpatrick, "Incremental Testing of Object-Oriented Class Structures," *Proceedings of the Fourteenth International Conference on Software Engineering,* Melbourne, Australia, May 11–15, 1992, pp. 68–79.

[HASH92] Hashemi, R., and R. J. Leach, "Issues in Porting Software from C to C++," *Software—Practice & Experience,* vol. 22, no. 7, 1992, pp. 599–602.

[HENN91] Hennel, M. A., "Testing for the Achievement of Software Reliability," in B. Littlewood and D. R. Miller, eds., *Software Reliability and Safety,* Elsevier Science Publishers (London), 1991.

[HENN95A] Henninger, S., "Developing Domain Knowledge through the Reuse of Project Experience," *Proceedings of the Symposium on Software Reusability,* SSR'95, Seattle, Washington, April 28–30, 1995, pp. 186–95.

[HENN95B] Henninger, S., "Information Access Tools for Software Reuse," *Journal of Systems Software,* vol. 30, 1995, pp. 231–47.

[HENR81] Henry S., and D. Kafura, "Software Metrics Based on Information Flow, *IEEE Transactions on Software Engineering,* SE-7, no. 5, September 1981, pp. 510–18.

[HOLL91] Hollingsworth, J. E., B. W. Weide, and S. H. Zweben, "Confessions of Some Used-Program Clients," *Proceedings of the Fourth Annual Workshop on Software Reuse,* Herndon, Virginia, November 1991.

[HOOP91] Hooper, J. W., and R. Chester, *Software Reuse: Guidelines and Methods,* Plenum Press (New York), 1991.

[HOWD87] Howden, W. E., *Functional Program Testing and Analysis,* McGraw-Hill (New York), 1987.

[HUMP89] Humphrey, W., *Managing the Software Process,* Addison-Wesley (Reading, Massachusetts), 1989.

[HUMP95] Humphrey, W., *A Discipline for Software Engineering,* Addison-Wesley (Reading, Massachusetts), 1995.

[ICHB86] Ichbiah, J. D., J. G. P. Barnes, R. J. Firth, and M. Woodger, *Rationale for the Design of the Ada Programming Language,* ALSYS, France, 1986. Reprinted by Cambridge University Press, Cambridge, UK, 1991.

[IEEE88] Institute of Electrical and Electronics Engineers, *IEEE Standard Dictionary of Measures to Produce Reliable Software,* IEEE STD 982.1-1988, 1988.

[IEEE92A] Institute of Electrical and Electronics Engineers, *Standards for Software Productivity Metrics,* IEEE Standard 1045-1992, 1992.

[IEEE92B] Institute of Electrical and Electronics Engineers, *Standard for a Software Engineering Methodology,* IEEE STD 1061-1992, 1992.

[ISO87A] International Standards Organization, *Quality Systems-Model for Quality Assurance in Design / Development, Production, Installation, and Servicing,* ISO 9001, 1987.

[ISO87B] International Standards Organization, *Quality Systems-Model for Quality Assurance in Production and Installation,* ISO 9002, 1987.

[ISO87C] International Standards Organization, *Quality Systems-Model for Quality Assurance in Final Inspection and Test,* ISO 9003, 1987.

[ISO87D] International Standards Organization, *Quality Management and Quality Assurance Standards—Guidelines for Selection and Use,* ISO 9000, 1987.

[ISO91A] International Standards Organization, *Information Technology—Open Systems Interconnection—Systems Management Overview,* ISO/IEC IS 10040, 1991.

[ISO91B] International Standards Organization, *Information Technology—Open Systems Interconnection—Systems Management,* ISO/IEC IS 10164, 1991.

[ISO91C] International Standards Organization, *Information Technology—Open Systems Interconnection—Structure of Management Information—Part 1: Management Information Model,* ISO/IEC IS 10165-1, 1991.

[ISO91D] International Standards Organization, *Information Technology—Open Systems Interconnection—Part 4: Guidelines for the Definition of Managed Objects,* ISO/IEC IS 10165-4, 1991.

[JELI72] Jelinski, F., and P. B. Moranda, "Software Reliability Research," in *Statistical Computer Performance Evaluation,* W. Freiberger, ed., Academic Press (New York), 1972, pp. 465–84.

[JENG95] Jeng, J-J., and B. H. C. Chen, "Specification Matching for Software Reuse: A Foundation," *Proceedings of the ACM-SIGSOFT Symposium on Software Reusability,* Seattle, Washington, April 28–30, 1995.

[JOHN92A] Johnson, B., S. Ornburn, and S. Rugaber, "A Quick Tools Strategy for Program Analysis and Software Maintenance," *Proceedings of the IEEE Conference on Software Maintenance,* Orlando, Florida, November 9–12, 1992, pp. 206–13.

[JOHN92B] Johnson, J. A., B. A. Nardi, C. L. Zarmer, and J. R. Miller, "ACE: An Application Construction Environment," *Proceedings of the Fifth Workshop on Software Reuse,* WISR-5, 1992.

[JOHN86] Johnson, L. F., and R. H. Cooper, *File Techniques for Data Base Organization in COBOL,* 2d ed., Prentice-Hall (Englewood Cliffs, New Jersey), 1986.

[JOHN88] Johnson, R. E., and B. Foote, "Designing Reusable Classes," *Journal of Object-Oriented Programming,* 1988, vol. 1, no. 2, pp. 22–35.

[JONE84] Jones, T. Capers, "Reusability in Programming: A Survey of the State of the Art," *IEEE Transactions on Software Engineering,* SE-10, no. 5, September 1984, pp. 488–94.

[JONE] Jones, T. Capers, "Assessment and Control of Software Risks,"

[JOOS94] Joos, R. "Software Reuse at Motorola," *IEEE Software,* vol. 11, no. 5, September 1994, pp. 42–47.

[JORG94] Jorgenson, P. C., and C. Erikson, "Object-Oriented Integration Testing," *Communications of the ACM,* vol. 37, no. 9, September 1994, pp. 30–38.

[KAFU81] Kafura, D., and S. Henry, "Software Quality Metrics Based on Interconnectivity," *Journal of System Software,* vol. 2, 1981, pp. 121–31.

[KAIS87] Kaiser, G. E., and D. Garland, "Melding Software Systems from Reusable Building Blocks," *IEEE Software,* vol. 4, no. 4, July 1987, pp. 17–24.

[KAMA93] Kamath, Y. H., R. E. Smilan, and J. G. Smith, "Reaping Benefits with Object-Oriented Technology," *AT&T Technical Journal,* vol. 72, no. 5, September/October 1993, pp. 14–24.

[KARL95] Karlsonn, E.-A., *Software Reuse: A Holistic Approach,* John Wiley & Sons (New York), 1995.

[KEIL83] Keiller, P. A., B. Littlewood, D. R. Miller, and A. Sofer, "Comparison of Software Reliability Predictions," *Proceedings of the Thirteenth International Symposium on Fault-Tolerant Computing,* IEEE Computer Society Press (Washington, D.C.), 1983, pp. 128–34.

[KEIL91] Keiller, P. A., and D. R. Miller, "Software Reliability Growth Models," in B. Littlewood and D. R. Miller, eds., *Software Reliability and Safety,* Elsevier Science Publishers (London), 1991.

[KERN82] Kernighan, B., and D. Ritchie, *The C Programming Language,* Prentice-Hall (Englewood Cliffs, New Jersey), 1982.

[KERN84] Kernighan, B., "The UNIX System and Software Reusability," *IEEE Transactions on Software Engineering,* SE-10, vol. 10, no. 5, September 1984, pp. 513–18.

[KERN88] Kernighan, B., and D. Ritchie, *The C Programming Language,* 2d ed., Prentice-Hall (Englewood Cliffs, New Jersey), 1988.

[KONT95] Kontio, J., "OTSO: A Systematic Process for Reusable Software Component Selection," University of Maryland, College Park, Technical Report CS-TR-3478, UMIACS-TR-95-63, December 1995.

[KRIS95] Krishnamurthy, B., *Practical Reusable UNIX Software,* John Wiley & Sons (New York), 1995.

[KRUE92] Krueger, C. W., "Software Reuse," *ACM Computing Surveys,* vol. 24, no. 2, June 1992, pp. 131–83.

[LAMO95] LaMonica, M., "Object Code Is Not Spurring Reuse by IS," *Infoworld,* vol. 17, no. 39, August 21, 1995, pp. 19–20.

[LEA92] Lea, D., and D. de Champeaux, "Object-Oriented Software Reuse Technical Opportunities," *Proceedings of the Fifth Workshop on Software Reuse,* WISR-5, 1992.

[LEAC93A] Leach, N., "Digitalk Moves PARTS Workbench to 32-bit Windows," *PC Week,* vol. 10, December 20, 1993, p. 45.

[LEAC94A] Leach, N., "KnowledgeWare Links with Digitalk Products," *PC Week,* vol. 11, April 18, 1994, p. 53.

[LEAC89] Leach, R. J., "Software Engineering Aspects of the Ada Repository," *Proceedings of the Seventh Annual National Conference on Ada Technology,* Atlantic City, New Jersey, March 13–16, 1989, pp. 270–77.

[LEAC93B] Leach, R. J., *Using C in Software Design,* Academic Press Professional (Boston), 1993.

[LEAC94B] Leach, R. J., *Advanced Topics in UNIX,* John Wiley & Sons (New York), 1994.

[LEAC95A] Leach, R. J., *Object-Oriented Design and Programming in C++,* Academic Press Professional (Boston), 1995.

[LEAC95B] Leach, R. J., and T. L. Fuller, "An Illustration of the Domain Analysis Process," *Software Engineering Notes,* ACM, vol. 20, no. 5, December 1995, pp. 79–82.

[LEAC97] Leach, R. J., and D. M. Coleman, "A Software Metric That Predicts Both Errors and Testing Effort," to appear.

[LEDB85] Ledbetter, L., and B. Cox, "Software-ICs: A Plan for Building Reusable Software Components," *BYTE,* June 1985, pp. 28–35.

[LEVE86] Leveson, N. G., "Software Safety: What, Why and How," *ACM Computing Surveys,* vol. 18, no. 2, 1986, pp. 125–63.

[LEVI92] Levine, J. R., T. Mason, and D. Brown, *lex and yacc,* 2d ed., O'Reilly & Associates (Sebastopol, California), 1992.

[LILL93] Lillie, C., "Software Reuse," *Proceedings of the Second Annual Reuse Education and Training Workshop,* Morgantown, West Virginia, October 1993.

[LIM94] Lim, W. C., "Effects of Reuse on Quality, Productivity, and Economics," *IEEE Software,* vol. 11, no. 5, September 1994, pp. 23–30.

[LIM95] Lim, W. C., *Managing Software Reuse,* Prentice-Hall (Englewood Cliffs, New Jersey), 1995.

[LIND94] Lindholm, E., "Snap-on Code," *Datamation,* vol. 40, February 1, 1994, p. 63.

[LITT91] Littlewood, B., and D. R. Miller, eds., *Software Reliability and Safety,* Elsevier Science Publishers (London), 1991. (Also in *Reliability Engineering and System Safety,* vol. 32, nos. 1 and 2, 1991.)

[LUQI88] Lugi, , and M. Ketabchi, "A Computer-Aided Prototyping System," *IEEE Software,* vol. 5, no. 2, March 1988, pp. 66–72.

[MACE94] Mace, S., "KnowledgeWare, Digitalk Building Link," *InfoWorld,* vol. 16, April 4, 1994, p. 26.

[MAHM93] Mahmot, R., *TPOCC: A Satellite Control Center System Kernel That Fosters High Reuse and Lower Cost,* NASA internal document, 1993.

[MAHM94] Mahmot, R., J. Koslosky, E. Beach, and B. Schwarz, "Transportable Payload Operations Control Center Reusable Software: Building Blocks for Quality Ground Data Systems," *Proceedings of the Third International Symposium on Space Mission Operations and Ground Data Systems,* vol. 2, November 15–18, 1994, NASA Goddard Space Flight Center, Greenbelt, Maryland, pp. 1161–1169, NASA Publication 3281.

[MALA93] Malan, R., "Motivating Software Reuse," *Proceedings of the Sixth Workshop on Software Reuse,* WISR-6, 1993.

[MATS89] Matsumoto, Y., and Y. Ohno, *Japanese Perspectives in Software Engineering,* Prentice-Hall (Englewood Cliffs, New Jersey), 1989.

[McCA76] McCabe, T. J., "A Complexity Measure," *IEEE Transactions on Software Engineering,* SE-2, December 1976, pp. 308–20.

[McCL92] McClure, C., *The Three R's of Software Automation: Reengineering, Repository, Reusability,* Prentice-Hall (Englewood Cliffs, New Jersey), 1992.

[McGA93] McGarry, F., R. Mahmot, J. Costenbader, K. Tasaki, B. Drake, E. Seidewitz, and B. Kelly, "Software Reuse in the Mission Operations and Data Systems Directorate (Code 500)," *Report of the Software Reuse Red Team,* NASA, April 1993.

[McGR94] McGregor, J. D., and T. D. Korson, "Integrating Object-Oriented Testing and Development Processes," *Communications of the ACM,* vol. 37, no. 9, September 1994, pp. 59–77.

[McIL68] McIlroy, M. D., "Mass Produced Software Components," in *Software Engineering Concepts and Techniques, Proceedings of the 1968 NATO Conference on Software Engineering,* Petrocelli/Charter, Brussels, Belgium, 1968, pp. 88–98.

[MEYE87] Meyer, B., "Reusability: The Case for Object-Oriented Design," *IEEE Software,* vol. 4, March 1987, pp. 50–63.

[MILI93] Mili, H., F. Mili, and A. Mili, "Reusing Software: Issues and Research Directions," *IEEE Transactions on Software Engineering,* SE-21, vol. 21, no. 6, June 1993, pp. 528–61.

[MILL78] Miller, E., and W. E. Howden, *Software Testing and Validation Techniques,* IEEE Computer Society (Long Beach, California), 1978.

[MILL83] Miller, E., and W. E. Howden, *Software Testing and Validation Techniques,* 2d ed., IEEE Computer Society (Long Beach, California), 1983.

[MILL87] Mills, H. D., M. Dyer, and R. C. Linger, "Cleanroom Software Engineering," *IEEE Software,* vol. 4, September 1987, pp. 19–24.

[MOD92] Waybright, R. L., *Mission Operations Division (MOD) Automated Information System (AIS) Security Handbook,* NASA Goddard Space Flight Center, Greenbelt, Maryland, Publication 510-ISHB/0192, 1992.

[MONT91] Montgomery, D. C., *Introduction to Statistical Quality Control,* John Wiley & Sons (New York), 1991.

[MOOR91] Moore, J. M., and S. C. Bailin, "Domain Analysis: Framework for Reuse," in *Domain Analysis and Software Systems Modeling,* R. Prieto-Diaz and G. Arango, eds., IEEE Press (Los Alamitos, California), 1991.

[MURP94] Murphy, G. C., P. Townsend, and P. S. Wong, "Experiences with Cluster and Class Testing," *Communications of the ACM,* vol. 37, no. 9, September 1994, pp. 39–47.

[MUSA87] Musa, J. D., A. Iannino, and K. Okumoto, *Software Reliability: Measurement, Prediction, Application,* McGraw-Hill (New York), 1987.

[MUSA93] Musa, J. D., "Operational Profiles in Software Reliability Engineering," *IEEE Software,* vol. 10, no. 2, March 1993, pp. 14–32.

[MUSE92] Musen, M. A., "Dimensions of Knowledge Sharing and Reuse," *Computers and Biomedical Research,* vol. 25, 1992, pp. 435–67.

[MYER76] Myers, J. G., *Software Reliability: Principles and Practices,* John Wiley & Sons (New York), 1976.

[MYER79] Myers, J. G., *The Art of Software Testing,* John Wiley & Sons (New York), 1979.

[MYER95] Myers, W., "Taligent's Common Point: The Promise of Objects," *IEEE Computer,* vol. 28, no. 3, March 1995, pp. 77–83.

[NASA88] National Aeronautics and Space Administration, "Software Reuse Issues," *Proceedings of the 1988 Workshop on Software Reuse,* NASA Langley Research Center, Melbourne, Florida, November 17–18, 1988.

[NASA92A] National Aeronautics and Space Administration, *Proceedings of the Second NASA Workshop on Software Reuse,* NASA (Research Triangle Park, North Carolina), May 5–6, 1992.

[NASA92B] National Aeronautics and Space Administration, "Software Engineering Program: Profile of Software within Code 500 at Goddard Space Flight Center," *NASA SEP Report R01-92,* December 1992.

[NAVA92] Navarro, J. J., "Organization Design for Software Reuse," *Proceedings of the Fifth Workshop on Software Reuse,* WISR-5, 1992.

[NIST92] National Institute for Standards and Technology, *Management Information Catalog,* Issue 1, June 1992, NIST, OIW, and Network Management Forum, Gaithersburg, Maryland. (There are subsequent catalogs.)

[NIST95] National Institute for Standards and Technology, *Glossary of Software Reuse Terms,* S. Katz, C. Dabrowski, K. Miles, and M. Law, eds., Gaithersburg, Maryland, 1995.

[PARN72] Parnas, D. L., "On the Criteria for Decomposing Systems into Modules," *Communications of the ACM,* vol. 15, no. 12, 1972, pp. 1052–58.

[PARN85] Parnas, D. L., P. C. Clements, and D. M. Weiss, "The Modular Structure of Complex Systems," *IEEE Transactions on Software Engineering,* March 1985, pp. 259–66.

[PERR90] Perry, D., and G. Kaiser, "Adequate Testing and Object-Oriented Programming," *Journal of Object-Oriented Programming,* vol. 3, no. 1, January/February 1990.

[PFLE89] Pfleeger, S. L., *Software Engineering: The Production of Quality Software,* 2d ed., Macmillan (New York), 1991.

[PFLE91] Pfleeger, S. L., "Model of Software Effort and Productivity," *Information Software and Technology,* vol. 33, no. 3, April 1991, pp. 224–31.

[PFLE94A] Pfleeger, S. L., and T. B. Bollinger, "The Economics of Reuse: New Approaches to Modelling and Assessing Cost," *Information and Software Technology,* vol. 36, no. 8, August 1994, pp. 475–84.

[PFLE94B] Pfleeger, S. L., N. Fenton, and S. Page, "Evaluating Software Engineering Standards," *IEEE Computer,* vol. 27, no. 9, September 1994, pp. 71–79.

[PFLE96] Pfleeger, S. L., "Measuring Reuse: A Cautionary Tale," *IEEE Software,* vol. 13, no. 4, July 1996, pp. 118–127.

[PLAU92] Plauger, P. J., *The Standard C Library,* Prentice-Hall (Englewood Cliffs, New Jersey), 1992.

[PLAU94] Plauger, P. J., *The Draft Standard C++ Library,* Prentice-Hall (Englewood Cliffs, New Jersey), 1994.

[PLES92] Pleszkoch, M. G., R. C. Linger, and A. R. Hevner, "Eliminating non-Transferable Paths from Structured Programs," *Proceedings of the IEEE Conference on Software Maintenance,* Orlando, Florida, November 9–12, 1992, pp. 156–164.

[POHL89] Pohl, I., *C++ for C Programmers,* Benjamin Cummings (Redwood City, California), 1989.

[POST94] Poston, R. M., "Automated Testing from Object Models," *Communications of the ACM,* vol. 37, no. 9, September 1994, pp. 48–58.

[POUL94] Poulin, J. S., "Measuring Software Reusability," *Proceedings of the Third International Workshop on Software Reuse,* November 1–4, 1994, Rio de Janeiro, Brazil.

[POUL95] Poulin, J. S., and K. J. Werkman, "Melding Structured Abstracts and the World Wide Web for Retrieval of Reusable Components," *Proceedings of the Symposium on Software Reusability,* SSR'95, Seattle, Washington, April 28–30, 1995, pp. 160–68.

[PRES92] Pressman, R., *Software Engineering: A Practitioner's Approach,* 3d ed., McGraw-Hill (New York), 1992.

[PRIE91A] Prieto-Diaz, R., "Implementing Faceted Classification for Software Reuse," *Communications of the ACM,* vol. 34, no. 5, May 1991, pp. 88–97.

[PRIE91B] Prieto-Diaz, R., and G. Arango, eds., *Domain Analysis and Software Systems Modeling,* IEEE Press (Los Alamitos, California), 1991.

[PRIE93A] Prieto-Diaz, R., "Status Report: Software Reusability," *IEEE Software,* May 1993, pp. 61–66.

[PRIE93B] Prieto-Diaz, R., "Some Experiences in Domain Analysis," *Proceedings of the Sixth Workshop on Software Reuse,* WISR-6, 1993.

[PUTN78] Putnam, L. H., "A General Empirical Solution to the Macro Software Size and Estimation Problem, *IEEE Transactions on Software Engineering,* SE-4, vol. 4, no. 4, July 1978, pp. 345–61.

[RADA95] Rada, R., *Software Reuse,* Intellect, Oxford, England, 1995.

[RAMA82] Ramamoorthy, C. V., and F. B. Bastiani, "Software Reliability—Status and Perspectives," *IEEE Transactions on Software Engineering,* SE-8, vol. 8, no. 4, July 1982, pp. 354–71.

[RAMA88] Ramamoorthy, C. V., V. Garg, and A. Prakash, "Support for Reusability: Genesis," *IEEE Transactions on Software Engineering,* SE-14, vol. 14, no. 8, 1988, pp. 1145–54.

[RATC90] Ratcliffe, B., and A. L. Rollo, "Adapting Function Point Analysis to the Jackson System Development," *Software Engineering Journal,* vol. 5, no. 1, 1990.

[RAY92] Ray, G., "Software Reuse Not a Panacea; Some Firms Pursue It As a Development Goal; Others Question Its Viability," *Computerworld,* vol. 26, December 21, 1992, p. 47.

[REIF95] Reifer, D. J., *Managing Software Reuse,* John Wiley & Sons (New York), 1995.

[RENS88] Renshaw, L., "Eliminating GOTOs While Preserving Program Structure," *Journal of the ACM,* vol. 35, no. 4, October 1988, pp. 893–920.

[RIX92] Rix, M., "Case Study of a Successful Firmware Reuse Program," *Proceedings of the Fifth Workshop on Software Reuse,* WISR-5, 1992.

[ROMB91] Rombach, H. D., "Software Reuse: A Key to the Maintenance Problem," *Information and Software Technology,* vol. 33, no. 1, January/February 1991, pp. 86–92.

[RUBI90] Rubin, H., *The Rubin Review,* vol. 3, no. 3, July 1990.

[SAMU94] Samuelson, P., "Self-Plagiarism or Fair Use?" *Communications of the ACM,* vol. 37, no. 8, August 1994, pp. 21–25.

[SAAT80] Saaty, T. L., *The Analytic Hierarchy Process,* McGraw-Hill, New York, 1980.

[SCHA94] Schaefer, W., R. Prieto-Diaz, and M. Matsumoto, eds., *Software Reusability,* Ellis-Horwood (New York), 1994.

[SCHN87] Schneidewind, N. F., "The State of Software Maintenance," *IEEE Transactions on Software Engineering,* SE-13, vol. 13, no. 3, 1987, pp. 303–10.

[SEAT95] Seaton, B. L., "Improving Software Project Estimation within the Missions Operation and Systems Development Division," Management Project for Course CSMN 690, University of Maryland University College Graduate School, College Park, Maryland, 1995.

[SEL91] Software Engineering Laboratory, *Proceedings of the Sixteenth Annual NASA / Goddard Software Engineering Workshop: Experiments in Software*

Engineering, NASA/Goddard Space Flight Center, Greenbelt, Maryland, December 1991.

[SEL94] Software Engineering Laboratory, *Software Measurement Handbook,* NASA/Goddard Space Flight Center, Greenbelt, Maryland, SEL-94-002, 1994.

[SEL95] Software Engineering Laboratory, *Impact of Ada and Object-Oriented Design in the Flight Dynamics Division at Goddard Space Flight Center,* NASA/Goddard Space Flight Center, Greenbelt, Maryland, March 1995.

[SHOO83] Shooman, M. L., *Software Engineering: Design, Reliability, and Management,* McGraw-Hill (New York), 1983.

[SHRI89] Shriver, B., and P. Wegner, *Research Directions in Object-Oriented Programming,* MIT Press (Cambridge, Massachusetts), March 1989.

[SINC94] Sinclair, G. C., and K. F. Jeletic, "Profile of Software Engineering within the National Aeronautics and Space Administration (NASA)," *Proceedings of the Nineteenth Annual Software Engineering Workshop,* Greenbelt, Maryland, November 30–December 1, 1994.

[SITA93] Sitaraman, M., L. R. Welch, and D. E. Harms, "On Specification of Reusable Software Components," *International Journal of Software Engineering and Knowledge Engineering,* vol. 3, June 1993, pp. 207–29.

[SORD78], Sordillo, D. A., *The Programmer's ANSI COBOL Reference Manual,* Prentice-Hall (Englewood Cliffs, New Jersey), 1978.

[SPIV88] Spivey, J. M., *The Z notation: A Reference Manual,* Prentice-Hall International (London), 1988.

[SRAH95] "Software Reengineering Assessment Handbook," Defense Logistics Agency, Fort Belvoir, Va., 1995.

[STEV92] Stevens, W. R., "Applications Programming in the UNIX Environment," Addison-Wesley, Reading, Mass., 1992.

[STRO82] Stroustrup, B., "Classes: An Abstract Data Type Faculty for the C Language," *ACM SIGPLAN Notices,* vol. 17, no. 1, January 1982, pp. 42–52.

[STRO84] Stroustrup, B., "Data Abstraction in C," *AT&T Bell Laboratories Technical Journal,* vol. 63, no. 8, October 1984, pp. 1701–32.

[STRO91] Stroustrup, B., *The C++ Programming Language,* 2d ed., Addison-Wesley (Reading, Massachusetts), 1991.

[STRO94] Stroustrup, B., *The Design and Evolution of C++,* Addison-Wesley (Reading, Massachusetts), 1994.

[TATE91] Tate, G., and J. M. Verner, "Approaches to Measuring Size of Application Products with CASE Tools," *Information and Software Technology,* vol. 33, no. 9, November 1991, pp. 622–28.

[TRAC88] Tracz, W., *Software Reuse: Emerging Technology,* IEEE Press (Washington, D.C.), 1988.

[TRAC95] Tracz, W., *Confessions of a Used Program Salesman: Institutionalizing Software Reuse,* Addison-Wesley (Reading, Massachusetts), 1995.

[UDEL94] Udell, J., "Componentware," *BYTE,* vol. 19, no. 5, May 1994, pp. 46–56.

[VERN89] Verner, J. M., G. Tate, B. Jackson, and R. G. Haywood, "Technology Dependence in Function Point Analysis: A Case Study and Critical Review," *Proceedings of the Twelfth International Conference on Software Engineering,* 1989, pp. 375–82.

[VOAS95A] Voas, J., J. Payne, J. R. Mills, and J. McManus, "Software Testability: An Experiment in Measuring Simulation Reusability," *Proceedings of the ACM-SIG-SOFT Symposium on Software Reusability,* Seattle, Washington, April 28–30, 1995.

[VOAS95B] Voas, J. M., and K. W. Miller, "Software Testability: The New Verification," *IEEE Software,* vol. 12, no. 3, May 1995, pp. 17–28.

[WALT95] Walton, G. H., J. H. Poore, and C. J. Trammell, "Statistical Testing of a Usage Model," *Software—Practice and Experience,* vol. 25, no. 1, January 1995, pp. 97–108.

[WARD89] Ward M., F. W. Calliss, and M. Munro, "The Maintainer's Assistant," *Proceedings of Conference on Software Maintenance 1989,* Miami, Florida, October 1989, pp. 307–15.

[WAUN95] Waund, C., "COTS Integration and Support Model," in *Systems Engineering in the Global Marketplace: NCOSE International Symposium,* St. Louis, Missouri, July 24–26, 1995.

[WENT92] Wentzel, K., "Software Reuse—It's a Business," *Proceedings of the Fifth Workshop on Software Reuse,* WISR-5, 1992.

[WEYU86] Weyuker, E., "Axiomatizing Software Test Data Adequacy," *IEEE Transactions on Software Engineering,* vol. 12, no. 12, December 1986, pp. 1128–38.

[WEYU88] Weyuker, E., "Evaluating Software Complexity Measures," *IEEE Transactions on Software Engineering,* SE-14, 1988, pp. 1357–65.

[WILK95] Wilkening, D. E., J. P. Loyall, M. J. Pitarys, and K. Littlejohn, "A Reuse Approach to Software Reengineering," *Journal of Systems Software,* vol. 30, nos. 1–2, July/August 1995, pp. 117–25.

[WOHL94] Wohlin, C., and P. Runeson, "Certification of Software Components," *IEEE Transactions on Software Engineering,* vol. 20, no. 6, June 1994, pp. 494–99.

[YOUR79] Yourdon, E., and L. Constantine, *Structured Design: Fundamentals of a Discipline of Computer Program and System Design,* Prentice-Hall (Englewood Cliffs, New Jersey), 1979.

[YOUR89] Yourdon, E., *Modern Structured Analysis,* Prentice-Hall (Englewood Cliffs, New Jersey), 1989.

[ZARE95] Zaremski, A. M., and J. M. Wing, "Signature Matching: A Tool for Using Software Libraries," *ACM Transactions on Software Engineering and Methodology,* vol. 4, no. 2, April 1995, pp. 146–70.

[ZWEB92] Zweben, S. H., and W. D. Heyn, "Systematic Testing of Data Abstractions Based on Software Specifications," *Journal of Software Testing, Verification, and Reliability,* vol. 1, no. 4 (1992), pp. 39–55.

Metrics

Description of Some Common Source Code Metrics

The *lines of code metric* (LOC) can be obtained in many ways, including a simple count of the number of lines in a file. The most useful metrics are those that are independent of the physical layout of the code and the coding standards used.

In the following well-known example, there are several ways of counting, depending on how delimiters, data declarations, and data definitions are treated. Even more variation can occur, depending upon how one counts the code for included files such as library headers.

```
#include <stdio.h>

main()
{
int i;

for (i = 0; i < 10; i++)
    printf("%d\n", i);
}
```

Commonly used computation methods give answers ranging from two to nine for the number of lines of code in this example. However, most organizations have counting standards that ignore source code lines containing only delimiters. Thus, the consensus is that there are at most five lines of code in this example: the `include` statement, the header of `main()`, the data statement, and the two statements comprising the `for`-loop.

Delivered source instructions (DSI) are a commonly used method of estimating the LOC metric. The DSI metric ignores `include` files, data declarations, and initializations that are part of data declarations. Thus, the DSI metric for this example has the value three. Further refinements can be made by determining how to count function headers such as `main()`. DSI is a useful measure that has a high-correlation LOC in most environments.

The *Halstead Software Science metrics* (effort, volume, length, among others) are based on the view that a program consists of a collection of operators and their operands and that the number of distinct operators and operands is important [HALS77]. The Halstead metrics are also based on the view that a program consists of operators and operands, with no other aspects such as control flow or module interconnection being relevant. These metrics seem to correlate well with the LOC metrics. They produce little information about the structure of the program.

These metrics are obtained by classifying all executable statements as being composed of operators such as : = , (,), *, +, and so on and operands such as x, 7, and the like. This classification is consistent with the syntax of many assembly languages.

Halstead defined several software metrics; one of the simpler ones is the so-called effort metric:

```
E = (N  + N ) * log (n  + n )
      1     2          1     2
```

Here n_1, n_2, N_1, and N_2 are the number of operators, operands, distinct operators, and distinct operands, respectively.

Note that this (and all other) Halstead measurement is invariant under changes of the names of all variables in a program. That is, the program fragments

```
a = a + 1;   and  b = b + 1;
```

are essentially the same, but

```
a = a + 1;   and  b = c + d;
```

are not because they have different Halstead metrics. In the first set of program fragments, there are three operators in each line (=, +, and ;) and three operands (a, a, and 1 in the first example and b, b, and 1 in the second example). The second example in the second program fragment has the operands b, c, and d.

The differences appear when we consider the numbers of distinct operands. If we consider only the two lines of code, there are two distinct operators in each line except for the statement

```
b = c + d;
```

which has three distinct operands.

Note that the value of the Halstead metrics for a program fragment depends upon the source code in which the program fragment appears. This is due to the computation of the unique operators and operands. The uniqueness of operators within a program fragment clearly depends on whether or not they appear in the fragment. Thus, these metrics are context sensitive.

Note that the Halstead metrics are also invariant under permutations of the order of operands in an expression. They ignore program structure and control flow and thus cannot provide a true picture of all of a program's complexity. The Halstead metrics can be applied to an entire program, to a single file, or to a single module.

The next type of source code metric we describe is the *McCabe cyclomatic complexity metric* [McCA76], which measures the complexity of the control flow. It creates a representation of the control flow graph of a program based on Euler's formula. All statements in a program are considered vertices of a graph. Edges are drawn between vertices if there is direct connection between two statements by a loop, conditional branch, or call to a subprogram or if the statements are in sequential order. McCabe's metric is $E - V + 2P$, where E is the number of edges, V is the number of vertices, and P is the number of separate parts (equal to the number of subprograms called, including the main program).

The cyclomatic complexity essentially reduces to the total number of logical predicates plus one. As such, it is invariant under changes of names of variables and under changes of the ordering of arguments in expressions. This metric is also invariant under any changes in the format of the control structure. Thus, changing a while-loop from the form

```
while (!found)
    {...
    }
```

to one of the form

```
while (found != 0)
    {...
    }
```

leaves the McCabe cyclomatic complexity unchanged.

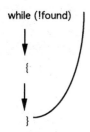

while (!found)

{

}

Figure A.1 A portion of a program graph.

Each of these program fragments has a graph similar to the one shown in Fig. A.1.

Both of these two loops have a McCabe cyclomatic complexity of 3 − 3 + 2, or 2. Adding nonbranching statements between the braces adds one to both the count of vertices and the count of edges, leaving the value of this metric unchanged. Changing a while-loop to an equivalent do-while-loop also leaves this metric invariant.

The cyclomatic complexity metric considers only control flow, ignoring the complexity of the number and occurrence of operators and operands or the general program structure and thus cannot be a complete measure of program complexity. Like the Halstead metrics, the McCabe cyclomatic complexity also can be applied to an entire program, to a single file, or to a single module.

However, unlike the lines of code and Halstead metrics, the McCabe cyclomatic complexity can be applied to detailed designs and to PDL (program design language) before a module is coded. It is one of the few metrics that can be applied at several places in the life cycle.

The McCabe cyclomatic complexity measure estimates the complexity of the control flow within a module. It counts the number of loops and branches in a program's control flow graph. The SPA tool that was used as part of the evaluation of the success of the NASA/Goddard TPOCC reuse plan produces both the cyclomatic complexity and the *"extended cyclomatic complexity,"* which adds an assessment of the complexity of a logical predicate such as

```
while ( (!a) || (b && c))
```

to the cyclomatic complexity. More information on the SPA tool can be obtained from SET Laboratories, which designed and markets this software.

The *coupling metrics* are based on a count of the number of arguments and global variables that can be accessed by a function. A more refined analysis distinguishes between arguments and global variables that can be modified within a module, control the flow of a module, or are merely used as data sources.

The *BVA metric* is based on an assessment of the number of cases required for testing of a module based on its interface and on results from testing theory that indicate that logical errors in software are most likely to occur at certain boundary values in the domain of the software. It is a measurement of modularity and testability. The BVA values associated with a function's arguments are defined as follows:

Arguments of type Boolean are given a weight of two (true, false)

Arguments of type int are given a weight of five (MININT, -1, 0, 1, MAXINT)

Arguments of type float are given a weight of five (MINFLOAT, -1.0, 0.0, 1.0, MAXFLOAT)

Arguments of type struct are given a weight that is the product of the weights of the components

Arguments of type pointer are given a weight of one plus the type of the object pointed to

Arguments of type array are given a weight of two plus the type of the element in the array. (The difference in treatment of arrays and pointers is a reflection of common usage, not syntax, since arrays and pointers are the same idea in C.)

Global variables that are visible to a function are treated the same way as function arguments

For a function with multiple arguments, the BVA value is the product of the BVA values associated with the individual arguments.

For a file, the BVA value is the sum of the BVA values of the individual functions.

We chose to omit qualifiers such as long, short, or unsigned since the first two do not change the BVA value. The qualifier unsigned restricts the integer to being nonnegative. This is a small decrease in the BVA value; we chose to ignore it because the qualifier is rarely used and is often used incorrectly. We would use a weight of three (0, 1, MAXINT) for function arguments with the type classification NATURAL in the Ada programming language, since the proper use of this type is more likely to be enforced by an Ada compiler.

The storage class qualifiers static, register, and extern were also ignored in our BVA computations since they specify where and how the data type is stored, not what the set of possible values is.

For simplicity of programming, structs were assigned an arbitrary value of 10 in the initial prototype used for data collection in this research. Also, any BVA contributions made by global variables were ignored. Thus, the BVA values reported in this appendix are all lower than the actual number of test cases based on boundary value analysis.

Data structure metrics are metrics that take into account how a particular data structure is used. Ideally, such metrics would be language independent.

Consider the C code

```
struct stack
 {
 int ITEM[MAXSTACK];
 int top ;
 };
```

There are two fields in this structured data type: an array of fixed size whose name is ITEM and whose entries are integers, and an integer variable named top. Any function that uses a parameter of this stack data type has to consider the two fields. The second field, top, has an infinite range (if we ignore the construction of a stack) and has several likely candidates to select for black-box testing. The five cases that we use are: −1, 0, 1, MAXSTACK, MAXSTACK + 1, assuming that top takes only values either inside or near the range of index values.

The array indices are tested at the upper and lower bounds plus or minus one; the test cases are 0, 1, 2, MAXSTACK − 1, MAXSTACK, MAXSTACK + 1. Thus, the total number of test cases to be added to the value of the BVA metric is 5 * 6, or 30.

The count of the number of cases for the BVA metric will be different in languages that support strong typing and run-time checking. For example, a definition of a stack in Ada might look like

```
record STACK is
      ITEM : array(1 .. MAXSTACK) of integer;
      TOP: integer range 0 .. MAXSTACK;
 end STACK;
```

There are still two fields in this structured data type that must be considered by any function that uses a parameter of this stack data type. The second field, TOP, has a finite range and has several obvious values to select for black-box testing. The four cases that we use are: 0, 1, MAXSTACK − 1, and MAXSTACK. This implementation of a stack in Ada has a BVA metric value of 4 * 4, or 16.

Note that neither count makes any use of the typical way in which a stack is used (access to the stack is usually limited to the top element of the stack, which should be done only by using functions to push and pop the stack). Therefore, the BVA metric may overstate the effect of the complexity of the data, particularly in an object-oriented environment in which access to the internal data of an object is restricted to specially written member functions of that object. Thus, the BVA metric is only a first approximation to a data structure-based metric.

Description of Common Requirements Metrics

The metrics considered in the previous section are primarily used for source code, although the McCabe cyclomatic complexity and the coupling metrics can be used with a detailed design. The *Albrecht function point metric* has the advantage that it can be used earlier in the software life cycle, even at the requirements phase.

This metric is based on the number and type of interfaces in the program. Interfaces can be either internal or external. The total number and size of interfaces are used as the basis for the collection of function points. Once this total is obtained, it is modified by several weighting factors, some of which are subjective and some of which are objective. The subjective factors include an assessment of the complexity of the interfaces and the overall complexity of the system.

More precisely, weights are assigned according to the following rules:

	simple	average	complex
external input or files	3	4	6
external outputs or reports	4	5	7
external queries or responses	3	4	6
external interfaces to other system	7	10	15
internal files	5	7	10

After the weights are assigned, a complexity factor is determined in the range 0 (no influence) to 5 (strong influence) for each of the following:

- Reliability backup and recovery
- Data communications
- Distributed functions
- Performance
- Heavily used system
- On-line data entry
- Ease of operation
- On-line updates
- Complex interfaces
- Complex processing

- Reusability
- Ease of installation
- Operation at multiple sites
- Modifiability

The objectively determined weights are obtained by determining if the program will be interactive or will execute without user interaction. The effect of the program executing concurrently with other applications is also included in these weights.

The function point metric is not directly associated with programming effort or system size. An organization using the function point metrics must define some of the subjective terms carefully, collect data, compare the data with other metrics that are directly computed using correlation and other methods, and then calibrate any models that use this metric. Only then can this metric be used with confidence in a particular environment.

Unfortunately, there is no single international standard that can be used for determining some of the definitions needed for consistent application of the function point method. Thus, there is little reason to expect exact correlations of your organization's experience using function points for cost and schedule estimation with another organization's use of function point data.

A simpler, less subjective metric is to simply count the number of distinct requirements used in a requirements document. This has the advantage of being quantifiable and is probably well defined as long as each distinct requirement is counted separately. A more elaborate metric would compute the number of distinct requirements at each identifiable level or subsystem in the requirements. As with the function point metrics, there is little reason to expect meaningful results from comparing the values of this metric on projects across different organizations.

Description of a Common Testing Metric

Testing metrics attempt to measure the degree to which a source code module's features are covered as part of the testing process. These metrics take several forms, depending on whether the testing process is black-box testing, white-box testing, or a combination.

In black-box testing, the internal structure of the source code module is visible to the tester, and thus he or she can determine the number of decision points, loops, or execution paths in the module. Thus, one possible testing metric is the percentage of decision points, loops, or execution paths that are exercised by the test suite.

In white-box testing, only the external interface of the source code module is visible to the tester. Thus, he or she must consider the number of possible cases in the domains of each of the functions in the source code module that is being tested. One possible testing metric for a function with a finite domain is therefore the percentage of the domain that has been exercised by the test suite. Unfortunately, functions whose only arguments are characters or booleans have finite domains; most function domains are extremely large or even infinite. Hence, a better approach might be to use a source code metric such as the BVA metric or another coupling metric to determine the number of test cases necessary for certain types of white-box testing and then determine the percentage of test coverage by the percentage of the potential coupling that is actually tested.

Other potential testing metrics are the amount of regression testing performed during testing and the number of errors found at each step in the testing process (for use in a reliability model).

Further Reading

Anyone wishing to start a systematic software metrics program should read the books by Grady and Caswell [GRAD87] and by Fenton [FENT91]. A second edition of Fenton's book, coauthored by S. Pfleeger, was published in 1996 [FENT96]. The paper by Basili and Rombach [BASI88] describes the Goal, Questions, Metrics paradigm that is often used to guide metric programs in some detail.

McCabe's original paper is well worth reading for the origins of the cyclomatic complexity metric [McCA76]. Coupling metrics are discussed in a paper by Kafura and Henry [KAFU81] and also in [LEAC95C].

Either Albrecht's original work [ALBR79] or a later paper by Albrecht and Gaffney [ALBR83] are essential reading for understanding the basis of function point metrics.

A recent paper by Voas and Miller describes some testing metrics [VOAS95B]. Two of Beizer's books also contain information on this subject [BEIZ83, BEIZ90].

2

Sources

General Information

Air Force Defense Repository System (AFDRS)

AFDRS Customer Assistance
  Center
U.S. Air Force Standard Systems
  Center
Building 856, Room 265
201 East Moore Drive
Maxwell AFB
Gunter Annex, AL 36114-3005

Army Reuse Center (ARC)

United States Army Information
  Systems Software Center
(USAISSC)
6000 6th Street
Fort Belvoir, VA 22060

ASMS Newsletter

Army Software Metrics System
  Newsletter
U.S. Army Operational Test and
  Evaluation Command

Attn: CTSE-MP-S
4501 Ford Avenue
Alexandria, VA 22303-1458
STEP@optec.army.mil

ASSET Catalog

This catalog is available both on line from the address

reuse@source.asset.com

and on a diskette formatted for an IBM PC compatible (3.5 inch, 720 MB). It includes the following:

STARS

Software Technology for Adaptable, Reliable Systems (STARS) program, sponsored by the Advanced Research Projects Agency (ARPA).

Order Number:	ASSET_A_725
Release Date:	30-JUN-94
Producer:	UNISYS
Author:	John Willison, Army CECOM SED, Judith A. Lettes, Unisys Corporation
Reference:	CDRL A011, STARS-VC-A011/001/01
Asset Type:	DOCUMENT
Size:	2476 Kbytes, 27 Files
Domains:	DOMAIN ANALYSIS AND ENGINEERING, SOFTWARE REUSE - DOMAIN SPECIFIC
Keywords:	DOMAIN ENGINEERING, DOMAIN-SPECIFIC ANALYSIS, KAPTUR, MEGAPROGRAMMING, RFL
Distribution:	Approved for public release, distribution is unlimited

STARS Technology Center
801 N. Randolph Street,
 Suite 400
Arlington, VA 22203-1714

CARDS

The acronym *CARDS* stands for the Central Archive for Reusable Defense Software. Version 2.0 of the library model is an encoding of the GCC (Generic Command Center) for Portable Reusable Integrated Software Modules (PRISM) program into the RLF (Reuse Library Framework) [ASSET_A_442], a part of the CARDS library infrastructure that can be thought of as both a tool and a formalism. A CARDS library model for a domain-specific reuse library is a formal encoding of information produced during domain engineering activities. The purpose of a CARDS domain-specific library model is to: capture critical information such as domain requirements and generic architectures that are produced by domain engineering activities based on requirements and architecture; describe criteria for qualification and insertion of reusable assets into the library; provide a basis for organizing ("classifying") reusable assets for search and retrieval applications; and provide a basis for constructing other kinds of reuse library applications.

Order Number:	ASSET_A_334
Alternate Name:	COMMAND CENTER DOMAIN MODEL DESCRIPTION - CARDS
Version:	12-92
Release Date:	25-NOV-92
Producer:	UNISYS
Author:	Catherine Smotherman, Christine Baker, Paul Kogut
Reference:	CDRL 04110, STARS-AC-04110/001/00
Asset Type:	DOCUMENT
Size:	2 Files, 515 Kbytes
Domains:	REUSE LIBRARY
Keywords:	CARDS, DOMAIN_SPECIFIC, RLF
Distribution:	Approved for public release, distribution is unlimited

Standards and Guidelines for Repository Deliverables

This technical report contains recommendations for guidelines and standards to be used in developing Ada programs and technical documents for delivery to a repository. It provides a proposal for standard prologues for Ada programs which are SGML-processable. A sample SGML DTD is provided that will validate an Ada prologue coded to this standard.

An overview of SGML tools is provided together with a discussion of processing graphics integrated with text.

This product was developed as part of the Software Technology for Adaptable, Reliable Systems (STARS) program, sponsored by the Advanced Research Projects Agency (ARPA).

Order Number:	ASSET_A_185
Release Date:	17-MAR-89
Producer:	BOEING DEFENSE AND SPACE GROUP

Reference: CDRL 0320, DTIC AD-A240478
Asset Type: DOCUMENT
Size: 1 File, 69 Kbytes
Domains: ADA PROGRAMMING LANGUAGE, REUSE LIBRARY,
                        SOFTWARE REUSE
Keywords: GUIDELINES, REPOSITORY, SGML, STYLE GUIDE
Distribution: Approved for public release, distribution is unlimited

SQL/Ada Module Extensions (SAME) Standard Packages

These software packages support the SAME (SQL/ADA MODULE EX-
TENSIONS) approach developed by the SAME-DC committee and
headed by Marc Graham of the SEI. They present strongly typed data
types to interface with the SQL Bindings. These packages are tailorable
to many applications. The "Installation" document gives complete instructions on how to tailor the packages for the specific database and
computer system used as well as how to compile the packages.

Order Number: ASSET_A_403
Alternate Name: SAME STANDARD PACKAGES
Version: CMU
Release Date: 02-DEC-88
Producer: SOFTWARE ENGINEERING INSTITUTE
Author: Marc H. Graham
Asset Type: SOFTWARE - BUNDLE
Size: 146 Kbytes, 26 Files
Domains: ADA STANDARDS AND BINDINGS, DATABASE
                        MANAGEMENT
Keywords: ADA, ADA BINDINGS, BINDING, DBMS, SAME, SQL
Distribution: Approved for public release, distribution is unlimited

State Machine Management Package

This package provides the types and operations necessary for manipulating a state machine over the exported state table. The package
abstracts the type State_Machine. The generic formal parameters
are as follows:

State => A discrete type that enumerates the possible states for a
state machine.

Input => A discrete type that enumerates the possible inputs to a
state machine.

Action => A discrete type that enumerates the possible actions that may be taken after a state machine makes a transition from one state to another.

Order Number:	ASSET_A_124
Version:	1.0
Release Date:	31-JUL-89
Producer:	SCIENCE APPLICATIONS INTERNATIONAL CORPO-RATION, SOFTWARE AND SYSTEMS INTEGRATION GROUP, ADA SOFTWARE DIVISION
Asset Type:	SOFTWARE - COMPONENT
Size:	11 Kbytes, 2 Files
Domains:	SOFTWARE DEVELOPMENT TOOLS
Keywords:	GENERIC
Distribution:	Approved for public release, distribution is unlimited

NSDIR

National Software Data and Information Repository (A strategic plan exists and is consistent with the NSDIR Order-I Prototype).

CAMP

Common Ada Missle Packages
(See *ASSET Catalog*)

DACS

This project is run by Kaman Sciences Corporation for the Air Force.

Data and Analysis Center
P.O. Box 120
Utica, NY 13503-0120
WWW: http://www.utica
.kaman.com:8001/
gopher.utica.kaman.com
ftp.utica.kaman.com
listserv@utica.kaman.com
dacs-info@utica.kaman.com
dacs@utica.kaman.com

Software Engineering Laboratory (SEL)

Software Engineering Branch
Code 552

NASA Goddard Space Flight
  Center
Greenbelt, MD 20771
(301) 286-3010
rose.pajerski@gsfc
  .nasa.gov

COSMIC

This is a software library. An electronic address for it is

http://www.cosmic.uga
  .edu/pub/online.cat.shtml

NETLIB

http://www.netlib.org/
  index.html
http://www.hensa.ac.uk/
  ftp/mirrors/netlib

Software Engineering Institute (SEI)

http://www.sei.cmu.edu
info@sei.cmu.edu

Software Engineering Institute
Carnegie Mellon University
5000 Forbes Avenue
Pittsburgh, PA, 15213

NTIS

National Technical Information
  Service
5285 Port Royal Road
Springfield, VA 22161
(703) 487-4808

Public Ada Library (PAL)

This information is available electronically on a set of two CD-ROM
disks from SIGAda (free to students) and commercially (at nominal
cost) from the Walnut Creek company. It includes the following:

Ada Software Repository

ASEET (Ada software engineering education and technology) educational software

Information from the AJPO (Ada Joint Program Office)

Ada compilers from the Free Software Foundation's GNAT project based on the familiar GNU system

Ada software development tools

Ada documentation tools

Ada courseware guides

The Ada Language Reference Manual

Bindings to various operating systems

Bindings to various GUIs

The ACVC (Ada compiler validation suite)

PRISM

The acronym *PRISM* stands for "Portable Reusable Integrated Software Modules." It is available from the ASSET catalog as

Asset number ASSET-A-34
CDRL B007,
 STARS-UC-B007/005/00

RBSE

Repository-Based Software Engineering
This project is based on a project at NASA/Langley Research Center in Langley, Virginia. As the name implies, it is an archive of reusable software components. David Eichmann is the principal investigator. Information is available from the Internet address

http://www.rbse.jsc.nasa.gov

RESSM

The acronym *RESSM* stands for "Reuse Economics Spreadsheet Model." This spreadsheet is available through both the Software Productivity Consortium and the ASSET catalog.

ASSET-A-490
SPC-92068-C

Reuse-based Spiral Process
 Model
ASSET-A-433
CDRL 03068-001
DTIC-AD-B157659
DTIC-AD-B157660
Publication Number:
GR-7670-1195-NP
STARS-SC-03068001/001/00

Internet Sources

Defense Software Repository System (DSRS)

This repository is run by the Defense Information Services Agency
(DISA) under its Software Reuse Program (SRP). The contents of this
repository are software components and may be architectures, designs, source code, test suites, tools, documentation, or any other software artifact. The term *asset* is used for the contents of this
repository. The electronic address is:

```
sw-eng.falls-church.va.us
```

The assets of the repository are classified as follows:

- Level 1: There is no attempt to evaluate the asset.
- Level 2: The asset has been compiled (if source code), and metrics
  have been collected.
- Level 3: The asset has been evaluated according to SRP standards
  for reusability, and functional V & V (verification and validation).
  Approved test suites are included.
- Level 4: Meets all standards at level 3 and meets additional stan-
  dards for documentation.

Defense Technical Information Center (DTIC)

Information Analysis Center

```
http://www.dtic.dla.mil/iac/
```

Ada Bases

```
http://www.informatik
 .uni-stuttgart.de/ifi/
 ps/ada-software/
 ada-software.html
```

E-mail: `adabases.informatik.`
`uni-stuttgart.de`

elib.cs.stanford.edu

This is a reuse tool intended for academic research.

ACM SIGAda

This organization supports several reuse activities, including its public Ada Catalog. Of special interest are the Reuse Acquisition Action Team (RAAT) and the Reuse Working Group. Relevant addresses are as follows:

AACM SigAda:
`http://www.acm.org/sigada/`
`listserv.wunet.wustl.edu`

(to subscribe send E-mail message with no subject)

Harry Joiner
System Resources Corporation
128 Wheeler Road
Burlington, MA 01803
(617) 270-9228
(617) 272-2889

General Reuse Information

Walnut Creek

4041 Pike Lane Suite D
Concord, CA 94520-9909
(800) 786-9907
Fax: (510) 674-0821

This is an excellent source for CD-ROM software. Their offerings include the Public Ada Catalog, the C User's Group Library, and inexpensive operating systems versions (primarily UNIX and UNIX clones), among others.

Code Farms, Inc.

(Source code for C/C++ libraries)
7214 Jack Trail
Richmond, Ontario, Canada
KOA2Z0

(613) 838-4829
jiri@debra.dgbt.doc.ca

EVB Software Engineering, Inc.

This company produces the Reuse Library Toolset, which includes an administrator, library manager, domain analysis tool, searcher, and browser. It also produces the GRACE components, which form a general-purpose science and engineering toolkit.

5320 Spectrum Drive
Frederick, MD 21701
(301) 695-6960
Fax: (301) 695-7734
info@evb.com

Rational Corporation

This company markets the Booch components, which form a set of general-purpose software packages.

http://www.rational.com
product_info@rational.com
ftp/ftp.rational.com/public

InQuisiX

Software Productivity Solutions, Inc.
122 Fourth Avenue
Indialantic, FL 32903
(407) 984-3370
Fax: (407) 728-3957
LWV@SPS.COM

Scandura Systems

This company produces software tools for automatic program translation for a variety of languages, including FORTRAN to Ada.

1249 Greentree Avenue
Narberth, PA 19072
(215) 664-1207

tools++

This is a set of C++ class libraries.

Rogue Wave Software
P.O. Box 2328
Corvallis, OR 97339
(503) 754-2311
support@roguewave.com

Generic++

This is a set of C++ class libraries.
(in North America)

Smart Object Technologies, Inc.
One Galleria Boulevard #905
Metairie, LA 700001
(504) 835-6706
Generic++@smobject.com

(elsewhere)

Siemens-Nixdorf
Otto-Hahn Ring 6
81730 Munich Germany
49 354 636 43578
cpplibs.service@mch.sni.edu

STL++

This is a set of C++ class libraries.

Modena Software
236 N. Santa Cruz Avenue,
 Suite 213
Los Gatos, CA 95032
(408) 354-5616
modena@netcom.com

3

Glossary

Many terms listed in the text but not defined in this appendix can be found in the NIST glossary [NIST95].

BVA An interconnection metric based on boundary value testing

COTS Commercial off-the-shelf

DSI Delivered source instructions

ESI Executable source instructions

LOC Lines of code

MTTF Mean time to failure

MTBF Mean time before failure

NCNB LOC Noncommented, nonblank lines of code

SLOC Source lines of code

(software) reliability Statistical estimates of the errors remaining in software after each checkpoint in the development life cycle.

stability The number of changes per unit time to a software system during development. A small number of changes reflects a stable system. See *volatility*.

volatility The number of changes per unit time to a software system during development. A large number of changes reflects a volatile, unstable system. See *stability*.

coupling metrics Metrics based on the interconnection between program subunits.

Halstead metrics   A set of metrics (effort, volume, length) based on the classification of individual program statements into either operators or operands.

McCabe metric   A metric based on the logical structure of a program. Can be computed as the number of logical predicates plus one.

cyclomatic complexity metric   See *McCabe metric.*

extended cyclomatic complexity   Related to the cyclometric complexity, but adds one for each logical condition within a compound logical statement that uses logical operators.

ACM   Association for Computing Machinery

ACVC   Ada compiler validation suite

ADSOFT   AT&T advanced software products group

AJPO   Ada Joint Program Office

ANSI   American National Standards Institute

ARM   Ada Language Reference Manual

ARPA   Advanced Research Projects Agency

ARTWEG   Ada Run-Time Environments Working Group

ASEET   Ada Software Engineering Education and Training

ASR   Ada Software Repository

BNF   Backus-Naur form

CADCS   AT&T's call attempt data collection system

CAMP   Common Ada Missile Packages

CARDS   Central archive for reusable defense software

ELPA   Emitter location and processing

GCC   Generic command and control

GQM   Goals, questions, methods paradigm

GUI   Graphical user interface

IEEE   Institute of Electrical and Electronics Engineers

ISO   International Standards Organization

KAPTUR   Knowledge Acquisition for Preservation of Trade-offs and Underlying Rationales tool

MSOCC   Mission Operations Control Center

NCSA   National Center for Supercomputing Applications

NTIS   National Technical Information Service

ODM   Organization domain modeling

PAL   Public Ada Library

PRISM   Portable reusable integrated software modules

RESSM   Reusable economics spreadsheet model

RLF   Reuse library framework

SOHO   Solar Heliographic Observer

STARS   Software Technology for Adaptable, Reliable Systems

UIL   User interface language

4

Suggested Term Projects

The purpose of these projects is to allow students to get experience in software reuse techniques, such as domain analysis, reuse library access and management, metrics-driven approaches, certification of reusable components, and reuse tools, if they are available. Each of these projects should be done by a group, if at all possible.

Each of the projects should include as a minimum experience in domain analysis, certification, and reuse library management. The size of the system should be the major variable in selection of student projects. Smaller groups of students should consider evaluating smaller software systems for their projects. Each student project should include a major report and presentation on the project activities. A list of suggested projects follows:

1. Build a system with the goal being to use the smallest amount of new code. The code should use available resources such as reuse libraries. Ideally, the system should reuse some existing tools such as parser generators. This is sufficient for a batch-oriented system, such as one that might use a UNIX command-line interface. For systems that are menu driven, use GUI tools if they are available to you.

An excellent project for an organization that does not already possess metrics tools is to develop its own. Such tools might include ones for the Halstead, McCabe, and some form of coupling analysis, such as the BVA metric.

After the system is built, new components of the system should be subjected to domain analysis and potentially reusable components should be placed into your own personal reuse library. The reuse library should consist of both source code and other software artifacts. Determine the system's modularity, using the coupling metrics dis-

cussed in this book. Assess the potential for reuse of each software artifact you create.

2. Review an existing system for reuse and determine any appropriate places where reuse could be applied. This will involve domain
analysis. The domain analysis should include both a classification
scheme and an assessment of each software artifact for potential
reusability.

The next step is to rewrite a major portion of the system in order to
make maximum use of reusable components from reuse libraries that
are available to you.

Compare the two systems and determine which is more modular
using the coupling metrics discussed in this book. Place each set of
components into a separate reuse library and compare the libraries.
Both reuse libraries should consist of both source code and other software artifacts.

3. Review an existing system for reuse and determine if the system
is of sufficient quality to warrant reuse. This means that the components of the system should be certified. This is only possible if you have
access to reliability information such as the number of software errors
determined at each appropriate milestone (external releases or internal
versions). Ideally, this would be done in conjunction with project 2.

Place all certified components into a separate reuse library. The reuse
library should consist of both source code and other software artifacts.
Assess the potential for reusability of each artifact you place into a
reuse library.

4. Review an existing system for its potential for reuse or for reengineering. Examine the use of the system and the current environment
to determine if the system is a good candidate for reengineering.
Evaluate the pros and cons of transforming all or part of the system
into an object-oriented one.

Also determine if some portions of the system are of sufficient quality
to warrant reuse. This means that the components of the system
should be certified. This is only possible if you have access to reliability
information such as the number of software errors determined at each
appropriate milestone (external releases or internal versions). Ideally,
this would be done in conjunction with project 2.

Place all certified components into a separate reuse library The reuse
library should consist of both source code and other software artifacts.

Notes to the instructor

If the students are not able to provide realistic systems for analysis
from their work environments, then they will have to make use of

some publicly available software. Unfortunately, these public systems are relatively large and have to be broken into more manageable subsystems. Therefore, it is feasible to have a class divided into several different groups evaluating the same system. A parallel development provides an opportunity for competition between the groups, especially to see who can develop the smallest amount of code or provide the most extensive analysis.

There are many opportunities for students to understand the role of metrics based on the GQM paradigm in a systematic metrics-based reuse program. In such an environment, a final class in which the students critique each other's systematic reuse program is extremely beneficial. (Try to have the actual demonstrations that the software works done at a different time.)

The experience of the students should be taken into account when assigning projects. Examinations and homework may be given and a literature survey may be performed, depending on the instructor's preferences and the level of student preparation. Special attention should be paid to student projects that are based on analysis of software systems that may be classified or otherwise restricted.

5

Checklist for Software Reuse in a Changing Environment

This checklist is intended to provide managers, both front line and higher level, with a set of actions that should be undertaken for most projects developed as part of a systematic program of software reuse. If a large number of the activities listed here are missing from the process it is very unlikely that the reuse process is systematic.

For ease of access, the checklist is grouped into sets of related activities.

Software Development Process

Systems engineering
Is the systems engineering process guided by software reuse?
Is there a domain expert on the systems engineering team?
Is there a domain analyst on the systems engineering team?
Is potential reuse used to influence the process?
Are system architectures placed in the reuse library after the system is built?

Technology assessment for COTS products
Is there continual assessment of relevant COTS products?
Does the assessment include functionality assessment?
Does the assessment include assessment of interface standards?

Development process
Which development process is used (waterfall, spiral, prototyping, reuse-driven requirements, other)?

Is potential reuse used to influence the process?

If the process is reuse-driven requirements, is an experienced systems integrator on the team?

If the process is reuse-driven requirements, is an experienced cost estimator on the team?

If the process is reuse-driven requirements, is an experienced negotiator on the team?

Are metrics collected as part of the development process?

If so, which ones?

Are metrics used to assess the development process?

Requirements process

Is the requirements engineering process guided by software reuse?

Does the requirements process include an assessment of available COTS products?

Is there a domain expert on the requirements team?

Have the requirements been subjected to domain analysis?

Have the requirements been placed into a reuse library?

Is a software technology expert available?

Are metrics collected as part of the requirements process?

If so, which ones?

Are metrics used to assess the requirements process?

Requirements traceability matrix

Has a requirements traceability matrix been set up?

If so, has it been used?

Domain analysis

Is a domain expert available?

Is a domain analyst available?

Is a domain analysis tool available?

Has the application domain been subjected to domain analysis?

Is a software technology expert available?

Designing for reuse

Does the design adhere to industry standards?

Does the design adhere to standard interfaces?

Does the design adhere to local standards and interfaces?

Is there a domain expert on the design team?

Is a software technology expert available?

Has the design been subjected to domain analysis?

Has the design been placed into a reuse library?

Are metrics collected as part of the design process?

If so, which ones?
Are metrics used to assess the design process?

Coding for reuse

Does the source code adhere to industry standards?
Does the source code adhere to standard interfaces?
Does the source code adhere to local standards and interfaces?
Is there a domain expert on the coding team?
Is a software technology expert available?
Has the source code been subjected to domain analysis?
Has the source code been placed into a reuse library?
Are metrics collected as part of the coding process?
If so, which ones?
Are metrics used to assess the coding process?

Configuration management

Are systems developed using configuration management?
Are tools used to help in the configuration management process?
Are metrics collected as part of the configuration management process?
If so, which ones?
Are metrics used to assess the configuration management process?

Test processes for reuse

Does the testing process adhere to industry standards?
Does the testing process determine that source code adheres to standard interfaces?
Does the testing process determine that source code adheres to local standards and interfaces?
Are test plans placed in a reuse library?
Are test results placed in a reuse library?
Has the test plan been subjected to domain analysis?
Has the test plan been placed into a reuse library?
Have the test results been subjected to domain analysis?
Have the test results been placed into a reuse library?
Are metrics collected as part of the test process?
If so, which ones?
Are metrics used to assess the test process?

Integration for reuse

Are any filters (glueware) needed to match interfaces between software components?
If so, have the filters (glueware) been placed in the reuse library?

Have all filters (glueware) been developed using configuration management?

Documentation for reuse

Has the documentation been subjected to domain analysis?
Has the documentation been placed into a reuse library?
Has the documentation been tested for readability?
Has the documentation been tested for usability?

Postmortem project assessment

Does every project have a postmortem project assessment done?
Are metrics used as part of the postmortem project assessment?

Overall software development process assessment

If applicable, how does the organization rank in the SEI Capability Maturity Model?
If applicable, how does the organization rank in the SEL Process Improvement Model?
Have the process rankings improved in recent projects?

Domain Analysis

Expertise

Is a domain analyst available?
Is a domain expert available?

Support and infrastructure

Is a domain analysis tool available?
If so, are the software artifacts in a form that can be read by the domain analysis tool?
If not, are converters available or easy to create?
Has domain analysis been done on many other artifacts in the organization?

Software architecture

Is the software architecture understood and well documented?
Are software architectures of other relevant systems understood and well documented?
What is the classification scheme used for describing the components?
Faceted?
Top-down?
Other? (List the scheme.)
Has a thesaurus been developed?

Classification scheme

Have the fundamental objects in the system been determined?
What are the fundamental objects in the system?
Have the fundamental actions in the system been determined?
What actions are applied to these objects?
Have the fundamental mediums in the system been determined?
Upon which mediums do the objects reside?
Have the fundamental subsystems in the system been determined?
Which subsystems are responsible for these actions and objects?
Has the system architecture been determined?
What is the maximum possible percentage of reuse?

Details of the classification scheme (repeat as many times as there are levels)

Is there another level to the classification scheme?
If so, have the objects, actions, mediums, and subsystems at that level been determined?
What are the objects in the system at that level?
What actions are applied to these objects at that level?
Upon which mediums do the objects reside at that level?
Which subsystems are responsible for these actions and objects at that level?
Has the subsystem architecture been determined?
What is the maximum possible percentage of reuse at that level?

Certification

Life cycle level

What is the life cycle phase of the software artifact (requirements, design, code, testing, integration, documentation)?
Is a CASE tool available?

Certification by previous usage

Has the software artifact been used successfully in several environments?
If yes, how many environments?
If yes, has the software artifact been of satisfactory quality?

Certification process

Are all software artifacts certified before they are entered into a reuse library?
If the certification process is "certify on demand" is there an ex-

ternal tag that can be examined to determine if a particular reuse library component has been certified previously without having to examine the component?

Certification of requirements

Have the requirements been subjected to domain analysis?

Has the size of the requirements been estimated?

If so, which metric was applied? (function point? other?)

Have the requirements been examined to determine opportunities for the reuse of existing architectures?

If a CASE tool is available, have the requirements been entered into it?

Certification of design

Has the design been subjected to domain analysis?

Has the complexity of the design been evaluated by a control flow-based metric such as the McCabe cyclomatic complexity metric?

Has the design been examined to determine opportunities for reuse of existing architectures or high-level components?

Has the design been examined to determine if subsystems have interfaces that encourage the use of reusable components?

Has the design been examined to determine if subsystems have interfaces that encourage the future reuse of the design?

If a CASE tool is available, has the design been entered into it?

Certification of source code

Has the source code been subjected to domain analysis?

Has the source code been developed using the appropriate coding standards?

Has the source code been evaluated for conformance to appropriate interface standards?

Has the source code been evaluated for size using a standard-lines-of-code or other measurement?

If so, which one?

Has the source code been evaluated for the size and complexity of its interfaces?

If so, which metric was used? (BVA? coupling metric? fan-in, fan-out? other metric?)

Has the source code been evaluated for having appropriate logical complexity using the McCabe cyclomatic complexity metric or equivalent?

If a CASE tool is available, has the source code been entered into it?

Certification of test plans
Have the test plans been subjected to domain analysis?
If a CASE tool is available, have the test plans been entered into it?

Certification of test cases
Have the test cases been subjected to domain analysis?
If a CASE tool is available, have the test cases been entered into it?

Certification of integration plans
Have the integration plans been subjected to domain analysis?
Is configuration management part of the integration plan?
If a CASE tool is available, have the integration plans been entered into it?

Certification of documentation
Has the documentation been subjected to domain analysis?
Have readability metrics been applied to the documentation?
Have usability tests been applied to the documentation?
If a CASE tool is available, has the documentation been entered into it?

Reuse Library Management

Creation
Does a reuse library already exist?
If not, what resources are needed?
Is a reuse library manager available?
If a reuse library manager is available, what portion of his or her time will be devoted to reuse library management?

Library management expertise
Is there a reuse library manager?
Is he or she experienced in library management?
Is he or she a domain expert?
If not, does he or she have access to a domain expert?
Is he or she a domain analyst?
If not, does he or she have access to a domain analyst?
Is he or she a software technology expert?
If not, does he or she have access to a software technology expert?

Library organization
Is the reuse library organized by the application domain of the asset?

Is the reuse library organized by functionality of its assets?

Is the reuse library organized by the tool used to create the asset?

Is the reuse library organized by life cycle phase of the assets?

Is the reuse library organized by some other technique?

Is the reuse library organized by a combination of the above-mentioned methods?

Search process

How large is the library?

Are automated search methods required or can searches be done manually?

What methods are used for searching the library?

What automated tools are available?

Are the automated tools efficient?

Does the search process provide too many partial matches if no exact match is found?

Does the search process provide all possible partial matches if no exact match is found?

Can searches locate assets by more than one of the following: functionality, tool used, life cycle phase?

Configuration management

Is the reuse library under configuration management?

If not, what procedures are in place to guarantee that the integrity of reusable components is assured?

Access issues

Will there be public access to the library?

If not, what criteria have been set up to determine who will be granted access?

How will access restrictions be enforced?

Public reuse library issues

Will public reuse libraries be used?

Will software assets from public reuse libraries be certified?

If yes, how will certification be done?

If yes, who will do the certification?

Encryption issues for electronic libraries

Is security necessary?

Is there any mechanism for library security?

Is the library encrypted?

Metrics

Will any measurement of reuse library usage be made?

If so, which metrics will be collected?

Will the metrics be used to improve reuse library organization?
Will the metrics be used to improve reuse library management?
Will measurements of reuse library access be used to influence the organization's software development process?

Systems Integration and Configuration Management for Reuse

Configuration interface matrix
Is there a configuration interface matrix?
Will it be updated as the systems are integrated?
Does it list all dependencies of software with COTS and other software?

Configuration of operating system
How much time is needed to make software consistent with a changed operating system?
What resources are needed to make software consistent with a changed operating system?
How frequent are new releases of the operating system?
Is the interface with the underlying operating system subject to configuration management?
Is a configuration interface matrix used?

Configuration of system utilities
How much time is needed to make software consistent with changed system utilities?
What resources are needed to make software consistent with changed system utilities?
How frequent are new releases of the system utilities?
Is the interface with all necessary system utilities subject to configuration management?
Is a configuration interface matrix used?

Configuration of general-purpose applications
How much time is needed to make software consistent with changed applications?
What resources are needed to make software consistent with changed applications?
How frequent are new releases of the general-purpose applications software?
Is the interface with all general-purpose applications subject to configuration management?
Is a configuration interface matrix used?
How frequent are new releases of the general-purpose applications software?

Configuration of special-purpose COTS

How much time is needed to make software consistent with changed special-purpose COTS?

What is the size of the external interfaces of the COTS product?

What resources are needed to make software consistent with changed special-purpose COTS?

How frequent are new releases of the COTS software?

Is the interface with all special-purpose COTS products subject to configuration management?

Is a configuration interface matrix used?

How frequent are new releases of the COTS software?

Configuration of locally developed systems

How much time is needed to make software consistent with changed locally developed systems?

What resources are needed to make software consistent with changed locally developed systems?

How frequent are new releases of locally developed systems?

Is the interface with all locally developed systems subject to configuration management?

Is a configuration interface matrix used?

Filters and glueware

Are any filters or glueware needed to match interfaces between software components?

Are any necessary filters or glueware developed under configuration management?

Are any filters or glueware proprietary software?

Do any filters or glueware need to be changed if the individual COTS products are changed?

What is the configuration management plan for filters or glueware?

Measurement

Quality improvement

Are metrics used to assess the quality of the software products developed?

Are metrics used to improve the quality of the software products developed?

Which metrics are collected?

How are metrics collected?

If metrics collection is automated, which measurement tools are used?

Process improvement

Are metrics used to assess the efficiency of the software development process?

Are metrics used to improve the efficiency of the software development process?

Which metrics are collected?

How are metrics collected?

If metrics collection is automated, which measurement tools are used?

Size of system

What is the size of the system?

How is it computed?

How are metrics collected?

If metrics collection is automated, which measurement tools are used?

Quality of system

What is the quality of the system?

How is it computed?

Is the system's quality acceptable?

Is there a reliability model?

How is it computed?

Is the system's reliability acceptable?

Is any special reliability or quality needed from COTS products?

How are metrics collected?

If metrics collection is automated, which measurement tools are used?

Function point complexity

What is the function point complexity of the system?

How is it computed? (In particular, how are subjective measurements made?)

Is the function point complexity acceptable?

How are metrics collected?

If metrics collection is automated, which measurement tools are used?

Control flow (McCabe cyclomatic) complexity

What is the control flow complexity of the system?

How is it computed?

Is the control flow complexity acceptable?
How are metrics collected?
If metrics collection is automated, which measurement tools are used?

Modularity (number and size of interfaces)
How many interfaces does the system have?
How is the modularity computed (number of interfaces, size of interfaces)?
If the number of data points communicated is used, how many data points are there per interface?
If the BVA metric is used, how many test cases are needed for complete black-box testing of the inputs, based on the BVA analysis?
If the coupling metric is used, how many test cases are needed for black-box testing of the inputs, based on the coupling analysis?
If the fan-out, fan-in metric is used, how many test cases are needed for black-box testing of the inputs based on the fan-out, fan-in analysis?
Is the modularity acceptable?
How are metrics collected?
If metrics collection is automated, which measurement tools are used?

Percentage of reuse
What is the percentage of reuse of the system?
How is it computed?
How are metrics collected?
If metrics collection is automated, which measurement tools are used?

Category of reuse
What is the type of reuse of the system?
How is it computed?

Number of times reused:
What is the number of times that the system is reused?
How is it computed?

Stability
What is the stability of the system?
Has the rate of change decreased over time?
How is it computed?
How are metrics collected?
If metrics collection is automated, which measurement tools are used?

Testing and Maintenance

Certification process
Have all software artifacts been certified?
Which software artifacts have been certified prior to placement into a reuse library?
Which software artifacts are subject to "certification on demand"?

Number of times used:
How many times has the software artifact been reused?
Was the software artifact reused in different environments each time?
What percentage of reuse occurred each time?

Learning activities for program understanding
Will the software require integration of any unfamiliar products?
Will there be any special difficulties in installing the system?
Are the installers familiar with the installation environment?

Continuing engineering analysis of evolving systems
Will the evolving system be examined regularly?
Will technology assessments of COTS be done regularly?
Will comparative quality assessments be made?
Will feedback be used to drive the development of new releases?
Will prospective users or customers be involved with the development process?
Will trends in process improvement be studied?

Cost

Software life cycle model
Which software life cycle model is used?
Is there a well-developed cost model for this software development process?
Is the cost estimating staff experienced in the life cycle model?
How accurate are existing cost models?

Percentage of reuse
What is the percentage of reuse?
How is it computed?
How is it used in the cost model?

Life cycle phase
Which life cycle phase is the software artifact being reused in?
If the software artifact is used in more than one phase, how are the costs charged?

Systems engineering
What are the systems engineering costs?
How are they computed?
How are they used in the cost model?

Software acquisition costs
What are the costs of software acquisition?
What are the maintenance costs?
How are they computed?
How are they used in the cost model?

Hardware acquisition costs
What are the costs of hardware acquisition?
What are the maintenance costs?
How are they computed?
How are they used in the cost model?
Other up-front costs
What are the other up-front costs?
How are they computed?
How are they used in the cost model?

Integration costs
What are the costs of system integration?
How are they computed?
How are they used in the cost model?

Operational costs
What are the expected training costs?
How are they computed?
How are they used in the cost model?
What are the expected operational costs after training?
How are they computed?
How are they used in the cost model?

Licensing agreements
What are the software licensing costs?
Are these licensing costs per use?
Are the licensing costs a fixed amount or a per platform charge?
How are they computed?
How are they used in the cost model?

Elaborate relationships with COTS vendors
Are special agreements needed in addition to licenses?
If so, how much will they cost?
How are the costs computed?
How are the costs used in the cost model?

Measurement costs

Is a comprehensive software measurement program in place?

What is the cost of a comprehensive software measurement program?

Do measurement and assessment drive the software process?

Number of potential reuses

How many times is the software artifact likely to be reused?

How is this number estimated?

Has the type of potential reuse been estimated?

If so, what is the type of potential reuse?

Cost charging issues

Are the costs of software measurement charged against specific projects or as general overhead?

If measurement costs are charged against specific projects, how are they computed?

Are the costs of systematic reuse charged against specific projects or as general overhead?

If costs of systematic reuse are charged against specific projects, how are they computed?

Are savings due to reuse assigned for specific projects or for a general cost saving?

Are costs of certifying reusable artifacts charged against the project that created the artifact?

Are costs of certifying reusable artifacts charged against all projects using the artifact?

Index

ABOUT THE AUTHOR

Ronald J. Leach is the Director of Graduate Studies in the Department of Systems and Computer Science, School of Engineering, at Howard University in Washington, D.C. He also works at the NASA/Goddard Space Flight Center, where he conducts research into reuse cost models and component certification. He holds B.S., M.A., and Ph.D. degrees in Mathematics from the University of Maryland, as well as an M.S. in Computer Science from Johns Hopkins University. His work has been widely published in professional journals worldwide, and he is the author of three earlier books. Dr. Leach lives in Baltimore, Maryland.